Poland
Today

Poland Today

THE STATE OF THE REPUBLIC

*Compiled by the "Experience
and the Future" Discussion Group*

*With an Introduction by
Jack Bielasiak*

M.E. Sharpe, Inc., Armonk, New York

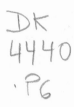

DK
4440
.P6

Translated by Andrew Swidlicki, Tadeusz Mollin, Michel Vale, and others.

This book is a translation of *Raport o stanie rzeczpospolitej i o drogach do jej naprawy —wersja wstępna* and *Jak z tego wyjść? (Opracowanie wyników ankiety)*, published by the Institut Literacki, Paris, 1980.

Published simultaneously as Vol. XI, No. 2-3, of *International Journal of Politics*.

Library of Congress Cataloging in Publication Data

Main entry under title:
    Poland today, the state of the Republic.

    Translated from the Polish.
    Contents: Report on the state of the Republic—Which way out?
    1. Poland—Politics and government—1945-   . 2. Poland—Social conditions. 3. Poland—Economic conditions—1945-   . I. Doświadczenie i Przyszłosć (Discussion Group: Poland) II. Report o stanie Rzeczypospolitej i o drogach do jej naprawy. English. c1981. III. Jak z tego wyjsć. English. c1981.
DK4440.P6   943.8'055   81-8782
ISBN 0-87332-201-0   AACR2

Printed in the United States of America

Table of Contents

Introduction

BY JACK BIELASIAK

The "Experience and the Future" discussion club was founded in October 1978 with the express purpose of analyzing the social, economic, and political conditions of Poland and of providing a program of reform to improve the situation of the country. The motivation for these tasks was found in the critical state of the Polish economic and social systems and in the perceived need to redress societal conditions in order to avoid a national crisis. On the basis of their work, members of "Experience and the Future," prominent professionals, scholars, and writers representing different social and political views, hoped to influence the political leadership to undertake fundamental reforms and thereby prevent the further deterioration of the national situation. The reports issued by the club in May 1979 and May 1980 provided an extensive and critical assessment of the social, economic, moral, and political climate of the nation, as well as a program for improvement. Failure to take immediate remedial action, the reports warned, could only result in some form of social eruption. In this prognosis, the "Experience and the Future" analysis proved prophetic, as the crisis of the summer of 1980 and the subsequent instability of the country demonstrate.

Historical Role of the Intelligentsia

The efforts of the "Experience and the Future" professionals and intellectuals to forewarn the authorities of the imminent danger of social breakdown are representative of the historical traditions of the Polish intelligentsia, who have consistently assumed a role of social responsibility in times of political crises

JACK BIELASIAK is Assistant Professor in the Department of Political Science and the Russian-East European Institute at Indiana University. In 1978-79 he was Visiting Associate Professor at the Institute of Political Sociology and the American Studies Center in Warsaw. During this period he conducted extensive research into the workers' movements and political crisis throughout Poland.

and national peril. In fact, this role of the intellectuals in Polish society has taken on a mythical quality that tends to perpetuate the self-identification of the intelligentsia as the social stratum representing the interests of the entire nation.[1] To a large extent this historical perception is the consequence of the long-term suppression of Polish sovereignty and the resultant function of the intellectuals in preserving and developing the national culture. This sense of responsibility for the maintenance of the national identity was in turn translated into a mission to safeguard the welfare of the country, especially during times of political or socioeconomic turmoil. The intellectuals acted not only to preserve the national identity but also to pressure the established political authorities to introduce changes and relieve the tensions prevailing in society. Accordingly, the traditions of the contemporary intellectuals reinforce their identification with the well-being of society and their advocacy of solutions to the problems of Poland. It is true, however, that strong disagreements among the Polish intelligentsia existed and continue to exist as to the best way to perform this social mission. The dilemma has been presented as a choice between romantic or idealistic actions, on the one hand, and realistic or positivistic acts, on the other hand.[2] The idealist conception was based on an open defiance of political rulers (in most instances occupying powers) regardless of the costs involved and the dangers experienced by the intelligentsia. The goal of national preservation was thought by the romanticists to justify the grave risks and the costs to society. In contrast, the realist school has argued for the need to accept accommodation with the political authority through a *modus vivendi* recognizing the limits of national or societal autonomy; the realists sought to assure the stable development of the country by minimizing risks and accepting compromises.

Revisionism and Neopositivism

The historical dilemma of idealism versus realism was present for the postwar Polish intelligentsia in a new form, for the choice involved accommodation or opposition to a political program of rapid social and economic transformation based on the Soviet model of socialism. The adaptation of this mode of national development signified not only the identification of Polish interests with Soviet preferences, but also the total penetration of society by the political authorities and the subjugation of civil society to the political state. The consequences for the Polish intellectuals, especially in the aftermath of de-Stalinization in the mid-1950s, was to determine whether the introduction of changes in the communist system could be achieved best through compromise with the political regime or through an open challenge to the state authorities.

The prevailing choice in the postwar years, made primarily in the hopes born during the innovations introduced by the Polish October of 1956, was that of realism, although two distinct variants of this strategy of change became visible.[3] One concept, that of revisionism, looked to the possibility of systemic evolution from within, based on the self-enlightenment of the Communist Party's leadership. The implementation of change, in this view, was to occur "from above" as a result of the penetration of new democratic ideas into the Communist Party, which would then affect the evolution of the entire society. Advocates of revisionism were primarily Marxist intellectuals who believed in both the possibility of reform within the communist organization and Marxist ideology and the ultimate triumph of socialist humanism in Poland. To influence societal development in this direction, the revisionists worked from within the system and through the party to convince the political establishment of the need for change and the positive consequences of such changes. This attitude on the part of the revisionist intellectuals did not mean the acceptance of the prevailing conditions in Poland. On the contrary, the revisionists took a critical stand toward the social and political systems and attempted to alter national conditions through their writings about the existing state of affairs in Poland. It is in this way that the revisionist school sought to influence the evolution of the political system, not by means of overt group opposition, organized social pressures, or appeals to public opinion. Revisionism operated within definite and self-imposed limits.

The other strand of realism in the 1950s and 1960s found expression in the neopositivism of Catholic intellectuals, grouped primarily around the Znak circle. This position rested on the recognition of the "geopolitical reality" of Poland and the necessity of an alliance with the Soviet Union, and thus accommodation with the Communist Party of Poland. At the same time, positivists rejected the applicability of Marxist ideology to the national culture, which they considered essentially Catholic. The efforts of the neopositivist adherents, therefore, were

aimed at preserving their cultural heritage through an understanding with the political authorities. In return for some degree
of support for the state, the Catholic intelligentsia was able to
safeguard the national culture and tradition that fell outside the
official interpretation of the Polish heritage. To facilitate this
task, clubs of the Catholic intelligentsia were formed, and
Catholic publications were allowed to appear. By these means
the neopositivist intellectuals sought to influence the course of
Polish developments. Their strategy, like that of the revisionists,
was limited to the pursuit of changes from above, by agreements
between the Catholic intelligentsia and the party leadership and
not by the application of pressure by the population on the
state. The attainment of the goals of the Catholic and secular
intelligentsia ultimately depended on the good will of the
political establishment and on the belief that state officials
would come to embrace positions more reflective of the intellectuals' stand.

Of course, not all the intellectuals in socialist Poland em-
braced the ideas represented by revisionism and neopositivism.
A substantial portion of the educated class in Poland, especially
the "new intelligentsia" formed after the advent of communist
power in the country, was integrated into the new sociopolitical
system and by-and-large gave its support to the communist regime. On the other end of the spectrum there remained intellectuals who continued to be irreconcilable to the new political authority in Poland. The intransigence of this group, however, was
expressed in the 1950s and 1960s in passivity rather than outright challenge. The main trends of intellectual thought at that
time, therefore, were the voices of the supporters of revisionist
and neopositivist views. Their commitment to the evolution of
social, economic, and political structures in Poland was not in
doubt, nor was their critical position vis-à-vis the prevailing social and political organization and activity. At the same time,
the belief of these intellectuals was that their criticism of the
present and their hopes for the future could be most effective if
expressed through a program of participation in the existing social structures, not by external pressures on the governing authorities.

This attitude prevailed for some years after the initial de-
Stalinization thaw of the mid-1950s, despite the "little stabilization" of the Gomulka regime, which consisted of a gradual erosion of the gains of the Polish October and the reimposition of
new limits on intellectual freedoms and on workers' self-orga-

nization. The policy of the Gomulka leadership departed from the initial liberalization programs and the restoration of a mutually beneficial relationship between state and society in favor of an authoritarian system of rule that neglected important problems of the country. The anticipated enlightened leadership in the political center failed to materialize, nor did the expected change in the organization of society. Despite this failure, nonetheless, the revisionist and positivist sentiments among large segments of the Polish intelligentsia persisted long after the official system revealed its commitment to the status quo. The explanation for the continuing positive expectations of the intellectuals is to be found in the differences between the pre- and post-October 1956 sociopolitical conditions, as well as in the fact that these changes were introduced by the party and reflected significant improvements in the conduct of political affairs by the official establishment. As a consequence, the belief that the party could be an instrument of positive social transformations continued, and hope for future alterations in favor of society prevailed among the intellectual community.

Limits to the attempt to transform Polish communism from above became evident during the crisis produced by the March 1968 events. A factional struggle within the party took the form of an anti-Zionist campaign that soon escalated into a stand marked by anti-intellectualism, especially its revisionist variant. The end result was a confrontation between the party bureaucracy and Marxist humanists that effectively demolished the hopes of the revisionist intellectuals for an enlightenment within the political apparatus. With this development the prospects for a democratization of the social environment initiated by the political authorities were dashed definitively. Although the positivist position was not as directly affected by the March 1968 crisis, for it did not depend as did the revisionists' on an internal ideological reformation within the party, the general tendency at the time to strengthen the authoritarian methods of political rule had its repercussions on the entire intellectual community. Furthermore, the fact that the 1968 conflict was restricted primarily to the upper strata of Polish society and involved issues of an intellectual nature meant that society as a whole did not get involved. In turn this intensified the isolation of the intelligentsia at the turn of the 1960s-70s decade, and the activism of the earlier years was replaced by a greater passivity on the part of the intellectuals. A case in point is the lack of involvement by intellectual circles in the labor unrests of December 1970, which remained essentially a defiance of the regime by the working class without support from the Polish educated strata. It appeared that a gulf had emerged not only between the political ruling elite and the intellectual circles, but also between the latter and the working masses.

The Democratic Opposition

The reemergence of the intelligentsia as a major force in the affairs of the nation occurred in the mid-1970s in circumstances reminiscent of developments following the Polish October of 1956. This time, however, the most visible aspect of the intellectual community's activities was the formation of a democratic opposition that attempted to influence the evolution of the Polish system through societal pressures on the political leadership. While certainly the majority of the nation's educated class continued to work within the official system, a growing number of the intelligentsia became associated in the second half of the 1970s with the democratic opposition. It was from this last sector that the loudest calls for change in the system of political rule emerged.

The rise of this intellectual movement in Poland can be traced to the governmental policies adapted in the aftermath of the workers' unrest in December 1970. The satisfaction of the workers' demands at that time could not be accomplished exclusively by a change of leadership, precisely because of the failure of Gomulka to fulfill the expectations of the nation in the post-1956 period. In addition, Gierek's new ruling team had to introduce substantive policy changes to end the social crisis. The conditions described by the "Experience and the Future" reports were formed by the regime's attempts to respond to and stabilize the situation after the 1970 events. In this regard a dual policy emerged: one side of it was directed at the socioeconomic satisfaction of the population, the other at strengthening the political position of the Gierek leadership vis-à-vis society.

The attempt to reconcile the civil community with the regime was characterized by efforts to improve the material wellbeing of the population and initiate a "new political style" based on a dialogue between state and society. In the short term, at least, based on policies of modernization, price stability, and social reconciliation, national conditions improved and popular satisfaction increased. At the same time, however, the Gierek leadership sought to consolidate its position within the system by making clear that the new political style did not mean a decline in the leading role of the party in the construction of socialism. In the belief that social stability had been attained, the authorities launched an ideological offensive in the mid-1970s to strengthen the power of the political center and the party apparatus. To emphasize the program of consolidation, the leadership chose the symbolic act of revising the Constitution so as to stress the party's guiding role in society and articulate firmly the authorities' dedication to the ideological transformation of the nation. The proposed amendments brought forth immediate opposition from intellectual circles, who were against the sanctification of the communist monopoly of power and the limitation of national sovereignty through linkage to the Soviet Union. The result was a confrontation between the political authorities and elite sectors of society that led to the reemergence of a strong critical attitude among the intelligentsia toward the state. The constitutional crisis most significantly affected the positivist position among Catholic intellectuals, whose accommodation with the state was founded on a recognition of social and cultural pluralism. Amendments legitimizing the dependence of society on the party and linking citizens' rights to duties to the secular state denied the validity of neopositivist assumptions.

The resurgence of a critical stand by some sectors of the intelligentsia was further accentuated by the events of June 1976. The workers' unrests of that summer were the result of the government's policy seeking to redress a rapidly deteriorating economy, a situation created by a continuing lag of supplies vis-à-vis consumer demand and an ever increasing national debt. The political remedy for this state of affairs was a program of reform within the existing institutions and processes of management that sought, in the main, to lessen the subsidies for foodstuffs. There was no question of policies that would introduce major structural reforms in the socioeconomic system. The commitment to centralization and political supervision of social and economic forces resulted instead in another attempt to raise prices on June 24, 1976, without prior consultations with or even information to the public. The reaction of the working class, which saw the move as a burden falling primarily on their shoulders, was immediate: work stoppages and street demonstrations took place and forced the government to rescind its policy within twenty-four hours.

The incident, coming on the heels of a public conflict over the Constitution, considerably affected the level of social tensions in Poland. The Gierek leadership suffered a growing loss of credibility, especially as it embarked on a campaign of repression and arrests of worker-activists in the second half of 1976. The result was a new impasse between the rulers and the ruled that altered the political reality of Poland. The regime's actions during the 1975-76 crises demonstrated to the nation once again that a communist leadership that had promised to govern in a new political style had violated the social compact between state and society. Furthermore, the policies and actions of the ruling team made obvious to large segments of Polish society the futility of pursuing a dialogue with the authorities. One consequence of this assessment was a growing dissatisfaction across all sectors of society that found expression in increasing distrust of the political establishment, social frustration and apathy, and the alienation of the population. The inability of the government to redress the situation led to a rapid deterioration in the national condition.

It was in the context of the growing gap between society and the state, and the failure to resolve the basic economic and social problems of the country, that a new movement was born, dedicated to pressuring the authorities to implement fundamental systemic changes. The silent response by the intelligentsia to the workers' revolt of 1970 was replaced in 1976 by a spirited defense of the labor class, as a number of intellectuals formed in September of that year the Committee for the Defense of Workers (KOR). Soon thereafter other voices from the intellectual circles, the working masses, and the Church establishment were heard in support of the mistreated workers and in defense of society's rights to better social, economic, and political conditions. The culmination of these developments was the establishment in the latter part of the 1970s of a democratic opposition among the intellectual community of Poland. Although a small minority among the educated strata, the movement witnessed a rapid proliferation of dissident groups that became the predominant voices in shaping the social thought of the nation through their discourse on the possibilities and directions of change in Poland.

The democratic opposition rejected the reformist strategy of revisionism and neopositivism and its reliance for systemic evolution on enlightened authorities. The crises of 1968 and

1976 had demonstrated that hopes for changes from above were unwarranted and resulted in the disappointment of the advocates of reform. Instead, the democratic opposition argued that it was essential to act outside the official system of rule and appeal to social forces to exert pressure on the authorities. Only through this form of agitation from below, and not by means of appeals to the regime, could the development of society be influenced. For that reason the mission of dissidents was to move beyond the existing political boundaries and openly advocate a program of change based on the confrontation of the political establishment by society. The intellectual opposition, in the main, recognized limits to its program of change and took into account the need to recognize the reality of the Soviet-Polish alliance and the primacy of the Communist Party within the political system. Nonetheless, the dissident movement believed that the style of rule of the authorities could be altered in favor of a more equal relationship between the state and civil society. To accomplish this change, however, social forces had to organize and openly present their demands for improvements, as well as to actively pressure the regime to implement the desired reforms.

The first task of the democratic opposition was to spread this belief from its own circles to society at large. This task was facilitated by the situation in Poland in the second half of the 1970s. Major social groups had by that time become well aware of the government's mismanagement of public affairs and the regime's inability and unwillingness to introduce necessary changes. Furthermore, society had seen in 1970 and 1976 that open expressions of discontent and challenges to the ruling circle's policies had forced changes in the government's programs. Therefore, the propensity of various social forces to express their interests and act in their defense expanded rapidly.

The aim of the democratic opposition was to facilitate the political activism of society by creating conditions enabling the free exchange of opinions and the self-organization of social forces. Only in such an environment could there exist an open expression of social concerns and the advocacy of different socioeconomic programs, and only through criticism, discussion, and protest could society influence the economic, social, and political development of the country. The activities of the dissident groups in the late 1970s were directed precisely at the creation of such a free and open atmosphere of political discourse. The strategy of the dissidents was to engage in legal conduct of social activity by observing and appealing to the civil rights provided in the Constitution and judicial statutes. This stand was further enhanced by emphasizing liberties relevant to the entire population, thus including the intelligentsia's own concern with freedom of expression alongside the workers' rights to the expression of their economic interests and the Church's advocacy of spiritual tolerance.

To channel the exertion of pressures on the political authorities, the democratic opposition also significantly extended the dissemination of information by publishing uncensored journals and books. The need for the free flow of knowledge was viewed as an essential component for eroding the state's hold over policy formulation and for entering into an open dialogue throughout society concerning the future course of the nation. Indeed, the uncensored publications have played a critical role in the sociopolitical debates in Poland over the last few years and have contributed strongly to the rise of political awareness among various strata of the population. In this way the democratic opposition in fact created a new reality in Poland on the eve of the 1980 workers' actions by penetrating public opinion with its views and activating social forces for the advocacy of change. The impact of the dissident activities went well beyond its own groups and resulted in discussions about the economic and social problems of the nation in a variety of official settings. Professional meetings, conferences, and discussion clubs where people of all backgrounds and views, including party members, met to discuss current issues and offer solutions had become a common feature of public life in Poland at the end of the 1970s.

Experience and the Future

The motivation for entering the public discussion on the state of the nation was made ever more urgent by the rapidly deteriorating economic and social conditions in Poland. In these circumstances intellectual circles not directly tied to the democratic opposition felt a sense of responsibility to society and attempted to engage the political establishment in a dialogue, thereby influencing the evolution of the sociopolitical system. Many of these efforts were unstructured and found expression in private exchanges of views or in meetings of professional societies whose primary activities were not relevant to the advocacy of reform. The need to go beyond these diffuse attempts was therefore felt by intellectuals and professionals who remained committed to the possibility of influencing the political regime not by means of the confrontation advocated by the democratic opposition but through accommodation between the state and society. A group of these individuals established the "Experience and the Future" club to provide a forum for the discussion of national conditions in a setting that would bring together the intellectual community and the political establishment.[4] The effort can thus be taken as an attempt to reintroduce into the educated circles of Poland the ideals associated with the earlier revisionist and neopositivist positions, namely, that change can be accomplished by addressing the political authorities and reasoning with them concerning the necessity of reform. In this sense the "Experience and the Future" view rejected the platform of the democratic opposition appeals to public opinion as pressure on the leadership and instead opted for a program meant to convince the authorities of the critical situation in the country and the urgent need to institute changes.

The "Experience and the Future" discussion club was founded by several prominent individuals in the intellectual community and had its inaugural plenary session on November 14, 1978, in Warsaw. The meeting brought together about 100 people, representing a variety of scientific, academic, professional, and creative fields, who had an extensive awareness of the conditions in Polish society. The participants also reflected different opinions; and while most were members of the Polish United Workers' Party, there were numerous politically unaffiliated and Catholic activists. Perhaps the most prominent feature of the membership was the high caliber of the participants, who were leading experts in their fields. Many of them were prominent members of the Communist Party; and even if some had taken critical positions toward the existing political conditions, they maintained close connections to the governing establishment. The association of such individuals with the club indicated that the group had no intention of overtly challenging the political authorities but was instead committed to improving the national situation through an examination of the country's socioeconomic and political problems. Further evidence of the establishment orientation of "Experience and the Future" was signaled by the sponsorship of the discussion club by the Collegium of the Society for the Free Diffusion of Knowledge, a state-run organization concerned with social issues. The ability of "Experience and the Future" to obtain the sanction of the latter institution indicated that official circles had granted approval for the meeting. Given the rising level of discontent among professional and intellectual groups, it is likely that the leadership sought to channel the discussion of national problems in a forum where it could exercise greater control through institutional and personal means. While such an arrangement would diffuse criticism, it could also demonstrate to the intellectual community the regime's readiness to engage in a dialogue and listen to suggestions for improvement. From the point of view of the authorities, the idea was to create the image of an enlightened establishment pursuing an exchange with social forces, but to control the environment of the interchange.

At the same time, the individuals associated with "Experience and the Future" made clear the limits of their activity. In particular, they disassociated the club from any political intent and emphasized that they were not interested in presenting a political program or pursuing political ends. The club was to act, therefore, as a think tank that could influence official programs through ideas rather than political infighting.

"Experience and the Future," in short, reflected the traditional role of the Polish intelligentsia as a medium for the expression of public concerns and the advocacy of solutions to political authorities. The intention of the participants in the club was to discuss overtly the important problems besieging the country, outline the possibilities for reform, and on the basis of the exchange of opinions, establish a consensus in society for the resolution of the difficulties. An analysis of the critical state of the nation was viewed as the point of departure for the articulation of a comprehensive reform program to be implemented on the basis of cooperation between the political establishment and the civil community. This perspective, as the editorial afterword to the reports makes clear, assumed willingness by both sides to accept compromises, the assurance of an institutional framework for the articulation of diverse views, and a commitment to implementing reforms. This signaled the rejection, at least initially, of the commonly held belief that while change was necessary, it was impossible to attain in the existing political conditions. The task of "Experience and the Future" was thus to demonstrate that the authorities could be receptive to ideas about change. The thoughtful presentation of a reform project by a circle of prominent experts was perceived by members of the club as a legitimate effort leading to an authoritative evaluation of its findings and the activization of some recommendations for change.

The hopes of "Experience and the Future," however, proved to be overly optimistic. After the first session the open forum for discussion necessary to carry out the intentions of the club was no longer in existence. Before the membership could gather again to revive the debate, the authorities withdrew the sponsorship by the Society for the Diffusion of Knowledge and in fact forbade the convening of the second session of "Experience and the Future" in January 1979. While there has been no official explanation for this action, it is apparent that the political leadership was stung by the severity of the criticism expressed at the first plenary meeting. After the November gathering the authorities became aware that their original expectations of moderating the articulation of discontent through official sanction of "Experience and the Future" was unwarranted. Faced with an outcry of opinion denouncing not only economic and social difficulties but also the failures of the political apparatus to resolve them, the government most likely became fearful that the nature of the "Experience and the Future" enterprise would legitimate criticism and facilitate its expansion throughout the system. Under the circumstances the ruling authorities felt that they had no other choice but to end the activities of the discussion club. Indeed, a few of the individuals with close connections to the establishment at that time severed their collaboration with "Experience and the Future."

Nevertheless the work of the club continued, although in a different form than that originally designed by its founders. These efforts proceeded despite the fact that the authorities' action had undermined the original intent of "Experience and the Future" to act as a conduit between the concerns of society and the political center and had in fact pointed to the regime's unwillingness to engage in a discussion based on a critical evaluation of official policies. It is true that members of "Experience and the Future" did not attempt to defy the political authorities by perpetuating the institutional existence of club, and after January 1979 there were no further attempts to meet in a discussion forum. Instead, an alternative method of serving the original purpose of a critical examination of the issues facing the nation was devised. An editorial committee of "Experience and the Future" was created to solicit from the intellectual and professional community written opinions about the state of the country. During the first half of 1979 the committee sent out a series of questions to gauge the opinion of various journalists, academics, and experts, in what became a major sociological survey concerning Poland's socioeconomic policy and political system.

The responses to the poll provided the committee with a comprehensive examination of the social, economic, and political conditions in the country, which the editorial team synthesized into an authoritative statement as the "Report on the State of the Republic," the first document translated in this volume. The "Report" presented detailed accounts of the causes of the national problems and of the manifestations of these problems in social life, quoting at length from the various individual responses to the original inquiry. The aim of the document, in the view of the basic philosophy of "Experience and the Future" to enter into a dialogue with the regime, was not to condemn the state but rather to describe the conditions in need of improvement. With this purpose in mind, the "Report" was forwarded in May 1979 to the authorities in the hope that some form of action would follow.

The official failure to react to this assessment and the continuing deterioration of the situation resulted in December 1979 in a second effort by the editorial committee. The pattern of inquiry was similar to the initial survey, although the spectrum of opinion and expertise was enlarged considerably in the follow-up study. The focus of this endeavor was on how to get out of the persistent sociopolitical crisis in Poland. Within a very short time the editorial committee received 141 answers to its initiative and, as in the previous case, issued a report based on the collected responses. The second document, entitled "Which Way Out?" and released in May 1980 (also translated here), was, like the first analysis, defined by the participation of prominent members of the cultural, scientific, academic, and sociopolitical establishment who were still hopeful of influencing the political leadership through the expression of their concerns. "Experience and the Future" continued to act as an internal critic that was not challenging the political establishment but rather addressing the governing circles in an attempt to initiate reforms and use its influence to improve the overall situation of the nation.

"Experience and the Future" argued that the dimensions of the crisis were so grave that only significant changes in the methods of governing could reverse the situation. The fundamental task was to create a rapprochement between the rulers and the ruled, which could be achieved only through a structural reform in policy-making. The program called for increasing the participation of social groups in the system, the revitalization of representative organs, the self-organization of group interests, adherence to legality and socialist values, and openness and truth in social relations. The implementation of these reforms could restore cooperation among different social forces and introduce a system of rule based on compromises and agreements. Only through such efforts at reform, the authors argued, could a more profound crisis be avoided, and therefore the political authorities had a responsibility to act on behalf of the entire nation and introduce changes to restore the vitality of society.

The response of the ruling team to the proposals set out by the "Experience and the Future" editors did not take the direction hoped for by the respondents to the surveys. Instead the primary concerns of the regime in the last years of the 1970s continued to be the preservation of its political power in the face of growing social discontent and demands for change. The apparent fear of the leadership was that the implementation of political reforms during a highly unstable situation would result in a permanent alteration of the status quo in favor of social forces. As a result the authorities remained strongly committed to the "leading role of the party" principle and the maintenance of party controls over social and political sphere. This attitude carried over to economic management, despite the further deterioration of economic conditions. The authorities thus resisted the introduction of structural reforms in favor of decentralization and enterprise autonomy as a way to improve the operation of the economic system. Instead, under the pressure of severe economic dislocations, the government preferred to rationalize the existing management process. In practice this signified the introduction of greater cost-efficiency through an increase in prices, curtailment of wage growth, and less reliance on Western products and credits. However, the leadership was well aware that such steps would have a negative impact on the welfare of the population and could result, as in 1970 and 1976, in open social discontent. To prevent the eruption of such a situation, the regime launched a program of "austerity and unity" in the campaign preceding the party congress of February 1980. The goal of the leadership was to make the people understand, through a description of the economic difficulties, the need for short-term austerity and material sacrifices. Furthermore, the propaganda campaign aimed at the creation of national unity as a solution to the economic difficulties. The resolve of the people to get together and work harder was depicted as a necessary condition for altering the economic situation. Evidently the Gierek team hoped that such appeals would result in the acceptance by the people of the deterioration in material well-being and enable the introduction of the desired economic rationalization.

These hopes, however, proved to be too optimistic, as the announcement of price increases on July 1, 1980, was met by popular resistance. The workers' strikes of the summer escalated rapidly from posing demands for economic satisfaction to pressures for changes in the sociopolitical environment. The events of the summer and fall of 1980 demonstrated to the entire world the fragility of Poland's social fabric. At the same time, the workers' actions and the resulting social upheaval proved the correctness of "Experience and the Future's" analysis. The latter had warned that failure by the authorities to take significant remedial action was likely to lead to a social eruption and the confrontation of the state by society, a pattern of social behavior evident in Poland since the workers' strikes. The reports had clearly proclaimed the impossibility of introducing economic reforms without simultaneously restructuring the political system and had condemned the policy of sociopolitical "muddling through" without addressing the critical disintegration of the system of rule. Changes, it was argued, could not take place without the active involvement of social forces and the participation of various groups in policy-making. The regime's failure to undertake these reforms and to establish a new authority through cooperation with society resulted in a massive and ardent resistance to the program of the leadership. Beyond that, the new activism of social groups has resulted in the surfacing of issues that were so well depicted by the respondents to the "Experience and the Future" questionnaire. The concern with social inequalities and the privileges of officials, the restoration of material well-being to all strata, and provisions for the free flow of information and adherence to legal norms have all formed the essence of the people's challenge to the political establishment. However, it is probably in the articulation of the need for the self-organization of social forces that "Experience and the Future" reports proved to be most prophetic. For without doubt the most significant aspect of the sociopolitical changes in Poland since August 1980 has been the movement for self-organization by numerous groups in society. The most important of these is the creation of an independent trade union, Solidarity, as a representative of the workers' interests. But other groups as well, students, farmers, and professionals, have declared their autonomy from institutions controlled by the Communist Party. This tendency to expand sociopolitical participation and open up the process of government, often through the continued pressure of society on the authorities, represents a fundamental alteration in the system of power in Poland. The hope must be that this process will lead to the restoration of cooperation among all forces of society that will promote resolution of the grave economic and social problems that continue to besiege Poland.

In the final analysis the sober assessment of national conditions by "Experience and the Future" did not divert the policies of the regime from the path leading to a clash of social forces. The aim of the intellectuals, experts, and professionals who took part in the activities of "Experience and the Future" was to influence the political leadership through a dialogue based on mutual concern over the sociopolitical and economic problems of the country. This position rested on the long tradition of the Polish intelligentsia to intervene at times of social turmoil and fulfill its social responsibility to the entire nation. As such the motivation for the work of the discussion club was to work for reform within the political system and to infuse the official establishment with ideas for change. In this activity "Experience and the Future" sought to distinguish its position from that of the democratic opposition, which attempted to directly address social groups as a way to increase pressures on the political authorities and force change in the system. Instead, the documents reprinted here were directed to the authorities of the country in the hope that the leadership would understand the seriousness of the national condition and implement the recommendations of the established intelligentsia. The events of the past year have shown that while the "Experience and the Future" evaluation of the social, political, and economic situations could not have been more correct, their strategy for change was ineffective. The current transformation of Polish society is not the result of reform from above but of extensive social pressures on the political authorities from below.

Notes

[1] For a discussion of the intelligentsia's historical role in Poland, see Alexander Gella, "The Life and Death of the Old Polish Intelligentsia," *Slavic*

Review, March 1971, and Maria Hirszowicz, "Intelligentsia versus Bureaucracy? The Revival of a Myth in Poland," *Soviet Studies* 30, July 1978.

[2] Adam Bromke, *Poland's Politics: Idealism vs. Realism* (Cambridge, Mass., 1967), and "Poland's Idealism and Realism in Retrospect," *Canadian Slavonic Papers* 31, March 1979.

[3] Adam Michnik, "The New Evolutionism," *Survey* 22, Summer/Autumn 1976, and Marek Tarniewski, *Ewolucja czy Rewolucja* (Paris, 1975).

[4] For background on "Experience and the Future," in addition to the documents reprinted here, see J. B. de Weydenthal, "The Unofficial Report on Polish Politics and Society," *Radio Free Europe Research*, Background Report 239, November 2, 1979, and "The Unofficial Program for Change in Poland," *Radio Free Europe Research*, Background Report 164, July 2, 1980.

Report on the State
of the Republic

Introductory Remarks

This document was drafted by the Editorial Committee of the "Experience and the Future" Discussion Group (set up as part of the Collegium of the Society for the Free Diffusion of Knowledge;[1] the first plenary meeting of the discussion group took place in Warsaw on November 14, 1978). The editorial committee included members of a service unit as well as those "Experience and the Future" members who expressed the desire to participate in the editorial work.

The study was based on responses to a survey in which fifty persons participated: representatives of various philosophical outlooks, various scholarly fields and the arts, journalists, and public figures.

Following the usual practice in this kind of poll, responses are quoted anonymously; the questionnaires were numbered in the order in which they were received.

Introductory Comments

The following text is a synthesis of poll responses on the topic "the state of the Republic and ways to rectify it." The survey covered problems first raised at the plenary session of the discussion group "Experience and the Future," and to which so many other meetings and discussions have been dedicated.

The discussion group was established in October of last year [1978] on the initiative of people from various walks of life who keenly felt the need for a more extended exchange of opinions on the most crucial problems facing the country, an exchange among people representing various professions, specialties, fields of learning, and viewpoints. This cross section included party members, Catholic activists, and specialists in a variety of fields, in some cases not those who are active in political or public life. The group had no political ambitions, and its meetings were inspired by the ideal of free and genuine discussion, the lack of which is acutely felt in our public life.

Unfortunately, the group was not able to hold plenary sessions. Hence it proved necessary to find another basis for an exchange of views. From this arose the idea of a poll made up of the following questions:

1. What are the crucial issues for our country in the social, political, economic, cultural, educational, and other realms?

2. What assets do we have to develop our country; how can we use them; and what negative and obstructive factors block their full utilization?

3. What threats, both immediate and long-term, are evident in the present political, social, economic, and cultural situation of the country?

4. What reforms are necessary for Poland to develop in the best possible way?

5. To what extent are contradictions in the interests of various social groups the source of current and potential conflicts?

6. What do I expect my own and other social strata to do now?

The questions were set up to frame the central issue without excluding the possibility of going beyond these limits. And the ranks of the people to whom the survey was addressed were broadened to include, besides members of "Experience and the Future," dozens of prominent specialists in various fields who were interested in the undertaking and expressed their readiness to take part.

Despite the short time allowed for answers, the responses displayed depth, breadth, and substance. We could not circulate all the material, which totaled several hundred pages, among all the respondents. Therefore this compilation was made in an effort to present the main points of view in all their variety and diversity. There was no attempt to avoid repetition in matters regarded as especially important.

The open nature of the questions and the wide-ranging subject matter with which they deal made it impossible to draw up a simple summary concisely presenting the results of the survey. Therefore, despite our concern to faithfully reflect the views expressed by our respondents and their major points of coincidence, this summary study is to some degree an independent effort, and to that extent the editors bear responsibility for it. Furthermore, in compiling the text we made use of other available material from discussions held in other forums.

The extent of the material forced us to be selective, so that some respondents are quoted more extensively than others. Nor should the text be construed as any sort of "joint platform," since the views of the "Experience and the Future" participants could not be discussed beforehand in a plenary meeting. If, nonetheless, the individual responses display a great degree of coincidence of views, it is not because they were made to fit, but because certain ideas imposed themselves with such unique force on almost all the "Experience and the Future" participants, regardless of their professional, age, or philosophical differences.

Neither the responses nor the study based on them represents any sort of expertise, and neither pretends to fill the information gaps caused by the negligence of institutions and services set up to provide information.

This text is not a petition to the authorities. It is simply an attempt to systematize the opinions of a broad cross section of people. Its purpose is to help crystallize views. It is addressed to all thinking people in Poland who are deeply concerned about the current state of the country and its future. It is addressed equally to those in power and those who are not, party members and nonmembers, those who believe in God and those who do not. Only through the collective efforts of all of us will we be able to secure for our country a better future and shield it from the dangers threatening it. The authors of the study would like to state emphatically that it is not a judgment on the state of the country as much as an explanation of the symptoms and roots of the crisis that, according to most of the respondents, has now appeared in various forms and in various areas of social life; we have therefore not dwelled extensively on the achievements of Polish society over the past thirty-five years.

We certainly do not expect everyone to agree with the whole of the study. We would, however, be pleased if it were to find the broadest possible use as a spur for new reflections. As regards the authorities, it obviously depends on them alone whether and to what extent they are willing to make use of the ideas presented here. We can only express our conviction that independent thought, like critical thought, about the important problems of the country should not be disregarded. It is, indeed, an inalienable right and civic duty to ponder these problems, to communicate, and to see that they do not go without an echo.

* * *

Before we go on to a more detailed presentation of the results of our survey, which we have arranged under several topical headings, it would first be useful to discuss some more general problems that bear on the origins of this survey and on the intentions and ideas that impelled us to do it.

Both the "Experience and the Future" editorial team and the poll itself were born of the conviction that the crisis our country is experiencing affects many basic areas of communal life and indeed is creating a highly alarming situation that will inevitably grow even worse. The hope that with the passage of time the symptoms of crisis would gradually give way to a readjustment and improvement in the methods of government and management did not materialize. The situation is exacerbated, on the one hand, by the ever more acute contradiction between the mounting tasks created by the development of an industrial society and the increasing complexity of public life, and on the other hand, by the ever more glaring inefficiency of the entire system of social interaction. In recent years we have witnessed a telling illustration of this contradiction, when, at the beginning of the seventies, unquestionable, objective, and fruitful economic, technical, and cultural progress, instead of quickening and consolidating improvements (as had been anticipated), only revealed even greater weaknesses and flaws in the system, thereby deepening the general sense of frustration.

The more or less clearly perceived dimensions of the crisis and their repeatedly dashed expectations and hopes have left in the minds of Poles lasting traces, reflected in the bitter conviction that radical changes in the way the social and political order functions are absolutely necessary and at the same time futile. Furthermore, resigned acceptance of this state of affairs leads to a variety of extreme and even contradictory attitudes, ranging from conformity and defense of the status quo, through various forms of escape into private life, to vacuous, hate-filled rebellion. Despite the quite different moral qualifications we can attribute to these attitudes, they have one trait in common: they all lead to disbelief in the meaning of any effort, to apathy, and to the paralysis of any constructive social thinking.

The first task of enlightened public opinion is to join battle with all these phenomena, regardless of what shape they assume and for what reasons they come about. Criticism of these benumbing attitudes must be resolute and uncompromising, which means it cannot rest content with that tendency, so common among Poles (albeit otherwise psychologically understandable) to seek out the guilty parties and make accusations. We must get at the manifold root causes and dispassionately explain the reasons for and background of the phenomena we criticize.

These phenomena can be described in various ways. One of the respondents (No. 9) called them "loss of nerve": "The most glaring problem of the country for me——and its origins can be found in every area of social life——is the state of social apathy . . . the fact that people have lost faith." Another respondent (No. 27) speaks of the "state of extreme moral and physical exhaustion of Polish society."

Counteracting these conditions requires getting to their roots. First, there must be an analysis and criticism of those organizational structures, those systems of dependence on and subordination to power that, by depriving people of their sense of responsibility and the meaning of their actions, lead to apathy and atrophy of civic pride. Many of the responses take up this problem in detail, pointing out that the instrumental subordination of the citizen and the progressive atrophy of any honest public life only apparently facilitate the task of the authorities, for in reality they lead to passive resistance and paralysis of the whole system of organization of communal life.

The criticism we are talking about here cannot shrink from an appraisal of the growing moods of opposition in the country. In an atmosphere of mounting criticism, besides justified condemnation of mistakes, faults, and negligence, one also hears the voice of what we referred to above as vacuous rebellion, which to a certain extent is inevitable in our situation, although it is a purely negative expression of the regrets, resentments, and grudges that have accumulated and clotted in the public mind. This is understandable, since the drift toward total conformity produces no less than total rebellion. An obtrusive apologetic leads to the denial of everything. However, the real threat does exist that these extreme attitudes, regardless of their opposing intentions, not only legitimate each other but also contribute, each in its own way, to the further deepening of the social crisis, revealing the unbridgeable gap that exists between aspirations and real opportunities to meet them, between what

seems on reflection to be necessary and what consistent and
resolute action can achieve. It is to be feared that under conditions in which a free exchange of views, so indispensable if public thinking and opinion are to mature, has become impossible,
muffled criticism will come to adopt increasingly extreme, and
what is worse, purely negative attitudes not conducive to a
sober assessment of the situation or to the search for realistic
ways out of it.

This brings us to a problem that is an important thread running through many of the responses: the role and function of
criticism, seen not as certain individuals' need to pour out their
own private complaints and grudges, but as an indispensable aspect of self-awareness in public life, a necessary condition for
the development and health of communal life. Respondent No.
29 has the following to say on this score: "No proper system of
organization can manage without regularly functioning corrective
mechanisms. The most important of them are an integral part of
the system itself, since they determine the openness and flexibility of adaptive measures and, indeed, the system's capacity to
undergo fundamental changes. . . . I submit that mechanisms for
intrinsic self-regulation are progressively disappearing from our
political order. I am thinking here of genuine forms of such self-
regulation, not sham ones. Institutional mechanisms for self-
regulation undoubtedly exist; but their obvious ineffectuality
must be interpreted either as faulty operation or as proper operation that nevertheless cannot overcome the resistance
mounted by the system itself. Unfortunately, the second explanation is probably closest to the truth. Everything indicates that
the regime in power has rigidified its structure, attempted to
stabilize and enshrine its elements, and protected its privileges.
The mere thought of needing improvement is both untactful
and dangerous in such a situation: resistance to such an idea becomes the natural reaction of virtually the whole system. This
unsound reaction stems from group instincts of self-defense and
egotism; hence attitudes are formed that are dangerous because
they are not tested daily but only from crisis to crisis. Growing
entrenchment of status, routine, avoidance of competition, and
fear of innovation are only the beginnings of a series of phenomena that produce the conservative faith in the superiority of
known stasis over risky, untested change."

A thorough discussion of the role and function that criticism
does and should perform under our social and economic conditions leads to the conclusion that that role must not be limited

merely to bringing to light the system's faults or its inefficiency, but must be accompanied by a search for ways to overcome the present crisis. Advancing the claims of the citizenry and social groups or exerting pressure on the authorities to broaden the limits of freedom are an important, but not the sole function of criticism. The authorities are, after all, not only a political apparatus and a system of constraint but also the organizers of the collective social effort. Thoughtful criticism must aim not at weakening but at reinforcing and improving this function of the authorities.

Without the active participation of a considerable segment of the existing apparatus there is no way to carry out the expected reforms. For even the best-conceived reforms would inevitably cause yet another disappointment if they did not get support, did not arouse hope and unleash social forces. From this follows the unavoidable conclusion, although it is alien to most Poles, that an independent public and civic opinion must undertake to provide and nurture conditions in which a partnership consensus can be instituted between the powers-that-be and society, in which, moreover, it would be possible to restore trust in the authorities. The poll contains a number of ideas about the conditions the authorities must meet to restore elementary trust in them.

From the responses of many participants it is clear that despite everything, they still see such a possibility if the public gives this trust another chance. But this chance would be short-term and would require real institutional guarantees. As time passes, the price of acquiring this chance will grow, and the conditions for it will become harsher. As respondent No. 33 writes: "This trust was carelessly squandered twice [in 1956 and 1970]. No one in Poland has earned such a new lease on trust, and it will not be easy to earn. However, I believe that trust can still be regained by providing honest and unembellished information, by opening all accounts to public scrutiny, by a credible description of the state of the nation, and finally, by showing who really rules whom in Poland, who decides what and why, and who is responsible for what."

The effort to restore provisional trust in the authorities and the state is all the more difficult in that it must be made against the wishes of many who, entrenched for thirty years in the wielding of power, consider the arguments presented here incomprehensible and revolting. It also flies in the face of a deeply rooted negative reaction from a public used to the arbitrary decisions of a state whose rapacity they take as justification, and sometimes even compulsion, to play their own games, a state they seek to outwit by any means at their disposal. This general type of attitude and behavior is also the result of many years of experience and propaganda in which the state is presented as a benefactor; such propaganda destroys civic responsibility and erodes the perception of the state as the repository of the common good, as a system of rights and duties linking all its citizens, and as the sum total of the accomplishments of all of us on whom its prosperity rests, and who bear the responsibility for its fate.

The awareness of these difficulties has not shaken the respondents' belief in the possibility of restoring civic pride, which, despite all the symptoms of exhaustion and discouragement, still exists and can be revitalized, not by even more appeals, but by creating conditions conducive to the development of an authentic public life.

CHAPTER 1

The Conduct of Politics

In this chapter we will attempt to answer the questions of how and why the country's present social, political, and economic situation has come about. Why, despite the valid plans that were drawn up for a major acceleration in the country's rate of economic growth, despite numerous tangible gains in the early seventies, despite public support for the program of reform, despite the favorable international boom in the early seventies, and despite massive credits—why despite all these things an acute crisis developed that touched the very foundations of social, political, and economic life. Was this crisis the result of specific mistakes by specific people, bad decisions with regard to economic growth, or was it the result of the worsening of the worldwide economic picture? Or were the reasons more deeply rooted; were the bad decisions—given the overall situation in 1979—caused by factors of a more general nature, factors deeply rooted in the social and political system as a whole? What are the causes, and what are the effects? These are the questions weighing on everyone today, not only because all of us are experiencing the effects of the crisis in our daily lives, but primarily because the period from 1971 to 1979 has brought to light totally new material that merits serious consideration.

If one looks carefully at the past eight years, one has to be struck by the scope and scale of the changes compared with previous years. There has been a change—to be sure, only at the theoretical level—in an axiom of the social order: the rise in the living standard and in production for the consumer market has been given precedence over the need to push the development of heavy industry. A policy based on stable prices and very slowly rising wages has given way to a policy of rapid growth and changing prices and wages. Balanced payments have given

way to a commitment to maximum use of foreign credits. A
cautious domestic policy has been replaced by, at times, extra-
ordinarily bold measures, such as opening the border to the German Democratic Republic, opening up the country in general,[2]
extending the social insurance system to the countryside,[3] and
a major reform in the administrative apparatus,[4] e.g., there has
been a massive rejuvenation of government and party personnel.
A general improvement in living standards was evident, and the
creation of jobs for the cohorts from the demographic explosion
was an unquestionable success.

Yet despite all these things, what is most impressive about
these eight years is not so much the changes as the similarity of
the years from 1971 to 1979 to the preceding period.

In the sphere of, as we will call it, the nation's household,
we find that after 1956, just as after 1970,[5] there was an improvement in the standard of living, a rash of dramatic and ambitious plans, and an upsurge in activity generally; but in each
case it was confined to the first few years. In both periods the
crisis struck at similar moments and for similar reasons: toward
the end of the first five-year planning period, and as a result of a
breakdown in investment policy.

As regards social policy in the broad sense and the conduct
of government, the scenario of change is virtually identical. In
both cases the first two years were marked by general liberalization, a relatively open cultural policy, improvement in the flow
of information, some curtailment of censorship, and increased
participation by party nonmembers in public life. In both cases
this was all followed by a quite rapid retreat from liberalization,
staunching of the information flow, and an emergent tendency
to concentrate authority in the hands of an increasingly narrow
group.

We also find such similarities in the changes that took place
in public consciousness. After an initial period of approbation
and a desire to do one's share, in both the midseventies and the
sixties we find growing apathy among the public, lack of identification with achievements—even those that were beyond
question—and mounting frustration bordering on open conflict.

Although the conditions, plans, and concepts in the two
periods were entirely different (despite the inevitable simplifi-
cations of our analysis), the upshot of the similarities, of the as-
tonishing repetitiveness—one is even tempted to say cyclical
nature—in the breakdowns in the economy and in domestic
policy is, we think, to confirm, almost beyond question, the

thesis that the country's present state stems from factors inherent in the system. These factors are not of an economic nature but rather have to do with matters that might be called ways to practice politics and wield power.

The Lack of Acceptable Compromises

The lack of acceptable compromises is also eloquently noted in the poll material. Regardless of the form chosen by the respondents, regardless of whether it is a subtle sociological analysis supported by empirical findings or simply the reflections of a sensitive, observant citizen, the general diagnosis is the same: throughout the entire postwar period we have never developed universally accepted and truly workable rules and norms to govern social life. It would be difficult at this time to point to even one area of social life in which we have been able to engineer adequate agreements or compromises in which the rules of the political game were recognized by all parties concerned. This applies to compromises outlining the framework within which goals are to be both set and implemented and to compromises accommodating the interests of different social groups or reconciling the interests of individuals with those of society.

Such acceptable compromises have been lacking on both the most general issues (e.g., attitudes concerning the way power is exercised, rules governing the distribution of national income, or how to assess the implications of Poland's geopolitical situation)[6] and more specific questions (such as attitudes toward the nation's cultural heritage, our own history, property and ownership, the legal system, work, consumption patterns, and so on).

What we have said does not mean that history has never witnessed a genuine coincidence of interests between the state and its citizens or the party and society in any of these areas. On the contrary, it has occurred innumerable times and in many essential matters. It occurred, for example, most importantly after 1956 and again after 1970, not to speak of the obvious period of postwar reconstruction. The years immediately following the political crises produced a number of decisions consonant with the interests of both the state and the nation as a whole. But even then they were, as a rule, *decisions* and not acceptable compromises. The point is all the more significant in that at least in 1956 and 1971, there existed the preconditions for establishing *principles for reaching understandings, agreements, and com-*

promises with the broadest segments of our population. As in other periods, some apt and well-thought out decisions were made. Invariably, however, they revealed three distinctive features:

   ✓—they were external to society, imposed, "forced," and not negotiated, which obviously did not make their acceptance by the general public—or at least a significant majority of it— any easier;

   ✓—the fact that they were not part of a process of reaching compromises often meant that the interests of particular groups were not taken into account sufficiently or as much as they could have been;

   ✓—the lack of compromises made it impossible to obtain the genuine support of all interested parties; what is worse, this was not conducive to creating a mechanism for public control that might have prevented subsequent inappropriate adjustments or real distortions of the original course of action.

   It is difficult to resist the impression that the disinclination to seek compromises with different segments and groups of the population has become one of the basic rules for conducting politics in our country. Such a policy has a major influence on what sociologists call the mechanism for distributing power, which in ordinary language could be defined as the principles and forms for taking part in the exercise of power. Such an influence produces habits of dependency, rather than partnership, in every sphere of public life.

   Describing the rules of the political game in our country, one of the respondents observed: "In examining the most important political decisions made over the course of the last five years, one gets the decided impression that in these decisions, criteria reflecting the interests and needs of the public were consistently passed over in favor of those dictated by the interests of the inner circles of power and of major pressure groups, regional as well as ministerial" (No. 7). Elsewhere the same respondent observes that in such important matters as work, relations between the group in power and the public, information and propaganda, and relations between producers and consumers there are conspicuous inequalities in the status of the two groupings.

   The consequences of this top-down decision-making and the failure to achieve understandings and prior agreement have necessarily been very grave as far as social change, progress in

culture and education, and the traditions of public life are concerned.

The situation is made even more serious by the fact that
the concept of regulating social relations by creating patterns of
dependency and inequality, rather than by means of compromises and consensus, has ruled out the development of mechanisms of self-regulation. It has also made it impossible to cultivate the skills of mediated agreement, and this obviously also
excluded any uncontrolled, spontaneous popular initiatives. All
these forms of social action would, of course, have contradicted
the operative principles for the exercise of power.

This lack of broad consensus on the most important issues,
the lack of mediating mechanisms and self-regulation of the system, the stifling of spontaneous popular initiatives, and finally,
a problem we have not yet mentioned—the secretiveness of
public life—all these issues were subjected to analysis in most
of the questionnaires. We have not quoted any of the individual
responses for lack of space. Many, however, will be cited elsewhere in our discussion. We would only like to point out that
most of the respondents believed the main reasons for the im-
penetrability and lack of interaction of both opposing elements
of the state lay in the ways—described above—that power was
exercised. This is clearly borne out by sociological studies which
show that today's average Pole does not consider the nation
synonymous with the state. After family and friends, for today's
Pole the nation, its history, and its present situation are most
important. The nation is a federation of families. On the other
hand, everything that exists in the gap between family and nation, the whole range of institutions operating there (political
organizations, trade unions, the civil service, etc.), elicits no sense
of identification. It is the world of "them."

Hence the question: How did this situation come about?
What lies at the root of the state of affairs we have described?

An analysis of the survey material permits at least a partial
answer to these questions. The respondents devoted particular
attention to four factors that they felt played a decisive part in
bringing about the present social, political, and economic situation.

They are:

—the interpretation we have given to the concept of the
"leading role of the party," particularly the way it has been implemented in the most important areas of public life;

——the legal system and the way it operates in practice;
——the secretiveness of public life and the associated issue
of propaganda;
      ——certain elements of social and cultural policy.
Let us but briefly examine these factors.

A Portrait of the Party

The picture of the party that emerges from the poll material
varies depending on whether the party is viewed from within or
from without. From without the party appears as an extremely   *p. 33-4*
isolated institution with its own goals, unconcerned with an understanding with the rest of society and uninterested in any
compromises that might let other groups share in wielding power.

The situation described above stems from the period when
the model of the party adopted in our country was forged; it
was a time of bitter struggle for power, and the party had only
one aim: to maintain and consolidate power. Perhaps the adoption of such a model was understandable then. However, this
model, aimed at domination rather than cooperation, intent on
monopolizing every decision in every domain of life, and mistrustful of any sort of control from without (and from within
the party itself, for that matter), has survived and endured. Perhaps, as some of the respondents suggest, it endured because it
fit the view of the way power should be exercised that the Polish
ruling groups had borrowed from their counterparts in neighbor-
ing countries without any regard for cultural differences or differences in political usages between, for example, Russians and
Poles or Germans and Poles. If these differences are ignored,
then, of course, by waiting long enough, crushing the opposition, and bending and manipulating historical consciousness and
education, the model will become a reality in Poland as well.
This presumably explains the tendency to shy away from any
step that to the public eye might signify democracy or liberalization.

On the other hand, the picture of the party from within is
quite different. It appears as a highly differentiated organization in which the persuasive power of ideological arguments is
considerably diminished, and the internal machinery suffers
from the same ailments as the society at large. From within we
see groups with varying interests, important distinctions among
the various categories of party members in terms of status and

access to power, and a tendency to concentrate a maximum of power in a narrowly defined, centrally situated group. Furthermore, the apparatus is highly bureaucratized and lacks democratic mechanisms for reaching compromises on both urgent matters and those that are less important.

One of the respondents (No. 39), however, pointed out the paradoxical fact that internal differentiation and the weakening or even outright eclipse of ideological arguments as motivations not only have not reduced the divisions between party and society but, on the contrary, have reinforced them. However, the paradox is only apparent: as ideological motives waned, power itself and its attendant benefits became the overriding motivation. Conflicts within the party grew more acrimonious—presumably a trait of any one-party system, especially if there are no mechanisms for delegating authority. When the existence of rival groups in the party is kept hidden, their actions inevitably begin to resemble clique behavior, while the legitimate work that needs to be done in the economy, culture, social life, and other areas recedes into the background, giving way to the most basic criterion of all, namely, how useful is any effort to the rival party groups for strengthening their own positions.

Under such circumstances these rival groups have no interest in lowering the barriers that separate the party and society. Indeed, this would mean making public the machinations we have described, which would have all sorts of hard to predict results.

Our description of the situation has necessarily been simplified, and it might even contain some exaggerations. However, these points were described many times by the respondents. They note that many extremely important decisions have been made not on the basis of real needs related to the building of a socialist society, but as a result of a momentary constellation of forces or the purely egotistical interests of particular groups within the party. This explains why some of the respondents so forcefully urged democratization of the party itself. They also mentioned the continued existence of the peculiar way of making decisions that one respondent called "negative compromise." He defined it as "reaching a compromise below the threshold at which any of the groups taking part in the transaction could sustain interest and identification." It is a principle that in the majority of conflicts between various groups within the party, makes reaching a compromise in which basically all the rival groups lose as far as the merits of the case are concerned "pay off." It is a compromise in which the most crucial objectives, those of substance, are abandoned in favor of maintaining tactical positions that are decisive for the odds in the power game. This principle of compromise seems to have become endemic; it rears its head wherever and whenever a decision is made, both within the party and outside it. An example is the fate of the educational reform;[7] a compromise was reached at a level at which none of the interested groups, neither teachers, nor the school administration, nor industry, nor parents, nor the pupils themselves, could hope to achieve satisfaction. And no one today has any interest in carrying out this reform. Similar examples are furnished by economic reforms in which a bold initial conception is so eviscerated in the course of reaching one of these "negative compromises" that attaining the basic objective, i.e., what the reforms were intended for in the first place, becomes an impossibility.

In the opinion of many of the respondents, the various "hidden principles and priorities," the gulf between the party and society, the absence of any cross-fertilization of ideas, values, and aspirations, the lack of established practices for seeking and reaching compromises on shared values and goals—all these things have had an injurious effect on the functioning of both the party and society. However, the tendency of the party to impose its decisions, its inclination to dominate, has clashed with deeply rooted values in our society, above all, with centuries of Polish republican tradition. As one of the respondents (No. 8) put it: "Poles have never in the course of history accepted a model of submission."

As a consequence, as most of the respondents believe, society has ceased being guided, and the central leadership, despite the semblance of unlimited possibilities, in reality has no effective way to wield power.

A Portrait of Law

One could point out any number of important reasons why the rule of law is one of the most essential conditions for the existence of viable social relations in our country. It is so because a sense of justice is so deeply engrained in public consciousness (although this may not always be so apparent in our daily life). Any infringements in this area are immediately recognized and judged very severely. The weight attached to these matters also derives from certain specific features of our system. In a one-party system, where the interests of many groups and individuals cannot be represented or defended, a legal system enjoying public confidence has an especially vital role to play. Finally, law is important because the state, which functions at once as legislator, administrator, and employer, has become such a strong partner (at least as the public sees it) that only a truly independent system of general and administrative justice could prevent a festering sense of inequality and even danger among the citizenry.

These circumstances lend dramatic significance to the fact that most of the respondents, as well as many sociological studies, put the problem of the deepening crisis in the rule of law in first place.

The nationwide studies conducted by Borucka and Arctowa on the legal consciousness of Polish society are particularly informative. These studies tell us that only 73.5 percent of the population believe that all people receive equal treatment under the laws of the land. A total of 10.9 percent of people with higher education, 18.2 percent of farm workers, 19.6 percent of unskilled workers, and 14 percent of white-collar workers with secondary education do not believe that the law is equal for all. A mere 52.6 percent of the population think that everyone has an equal opportunity to bring their personal affairs before the courts, and only 56.7 percent think that everyone receives equal treatment in our courts. Furthermore, and what is perhaps most important, the studies revealed a stereotyped image, quite deeply rooted in our society, of people who enjoy immunity before the law. In the opinion of those surveyed, they are people with higher education, status, connections, and money.

In a society with very deep class differences, and ruled with no regard for laws, these findings would be understandable; but only then. The fact that they come from recent studies conducted in our country shows that many people in our society feel that flagrant violations of the standards of social justice occur regularly in our country.

One of the respondents put it this way: "It is difficult to avoid the impression that the law has in many cases begun to play a quasi-class role in our country. It serves to maintain privileges and inequality, and it is an instrument for dictating by groups and individuals, dictating whose objective is uncontrolled power exercised for the sake of egotistical gain."

Many of the respondents intimate in various ways that the law is bent to suit momentary ends; they point out examples from tax policy or the practice of expropriations; the authorities do not feel themselves bound by the laws that they themselves have passed. Such attitudes toward law have spread throughout the entire ruling apparatus, as a result of which, twisting and breaking the law have penetrated to the very lowest levels of local politics, and in the process have caused a wholesale undermining of all confidence in the authorities.

Treatment of the law as a tool of political expediency or to serve the momentary ends of a multitude of interest groups has perverted both the making and the application of the law in many ways; it causes grave disturbances in every area of life where law is, or should be, a regulatory force.

Law-making is flawed by disorder and arbitrariness on a vast scale. The criteria for judging what is law and what is not have become blurred. There are no controls to determine whether administrative rules and regulations conform with statutory laws. Regulations violating one of the oldest legal principles, namely, that the law shall not be retroactive, are commonplace. And there are regulations that contradict other regulations, as well as some simply comical ones that interfere in the pettiest of people's private affairs, even those that clearly should not be subject to regulation. This has ceased to surprise anyone. "In the public mind," writes one of the respondents (No. 15), "the distinction between an ever growing number of often mutually contradictory rules and regulations issued by miscellaneous institutions and the law, i.e., legislation enacted by law-making bodies, has been lost. The growing multitude of rules and prescriptions is deemed to carry the force of law, whereas in the majority of cases they are no more than arbitrary decisions, despite the fact that the essence of any legal order is precisely to restrain arbitrariness."

The situation is much more serious with regard to the application of the law, especially with regard to the administration of justice and the independence of the courts.

Information reaches the public from time to time about manipulation in the administration of justice in violation of the principles of legality. Characteristically, although we have for years ranked among those countries in which political show-trials have been almost nonexistent, we have not made this into an iron rule. As one of the respondents described it (No. 13), "although in general the practice of false witnesses and faked evidence has been abandoned, this has never been made a principle brooking no exceptions. As the trials in Radom and Ursus[8] have shown, the possibility of a recrudescence of such practices still exists, however much we have experienced the harmful effects of such regressions." The Hankus versus Petrys[9] case a few years ago demonstrated in an almost clinical way all the faults in our system of administration of justice. This was not only because during the trial, which lasted several years, every rule of material and procedural law, as well as every elementary principle of justice and even decency, was violated. It was also because, as it turned out, the machinery of justice, once set into motion at the lowest rung, could not be contained; there were individuals who contrived (it is unclear how) to obtain verdicts that were contrary to the law at the first judicial level. Furthermore, they were able to exert influence—again, by what means is unknown—throughout the entire process of appeal, up to and including the Supreme Court. It was particularly depressing that justice was achieved only after an extraordinary *second* review, which was contrary to existing penal procedure.

Such "corrections" of unjust administrative decisions, and sometimes even court verdicts—to be sure, in the name of justice, but nonetheless by extralegal means—are not at all rare. Justice is served in the particular case, but at the price of a further lowering of general respect for the law.

These are only a few examples demonstrating erosion of the rule of law. We could provide an endless list, ranging from coverups by the most varied methods to flagrant violations of the law, instances of disregard for the law, illegal privileges like the infamous "R" stickers[10] entitling people to break traffic laws, and the existence of a secret law (unpublished regulations).

In our country we are experiencing a paradoxical and disturbing situation in which it is difficult to say who is actually in control of legislative and quasi-legislative activity, or who is in control of applying the law. No one is doing it, at least in accordance with clear-cut and universally valid rules.

✓This way of "playing politics" in the realm of the law ultimately does grave harm. It produces such absurdities as a Supreme Chamber of Control,[11] subordinate to the very government it is supposed to control, or the deterioration in workers' status in the new labor code,[12] which is a regression in comparison with the 1928 code. Both may have been expedient for someone at the time, indeed genuinely so. But the effect of this expediency was in the first case to create impunity for persons who are remiss in their duties and the squandering of public resources by government agencies, and in the second case, an increase in social tensions and a sharpening of antagonisms in labor relations. ✓

Or to take another example: housing cooperatives.[13] Here, in a frivolous and totally irresponsible manner, respect for the law was destroyed for millions of young people simply to cover up the crisis in construction, thus making cooperative agreements into worthless pieces of paper.

A typical quotation from one of the respondents (No. 39) will illustrate the point: "Abandonment of the principle of fair play in relations between the authorities and the citizenry, and even between different groups within the authorities themselves, has deprived those in power of the opportunity to acquire any real purchase on economic and social conditions and has produced in our citizens an ever present feeling of apprehension. People are thus led to defend their rights by any means, legal or illegal, moral or immoral, and to neglect their duties. The scars this has left on the minds of more than one generation are hard to remove."

The situation with regard to the realm of law and order has had an especially deep impact on moral attitudes in our society. This is a recurrent theme in most of the responses. The respondents note the damage that has been done, damage difficult to repair, and the broad erosion of moral standards. Furthermore, they point out that the public has developed the fixed and dangerous idea that moral and legal principles can be flaunted and violated in all fields and in various ways. People believe that the chance to do this sort of thing depends on having a hand in the exercise of power, having "access to power,"—or to put it more bluntly, on corruption. The studies by A. Tymowski are a case in point: he shows that it is commonly believed that violation of the law and the rules of morality is a mass phenomenon.

"Corruption entails economic losses the extent of which no one can assess; but whatever their scope, the havoc they wreak in the minds of the population is certainly greater. It is the general belief that everyone is 'on the take'—an official for his signature, a doctor to get hospital treatment for a patient, a professor for admission to school. There is of course some exaggeration in this general view, but it must be accepted as a fact of social pathology. All of us know that it has some basis in existing realities" (respondent No. 20).

Tymowski's studies show that more and more, immoral and even outright criminal conduct is not even regarded as objectionable. This applies in equal degree to areas such as attitudes toward work, respect for public property, and the ethical codes of the various professions. Furthermore, Tymowski's study shows that the main argument people use to justify their own conduct contrary to law and morality is that those in power misuse it for their own ends; the system of acknowledged and concealed privileges for certain social groups is also pointed out. There is today a very strong tendency toward "evening things out": since some people get certain advantages from their privileges, it is natural for others to want similar privileges for themselves, even though they must get them by breaking the law.

To sum up the opinions about the situation with regard to the law and morality, everyone agreed that this way of treating the law:

——has been of no benefit in the exercise of power; on the contrary, it has in a very fundamental way reduced opportunities to effectively wield power in every area, from the economy to local administration to the administration of justice;

——has thoroughly undermined public trust in and respect for the authorities;

——has given rise to asocial attitudes among broad segments of the population.

Openness and Information

The openness of public life, or rather the absence of such openness, is one of the most frequent topics of conversation in many quarters throughout the country. The issue does not stop with censorship, although undoubtedly the Main Office for Control of the Press, Publications, and Performances has become a symbol of secretiveness in public life. The issue is broader. It really concerns the fact that a vast proportion of the information necessary for someone to form any sort of opinion on the functioning of the state and its agencies, on the state of the economy and social processes, on domestic and foreign policy, or on worldwide political and economic changes is not available to the public. Indeed, this is an understatement. Much of this information does not even get to those persons and institutions which, by virtue of their position and function, should have access to it, since it is indispensable for their work and the performance of their duties. Many statistical data never get beyond the Main Statistical Office, even though this information is indispensable to thousands of persons, including those governing the country, if their work is to make any sense and their decisions are to have any bearing on the real, not an imaginary, world.

"Thirty-four years ago the Polish people were declared the collective proprietors of banks, factories, railroads, state farms, and all state property. However, it is a peculiar sort of proprietor who has no one of whom he can inquire about the state of his own assets and holdings, who cannot make his administrators give an account of their stewardship. The Polish people are a proprietor who does not know and does not have the right to know whom and how much it owes nor what it is owed and from whom.

"Rumor has it that early this year, representatives of a Western bank consortium came to Warsaw to arrange the refinancing of the Polish public debt. On this occasion one could read in certain Western papers information, supposedly furnished by the Polish government, on the size of the debt (stated only in convertible currencies, translatable into dollars). Yet nowhere *inside* the country had any data been published on the Polish debt. If indeed this story is true, we can formulate a new definition of the concept of state secrets: 'State secrets are information concerning the state of our country that the entire world is entitled to know, with the exception of the Polish people themselves.' "

We have quoted only a fragment of a response completely devoted to the problem of openness in public life (No. 33). The case of the loan would be amusing if it were not true that until recently no one actually knew these figures. But a few years ago, even those persons who arranged purchases of licenses and machinery, those who spent this borrowed money, did not know the figures . . .

"The belief is quite widespread," we read in questionnaire No. 18, "that flagrant mistakes in the steering of social processes and the management of economic life are made simply out of incompetence, lack of qualifications, and the ineptitude of people involved in making decisions. In fact the matter is far more serious: the system of information in its present form, which mystifies an accurate picture of reality, ensures that the fundamental premises for any decision are mistaken. The whole system can be seen as a gigantic plot meant to compromise the authorities, undermine confidence in them, and encourage attitudes of opposition and rebellion. In reality this complex apparatus is guided by its own goals, which lie with the interests of groups that have a stake in providing misinformation and eroding the entire system of social cooperation."

But obviously information is not only necessary to make proper decisions. It is the basic material out of which each citizen shapes his own views. Without it there can be no public opinion, and without it no citizen in our country can feel himself a full-fledged citizen bearing his own share of responsibility. Let us return to respondent No. 33; the following passage perhaps captures most accurately the essence of everything our respondents had to say on this matter:

"The system of almost total secretiveness in the public domain, the domain which by virtue of its very name and definition should be the most open, is responsible for the indifference among the majority of the so-called citizens of the so-called Republic toward almost everything that has to do with the state politically and economically. The effects of politics and economic policies we experience literally every day, but we feel ourselves left out of the decision-making processes, not only as active subjects but even as mere observers. We are left out and hence cut off from responsibility. A Polish citizen experiences the meanderings of politics and planning more or less as he experiences changes in the weather: as important changes he must adapt to but whose causes——wholly external——are not worth exploring more deeply, since he has no way of influencing them. . . ."

What is more, this system has created something that is more dangerous than indifference and cynicism, something that surely was not intened: it has created a state of collective *informational* psychosis. One week a couple of fires break out in a capital city of one and a half million people:[14] well then, some mysterious arsonist must be on the prowl! Perhaps it is a sign of a power struggle! Posters are put up——as they are every year—— announcing a call-up for military service: well then, it must be a general mobilization; they are sending our boys to Vietnam! Or what about the explosion in the General Savings Bank at the Rotunda?[15] Obviously a time bomb, dynamite, sabotage, a provocation.

It was not the explosion in the Rotunda but rather the public reaction to it that ought to serve as a warning to our authorities. . . . People who for decades have not been informed, or who have been misinformed, about the critical issues facing our country, people who see only the results of actions taken by the leadership (and to see them it is enough today just to walk into a shop), but who know neither the motives nor the reasons for those actions, have a reflex reaction to every piece of news: "They can't fool us!" If they cannot determine how many people died in Poland in last winter's storms[16] (although they know how many in the Federal Republic of Germany), then why should they believe that exactly forty-eight people died at the Polish Savings Bank, and not, for example, three times as many? If the real machinery of politics remains hidden, then people will look for a secret mechanism, somebody's invisible hand behind every event. Poles have ceased believing in coincidences and have also ceased believing, it seems, in the possibility of spontaneous acts, that is, social action undertaken by someone out of his own genuine conviction. Anytime anyone says or does anything, we try to find out what spectre is lurking in the shadows, who is doing the manipulating, provoking, paying out rubles or dollars, who is giving advice, who is pulling the strings. "They can't fool us!" That gas explosion is suspicious. Every accident is suspicious, every catastrophe. Any article is suspect. Any letter. The government is suspect, and so is the "opposition." Every act and every plan of action is suspicious.

No, this is not even understandable skepticism. It is naive credulity in reverse. People who trust no one and believe nothing will tomorrow accept the most improbable rumors and trust the first clever demagogue who comes along. A society that has no trustworthy political figure can easily become, in times of crisis and panic, an unpredictable society, a "blind force."

This brings us to some matters very closely linked to propaganda policies in our country. Propaganda is guided in its activities primarily by the principle of secretiveness in public life, and it carries that principle almost to the point of absurdity. Not only does it hush up, it consciously misinforms. It creates an image of the world with no concern at all for how that image fits reality. It propagates a mythology of success in situations of deep crisis, talks about enthusiasm where a state of apathy reigns supreme. In other words, it maximizes the distance between reality and the way it presents that reality, not realizing that in doing so it serves only to deepen each crisis. We will return to these matters later in our discussion.

Some Remarks

Social and cultural policy are taken up more broadly in other parts of this discussion. Here we would just like to call attention to a few matters that evidently are particularly symptomatic of the preferred ways of practicing politics in our country.

On cultural policy

In recent years a highly disturbing tendency to manipulate culture has appeared at the same time as real cultural needs have been neglected. This has considerably sharpened the conflict with creative circles and led to a recurrence of the situation at the end of the '60s, when many of our most outstanding creative figures simply withdrew from the cultural life of the country.[17] There has been a return to practices that preclude the possibility of creative figures acting as partners, as subjects in public life. Protest against such a policy and you run the risk of finding yourself on the list of cultural undesirables, which first bars access to the mass media and then often makes it generally impossible to practice one's profession.

The effect of the current situation is growing apathy and "a progressive disintegration of intellectual and creative circles. Creative circles have been stricken with a feeling of impotency, that they have no influence on the profound social changes that are taking place" (No. 30). These attitudes are intensified by the overall situation in our culture (small editions of valuable books; books that cannot be published at all because of their contents or their authors; films that are suppressed in the process of their being made, including excellent documentary films that could play a major role in shaping public opinion and stimulating discussions about vital current topics). The free exchange of views is blocked—states respondent No. 30—making continuity and accumulation of experience and the confrontation of views impossible. A situation has come about in which, on the one hand, a genuine need for participation in culture has been awakened in us (truly one of the major accomplishments of the past thirty-five years)—we do indeed have talented artists. On the other hand, there is a tendency toward manipulation, replacing genuine participation in cultural life with fictitious spectacles that are for the most part stage-managed galas made up mainly of preludes, talks, banquets, reports—in other words, "ceremonies."

On social policy

We come now to the question of *social policy*. Reports from so-

ciological studies on attitudes and problems in matters of law
and morality, as well as some of the responses, indicate that a
rather alarming tendency has arisen in the way material incentives
are understood and used. Material advantages in the form of
money itself or as open or, more often, hidden privileges have
become an essential element in political life. They can be seen
everywhere in the form of epidemic unjustified payments, especially in large enterprises. The impression is created that every
means of mediating employee conflicts has been abandoned in
favor of money, which is quite simply used to buy temporary
peace. The result is disorganization throughout the economy,
accelerated inflation, and what is worse, lack of respect for work.
This problem——respect for work——is specifically addressed by
many of the respondents. It is paradoxical that precisely in a socialist system, where work, any work, should enjoy universal respect, work has become generally debased. The attitude toward
work that sees it solely in terms of monetary rewards has even
further intensified this process.

At the same time, money and the system of privileges have
become the preferred means for exercising power, in the literal
sense. One of the respondents (No. 27) even asserts that these
conditions have given birth to a group of individuals who have a
direct interest in seeing that an ailing economy and unhealthy
social relations remain untouched. It is a group that by virtue of
the functions it performs, "has access to a second economy[18] for
procuring supplies, housing, health services, and scarce goods."
In other words, it is a group whose loyalty is quite simply
bought. Yet their's is only a specious loyalty, since it amounts
to just one function——direct help in maintaining power. It certainly does not include participation in activities that might restore health to the country's social and economic situation——
that would be contrary to the interests of the group. It is evident from this that the central authorities, by tolerating this situation and continuing to treat money and privilege as an important element in the practice of politics, diminish further their
own chances to influence the country's future posture, to say
nothing of the fact that the practices we have described are sure
to lead to serious divisions in society, to tensions and conflicts,
and to grave violations of the principles of social justice.

The Price We Pay

Genuine principles for the practice of politics and the exercise of power, legal institutions that work, and a broadly conceived social and cultural policy are matters of paramount concern for all of society. Similarly, for society to function properly, public life must be open, and there must exist clear rules accepted by the majority of the citizenry.

Let us quote respondent No. 39 on the consequences of this situation: "The choice of just this interpretation of 'the leading role of the party' and the abandonment of any attempt to draw broad segments of the population into sharing in the exercise of power are tantamount to forfeiting real leadership that derives its legitimacy from the support of society at large. It appears that the party has consciously accepted this price.

"The abandonment of any effort to negotiate an understanding with society about the consequences of our economic situation, our interests as a nation, and the interests of our allies has made it impossible for the leadership of the state to forge healthy relations with our neighbors. And the leadership has decided to pay that price.

"The price we have paid for the absence of the rule of law has been the grave demoralization of a large part of society, the unbridled spread of corruption, and the impossibility of using the law for social mediation and managing the economy. This price, too, was paid.

"The abandonment of compromise as a way to arrive at principles acceptable to the majority for distributing social income has led to further social divisions (as demonstrated in innumerable sociological studies) and to, not so much the violation of the principles of egalitarianism, as the abandonment of social justice altogether. Furthermore, it has led to the spread of conspicuous consumption and the emergence of numerous groups of individuals who have a vested interest in keeping the economy in ill health, since only that lets them make huge profits, usually illegal. All this threatens major social conflicts or even an uncontrolled explosion. This price, too, has been accepted.

"The refusal to allow representatives of rural Poland to participate on an equal footing in setting agricultural policy has led to recurrent crises in agriculture and a severe food crisis. Here, too, the price was paid.

"The rejection of clearly defined rules for making economic decisions and for letting the public review and oversee these decisions has led to a paradoxical situation: shady pressure groups (regional or institutional) are able to push through decisions advantageous to themselves for which they cannot be called to

account, no matter how great the harm done to society by
those decisions. Investment and wage policies are good examples. In such a situation management of the economy is a
practical impossibility. Here too, however, the price was paid.

"Then comes 1976. No attempt was made to bring to account the people responsible for the decision to raise prices.[19]
It was obvious that a large segment of society saw it as a breach
of the understandings of 1971. It was equally obvious that this
breach would have grave consequences, if only in the form of
society's withdrawal of cooperation and turning a deaf ear to
any appeal for help. Nevertheless, this price was paid."

This list could be continued, noting other areas of life in
which we are paying a tremendous price for the way politics
is conducted. The poll participants say that because there are no
mediating mechanisms, serious social conflicts will often end in
uncontrolled eruptions of discontent. The economic consequences of the system's lack of self-regulating mechanisms are
pointed out; attention is called to the spread of sham and facade
throughout all spheres of life, which one of the respondents describes as follows (No. 32): "So we have sham planning and
sham fulfillment and even overfulfillment of plans, sham
achievements in industry, science, culture, and education, sham
legislation, and sham performance of duties, a sham show of
concern for the social good and sham government, sham socialism and social works, sham voting and elections, sham morality,
sham modernity and progress, the opening of supposedly complete factories and social facilities with great fanfare, sham struggle against social evils and sham claims of a contented citizenry,
sham freedom of conviction, and sham justice, and so on. Playing this game of pretence and sham has become so universal that
no one, not even at the highest levels of power, can distinguish
any longer between what is real and what is not. The objective
indicators are either totally false or too fragmentary, and they
do not provide an adequate picture of the real situation in society and the state. Under such conditions making a decision is a
purely random matter, based on no sound method nor a knowledge of realities. Even an empirical verification of the results of
actions, the drawing of concrete conclusions from successful or
unsuccessful actions, has become impossible."

One of the most important consequences of this situation
is the fact that cyclical social crises have become an accepted
phenomenon in practical political life——their inevitability goes
unquestioned. For the third time in the past twenty-five years,

events seem to be taking the same turn: eruptions of discontent, changes in the government team, temporary liberalization, another eruption of discontent, another change in the governing team, and so on.

The situation is all the more dangerous in that any such eruption of discontent can degenerate into a national tragedy. So far we have been able to avoid such a tragedy, thanks mainly to the deep sense of responsibility of our society and our citizens, but also because the tensions between the apparatus of power (particularly the secret police and the military) and society have never passed the critical point. In 1956 the conflict between the police apparatus and society was smoothed over by the changes that occurred in the police in 1954 and 1955. The 1968 conflict had already petered out in many respects by 1970;[20] however, that conflict had mainly economic roots. The current situation is more complicated—one has only to think of the aftermath of 1976—and the tensions go deeper. All the more reason therefore that we cannot afford social warfare. But avoiding conflict depends not only on the public and society but also—and above all—on the authorities.

* * *

In this part of our discussion we have taken up some of the principles governing the practice of politics and the exercise of power in our country. Later we will return to many of the problems touched on here. At this point we would like to call attention to another of the respondents' viewpoints—none of the aforementioned "principles" is essential to strengthen the state and society.

And no ideological considerations justify the political practices we have discussed. Most "principles" that have been subjected to critical analysis have at one time or another—after one of the recurrent crises—been a subject of public discussion and have been among the issues the party has declared itself willing to negotiate.

In 1956 the list of negotiable issues put forward by Gomulka included:

—redefinition of the alliance with the USSR;

—democratic relations within the party;

—the initiation of a broad dialogue with society at large;

—increased participation by society in government (the Sejm, workers' councils, etc.).

In 1971 the list of new principles of public life included:

——abolition of privileges and discrimination (directed to party members and nonmembers, the religious and nonreligious);

——the elimination of poverty (the problem of extremely low wages and retirement pensions);

——a different attitude toward national culture and history (reform of education, the rebuilding of the Royal Palace in Warsaw, etc.);

——increased participation by the public (especially the workers) in running the government;

——greater democracy within the party;

——an open cultural policy (initiation of a dialogue with creative circles).

We should add that both in 1966 and in 1971, society eagerly accepted the proposed settlement. It was no fault of the public that the party proposal did not play the role that it should and could have played. Be that as it may, the important thing is that never again should such a situation——or even its mere possibility——be permitted to occur.

CHAPTER 2

Structures and Mechanisms
in the System

The philosophy underlying the practice of politics in our country, which was outlined in the preceding chapter, has its logical counterpart in the structures and mechanisms of the system of power and the institutions of public life.

Since Poland after World War II neither could nor wanted to mechanically adopt the pattern of a parliamentary republic, nor was it able to fashion its own system for running government, the system of power was in the end shaped by a process of trial and error. At most it adapted the institutions and assimilated the experiences of the similarly shaped system of power in the Soviet Union, which, however, had developed out of other traditions and in other circumstances. Thus the "system of power in Poland, requiring above all legitimacy, as do many revolutionary powers, deprived itself of the chance to analyze its own performance," observes respondent No. 36. "As a result we had to deal with a series of tendencies, ideas, and successive attempts at makeshift remedies, which time and again did more harm than good. Even today we still have no coherent theoretical model for a system of power toward which the successive reforms might have worked. Even though the reform of the local administrations in 1975 might have been justified in practical terms, it was later interpreted as a political maneuver. . . ."[21]

Respondent No. 46 described the operative system of power in Poland in this way:

"The exercise of political and economic power is based on a centralized administrative, party, and government apparatus with a series of appended facades in the form of the Sejm and the local people's councils, which are dominated by the administration. . . . The integrating link in the bureaucracy of power is the party, which runs the state and pervades all levels of its or-

ganization, but is, however, not able to overcome or even consistently check any dualism created by the existence of these
two interpenetrating apparatuses: the party and the government
(the state). Competition between these apparatuses, despite the
fact that a number of leading posts in both are occupied by the
same people, is thus a certain guarantee of steady disintegration,
although its intensity may vary. At the same time, the increasingly blurred distinction between the functions of the party and
the functions of the government administration and of other
agencies of the state, the party's obvious abandonment of its
functions of supervision and control over ongoing governmental
and administrative affairs——all these things have contributed to
a conceptual confusion within the apparatus of power and a
contempt for law both within the party and by the public, and
hence to the abandonment of statutory procedures and general
methods for the exercise of power in favor of makeshift, ad hoc,
and uncoordinated instructions."

How the Authorities Function

It is commonly believed that there is an omnipotent group of
individuals who rule the party; but respondent No. 41 describes
it as a "group that is under the impression that it is exercising
power." At the first plenary meeting of the "Experience and
the Future" group, one of the participants in the discussion
graphically described how decisions that the ruling group within
the party considers its "own" and for which it assumes responsibility were manipulated by interest groups within the power
apparatus. Even the expert opinions provided the ruling group
did not come from an independent consultant; rather, close ad-
visors and associates of members of the ruling group skillfully
channeled the inflow of information and opinions. Respondent
No. 34 writes: "In the real social and economic world there is
no such thing as a 'central planner.' Rather there is heteroge-
neous collection of central institutions using a wide range of different standards to arrive at their decisions. We know very little
about how the center operates, about how it drafts and adopts
macroeconomic decisions. What we do know is based on the external and more ceremonial forms of the activities of various
central institutions and, of course, on the results of these actions. But we still do not know where the initiatives come from
for specific macroeconomic planning decisions; what kind of

role is played in them by specific offices in the center; what is the scope of the rights and responsibilities of these offices in shaping these decisions; whether decisions are made after an analysis and rejection of alternative solutions, or whether only one version is examined; who is in charge of checking the internal consistency of that version; whether anyone is aware of the inevitable tensions a decision will produce; who decided and on what grounds that it was a good idea to subject the economy to any strains; through what channels and after how much delay information reaches the center, alerting it to growing disproportions in the development of the economy; why it takes just so much and not some other length of time for the center to decide to revise a plan; to what extent decisions about plan revision help clear up problems entailed in the original decisions, and so on. Not only the average citizen but even many professional economists and economic policy-makers cannot answer these questions."

Let us continue the same respondent's answer: "The issue of the importance of relations within the center for the proper functioning of the system was officially raised in Poland after the political upheavals in 1956 and 1970. At the February 1971 meeting of the Central Committee of the United Workers' Party, it was even explicitly stated that a more clearly defined delimitation of powers between the leadership of the party, the government, and the Sejm had to be introduced. A special party-government committee was created to overhaul the economy. All this was forgotten, although the matter is no less urgent today than then.

"There are two conclusions to be drawn from this. First, seen from both outside and inside the center, there is a glaring lack of a clear delimitation of rights, duties, and responsibilities of the various offices of the center. Second, these shortcomings are officially brought into the open only under the pressure of conflicts between the authorities and society. And almost immediately after the conflicts have been resolved, the whole matter is pushed aside. This in turn means that the center is unwilling or unable to keep its own internal relations in order. It is probably both.

"This unwillingness to alter the status quo is not difficult to understand. Any sort of regulation of the division of powers would lead either to a partial curtailment of the authority of those offices that are the most powerful, or to the formal exclusion from responsibility of those other offices that are not so powerful, something that would not suit the leading offices. This brings us to the second characteristic feature of the center ——its hierarchical organization.

"It is not the usual kind of hierarchical structure. Its uniqueness derives from the fact that the de facto pattern of command and subordination deviates markedly from what is formally prescribed by law.

"This condition has clearly become a permanent one. The actual division of power cannot be given a formal legal status. Attempts to do so would not meet with society's approval. On the other hand, the center, endowed with overriding authority, is little inclined to agree to any limitations imposed on it by bringing the real order of things at the center into line with the order formally prescribed in law. This creates an impasse, manifested in the entrenchment of a dual order——the party and the state.

"The discrepancy between the real and the formal division of power at the center varies. It is greater the less the center performs its nominal functions. The gaps that arise are filled by sham and ceremony. Indeed, an increase in the latter may serve as a good indicator of the extent to which institutions do not perform the tasks they are formally assigned."

A corollary of what has been described is the common, although little noted and analyzed, practice of cultivating personal relationships between people holding positions at various levels of power.

There is a constant flow of personnel among posts in the political, managerial, and administrative apparatuses——the same person may either alternately, or at the same time, hold posts in all of these structures. Sixty percent of managing directors of enterprises are members of the party hierarchy. Often posts at the various levels of power are filled on the basis of informal group relations among colleagues. Entry to or a fall from the power apparatus depends on whether some such group, in which one member protects another, is able to hold its ground.

"Relations between the party apparatus and the economic administration are formed in such a way that the party apparatus, where power resides, exercises this power through recommendations and directives ranging from the political to the personal (patronage, favors, jobs, etc.); yet it has to defend the actions of its subordinates, who therefore have developed impressive skill in manipulating their superiors, using them as "covers" or "battering rams" to clear the way for their projects. This is not a value judgment. People whose roles are interdependent have to get along with each other," notes respondent No. 37.

The relationships in this setup are not defined by any practical requirements; they depend on the attitudes, positions, and influence of the parties involved.

Some of our respondents noted that the executive has a tendency to grow. Respondent No. 36 describes where this could lead:

"Economic growth in the twentieth century has inevitably led to the marked preponderance of the executive branch in all systems of power. This is a consequence of growth itself: growth, indeed, implies 'tasks' that have to be performed, and not the steady grinding away of bureaucratic machinery. However, this preponderance of the executive, which in our country has reached an extreme, turns power structures into feudal systems——and not just in our country; this is now the most serious ailment besetting quite a number of huge corporations in the capitalist world.

"Consequently representative bodies in our country perform no real functions either of a representative nature or as instruments of control and supervision over executive practices. While the status of a member of the Sejm is quite 'high' as far as personal prestige goes (for instance, no minister or other central official can afford not to meet a member of the Sejm), council members are usually treated worse than provincial or local government officials. The fact that a provincial party council is chaired by the first secretary of the provincial party council[22] in no way increases the prestige of that position because the position itself does not guarantee power. His participation in council affairs is considered merely 'lip service to democracy.' Provincial and local governors[23] have obviously become formally independent of the council because they are appointed by higher administrative authorities. Even officials under provincial or local governors feel not the least sense of dependence on their councils. When it comes to manipulating the Sejm or other representative bodies, we see a total disregard for all those imponderables that are so important in Poland. When in 1976 the Sejm had to vote unanimously on two consecutive days on two completely contradictory bills,[24] it 'lost face' in a way that left no room for doubt about its true role. On the other hand, public opinion has no knowledge of the real discussions that take place among Sejm groups or about the debates in the various committees; furthermore, public opinion knows nothing about

how over the years the Sejm has systematically blocked the passage of bills that would have had socially damaging effects. That
is, however, all the Sejm can do. Even its official prerogatives
leave no room for illusions about the supplementary role it has
been assigned.''

The lastest changes in the Constitution subordinated the
Supreme Chamber of Control,[25] with its specialized functions,
to the chairman of the Council of Ministers. The record of the
Supreme Chamber of Control is not unambiguous. In the course
of its supervision of how the activities of administrators and
economic units conform to the law, the Supreme Chamber of
Control has often had to rely in its analyses on norms that were
either impractical or simply absurd. The formalism of the recommendations it makes after its enquiries have rendered many
of them useless in any practical sense. All the same, the relatively
independent functioning of the chamber has to a considerable
degree served as a brake on excesses and abuses, and in general
the chamber has gained the reputation of being an incorruptible
body not easily manipulated. The constitutional changes of
1976, about which the Polish legal profession had voiced grave
doubts, made the Supreme Chamber of Control into yet another appendage of the political authorities.

How the Law Functions

The change in the status of the Supreme Chamber of Control
was only the crowning moment in a process of eliminating all
practical controls over the administration. Respondent No. 46
puts it succinctly: ''There is a lack of judicial or any other form
of control or supervision over the legality of what the administration does and over the observance and safeguarding of the
Constitution, for instance, with regard to protecting the rights
and freedoms of the individual; a lack of any means whereby
the Sejm could exercise this control or the elimination of any
powers that it did have (the Supreme Chamber of Control being
a case in point); a lack of any of the institutions of direct democracy that have long flourished in other countries; and a lack
of an effectively functioning system for participation by organizations and individual citizens in government and the administration of state affairs, apart from the traditional and officially
recognized representative bodies.''

In the light of the lack of an effective system for monitoring the legality of administrative decisions, other methods for maintaining checks on the administration have developed: letters and complaints to the party or reports in the press, which, however, rarely go beyond the lower levels of power. When they do, they are usually ineffective.

Aside from——in the public view reprehensible——phenomena of unpunished violations of and disregard for the law, the decay in the legal system and, indeed, the lack of a legal order engender a situation in which both public opinion and the authorities themselves come to consider abuse of and disregard for the law justified. Lost in a chaos of unnecessary or poorly conceived regulations, the authorities have to tolerate the erosion in practice of these rules. This results in the general phenomenon we discussed earlier——the sense that legal requirements are relative and the habit of disregarding regulations. The view that lack of respect for the law is part of the Polish cultural heritage, dating from the period of foreign occupation when the law was made by usurpers and occupiers, is only partly borne out by studies and public opinion. If the law in Poland is not respected, it is disregarded mainly by those who make it.

Legal chaos on the one hand encourages excesses and on the other makes it necessary to involve the law enforcement apparatus where administrative and economic measures would ordinarily be sufficient. Given the lack in the economy of an effective system of controls and supervision and the lack of feedback mechanism that automatically correct any aberrations or anomalies, these functions must be assumed by law enforcement agencies. For years the public prosecutor's office in its statements and the Supreme Chamber of Control in its reports on its findings have called attention to this phenomenon, but, alas, in vain. Finally, public life in Poland has witnessed the growth of a whole area of extralegal activity by the power apparatus that is subject to no regulation (e.g., the functioning of censorship, which makes arbitrary interventions that cannot be appealed, often without even informing the author of the reasons for the intervention; moreover, the censor frequently does not decide what is to be protected by censorship; often the personal interests of prominent individuals in the power apparatus are involved).

The police apparatus is de facto subordinated at all levels to the parallel party cells. This arrangement was designed to guard against a return to a situation in which an independent political police apparatus dominated the party.[26] It has, how-

ever, in its turn given rise to manipulation of the law enforcement apparatus to meet the needs of the moment (which are
not necessarily political in nature). At the same time, the range
of activities that the law enforcement apparatus is forced to
carry out in the economic domain has been enlarged beyond
measure by the legal muddle, and as a result, the size of the police apparatus has been increased to proportions more in keeping with a police state.

Unfortunately, supervision of the police diminished
markedly after 1956. The prosecutor's offices, which were empowered to perform that supervision, are in a much weaker position today with regard to the apparatus they are supposed to
oversee, particularly the internal security service.[27] Thanks to
the lack of control over the police apparatus there has been a
growth of criminality within that apparatus itself, ranging from
the extraction of material advantages from the exercise of power (the Matejewski affair,[28] for example, or the acceptance of
bribes by the highway police), to the ever more frequent cases
of robbery and beatings committed by members of the police.
The prosecutor's office usually tries to keep itself at a distance
from these phenomena. However, events—and not only those
recorded during times of political tension, such as in 1976—
have shown how easy it is for even it to turn to oppressive measures.[29]

The agencies of public order have, for their part, never
worked out a moral code of conduct toward the public. Their
value, after all, is judged exclusively in terms of their usefulness
to the political apparatus. If one nevertheless encounters among
them attitudes that indicate respect for law and for the social
function of those exercising it, this is exclusively a product of
the good will of those involved.

The judiciary fares no better in the eyes of society. This is
partly the effect of the penal policies adopted in the seventies.
Courts began to demonstrate a consistent bias toward severe
sentences even for minor offenses, despite the fact that the
crime rate was not on the increase in Poland. This raised and
continues to raise serious doubts in the minds of many lawyers,
in whose opinion consistency in the prosecution of criminal acts
is more effective than increasing the repressive uses of the law.
In the midseventies Poland had approximately the same number
of prisoners per hundred thousand population as did the United
States, a country where crime is much more common and the
crime rate higher, sometimes much higher, than in many Euro-

pean countries, although there is nothing in the social situation in Poland that could justify such a statistic.

[The Polish judiciary, very poorly paid for many years, its various posts filled by political appointees, subject to political directives and manipulation, constantly overburdened by too much work, nonetheless does on the whole try to perform its functions in a socially worthy manner, despite the lack of satisfactory incentives.] Judges who are particularly susceptible to pressure from the party and administrative apparatus do not have a good name in their own professional circles. Unfortunately, susceptibility to those pressure has not diminished. The period of repression following the events of June 1976 showed how easy it is in Poland to return to the old system of show-trials, which in reality were political, by exerting the requisite pressure on the courts.

Despite the fact that there are for all practical purposes no political prisoners in Poland, various negative phenomena attendent on the activities of prosecutorial and judiciary bodies appear political to the public. The same applies to the shortcomings in the legal system. The right to defense in a criminal proceeding and the right of the defender to have a say in the investigation, although new and positive additions to the Polish penal code, were restricted and made dependent on a decision by the prosecutor's office, thereby depriving the suspect of adequate protection during the investigatory phase. To the public it seemed political reasons alone were responsible for this turnabout. Similar doubts have been expressed about the labor code[30] introduced in the 1970s, which, although it eliminated many of the inequalities in the rights of different occupational groups, still does not guarantee employees partnership relations with their employers.

Despite all these negative phenomena, our judicial system has not yet experienced total and open decay as a result of corruption and pressure from the political authorities. Though our respondents do not totally dismiss our judicial system, from their statements it seems clear that they feel this disintegration is obviously under way. The scale of manipulation will vary depending on the place, the time, and the circumstances, but worst of all, it has become a habit for either side, both the judges and the party, and has become such an ordinary, everyday practice that it no longer shocks anyone. The press does not even bother to conceal the fact that judges confer about implementing the recommendations of the latest party Central

Committee plenums, which leads public opinion to doubt that any regard at all is paid to the principle of the independence of the courts.

The dropping of proceedings against privileged persons, the more severe treatment of people who cannot afford professional counsel—these things have become common phenomena. To sum up: neither the prosecutorial bodies nor the judiciary perform their tasks in our country in a way that inspires public confidence that the rule of law is being observed and that the most elementary requirements of the system itself are being met.

How Interest Groups Function

Society does not tolerate a vacuum. As a result of the atrophy of effective legal mechanisms, the seventies have seen the rise to prominence (although they existed before) of various interest groups, particularly among the authorities. A typical example is the industrial lobbies that have emerged to the extent that the economic management system has fallen apart (we will discuss this in more detail later). For example, by forcing up prices on new items, the branches, combines, and individual enterprises are looking to their own interests, are seeking privileges for their work forces to buy peace and stability, are trying to get their share of scarce labor, etc. The price of all this is paid only by the customer, who in Poland does not have a lobby of his own, such as a consumer defense movement.

There is nothing wrong with the existence of industrial lobbies in themselves. They are not unique to Poland. Indeed, even the term "industrial lobby" is borrowed from abroad. However, in our country the power of a particular lobby is not determined by the real value and importance it has in the economy as a whole, but by the reigning dogma, or the current notions of the party and state leadership about what constitutes modernity and progress, or finally, by incidental personal connections. So, because of a dogma whose anachronism has been proved and even acknowledged many times over, we know in advance that certain lobbies from heavy industry or the machine-tool sector carry much greater weight than those representing light industry, the food industry, or, for instance, the pharmaceutical industry. This often has a decisive influence on the allocation of resources, including hard currencies, among these various sectors.

Sometimes the importance of a particular lobby is difficult

to assess, as in the case of the mining lobby. When the Polish coal-mining industry was going through hard times, this lobby was able to make an effective stand against pernicious tendencies that would have led to its demise.[31] On the other hand, because it is now so powerful, it is able to force the expansion of mining sites that from a technical point of view are inadequately prepared, and that from an economic point of view are often unjustified. This invariably entails taking good farmland away from the private farmer, who does not have a strong interest group of his own.

It might appear from what we have said that the problem is one of industrial lobbies and sparring between different ministries or sectors of industry. This, however, is absolutely not the case.

There are, for instance, regional lobbies that during the thirty-five years since the war, have played a quite varied role. In a number of cases they have been able to avoid implementing decisions made centrally——sometimes even to their credit, although in itself this exposes an illness of the system. Sometimes they have been able to give priority to investment projects that, again, were often truly essential for the particular region but were often equally unjustified from the point of view of the economy as a whole, or were undertaken purely for reasons of prestige.

The ruling party——the Polish United Workers' Party——like most political parties, is not a uniform interest group. Quite the contrary; because it has a monopoly on power, it is traditionally all the more prone to factional infighting between different pressure groups and interests that in turn are supported by groups outside the party and by various lobbies.

Although today the situation is less glaring than, say, in 1968, the Polish United Workers' Party is not a monolith. There are clear signs of friction and internal struggle, which we discussed in the preceding chapter.

The existence of interest groups in Poland is, as everywhere, a natural phenomenon and hence cannot be assessed unambiguously as either entirely negative or entirely positive. As we have already said, interest groups fill a certain vacuum in the legal order. They can play a variety of roles, even positive ones. But given the secretiveness of our political life, they can also constitute a grave danger.

How the Economy Functions

Our economy suffers from ailments of a very special nature.

The present situation is described by respondent No. 34: "Our 'great leap forward' in the early years of the present decade has left in its wake greater disproportions between the various sectors and branches of our economy than had existed before. This is a great burden. The resulting bottlenecks prevent us from making proper use of our expanded and considerably modernized economic potential. What is more, we have no chance to fill the existing gaps in supply by increasing our imports. Quite the opposite—the present growth in imports must be arrested. This is the result of our taking foreign loans without considering the export potential of our economy and investing these monies in branches of the economy that were import intensive. The consequence is the prospect of a long-term balance-of-payments problem. The disproportions have lowered the overall efficiency of the economy, and blatant signs of wastefulness in our economy have rampantly increased.]

"The creation of incomes bearing no relation to the scale and structure of investment has thrown the consumer market into disarray. People are irritated by the never-ending stream of hassles, which, although their importance may vary, affect the populace at every turn: in public transport, in the shops, at the workplace, and in hospitals and offices.

"Attempts by the authorities to lead the country out of the situation we have described have so far not met with success. The shift in economic program, the adoption of the celebrated 'economic maneuver,'[32] has been a failure. This is evident in the results of the economic plans, which fall far short of the targets set. The flood of erratic and makeshift recommendations and restrictions only adds to the chaos because they bear no intrinsic relationship to one another, nor indeed could they. In view of the failure of these measures, appeals for general austerity are unconvincing as a way out of our difficulties."

The crisis in economic management was evident to all the respondents. Let us quote respondent No. 16 as an illustration:

"Our system of managing the economy has failed to meet the requirements of accelerated growth. It is beyond comprehension how in a planned and centralized economy it is possible year in and year out to overfulfill the investment targets or to make unnecessary or premature purchases abroad of industrial plant and unneeded licenses—which the government reports and the press tells us about every day. It is beyond comprehension how the task of moving goods through the ports has apparently been assumed by Polish television, which, it seems, has even been able to get the local directors of the Polish State Railways and Coach Services to do the job and explain how it is done. The press constantly tells us about numerous absurdities—easily dealt with—after which everything remains unchanged . . .

"Top-level administrators in the various branches of the economy have ceased, so it seems, to react to external incentives and appear incapable of amending their own decisions."

"Practically all the elements in our system of management are ailing," writes respondent No. 36. "Planning has ceased to deserve the name of planning, coordination has become impossible, while any check on performance is a total illusion."

This diagnosis is seconded by respondent No. 4, who points out the curious phenomenon of chaos spreading automatically:

"Our system of management is highly bureaucratized. It has an inherent tendency to create monopolies that are then able, by constantly raising prices, to meet plan targets without a real increase in production, without bringing their product mix into line with the needs of the consumer market, or finally, without any improvement in quality. This system has not been reformed. The reform that involved the creation of so-called Large Economic Units[33] was so bungled that it is not even possible to assess its results.

"On the other hand, any reorganization that does take place is carried out in a totally arbitrary manner. For instance, a couple of years ago small-scale manufacturing was abolished, and local enterprises were joined to production associations[34] in key industries, only to rediscover later the need for small industry. With a nonchalance that disregards all existing statutes and common sense, every now and then the cooperative movement is reorganized."

The only medicine that our system of management was able to find for the inadequacies of our economy has no effect on that system itself (the "innocence" of the system, as respondent No. 37 puts it). This medicine is of two kinds, as respondents No. 42 and No. 43 describe it:

"The first consists of appeals, slogans, exhortations, which as practice shows are largely fruitless and cannot assure any consistency of action. An example is the catchy slogan stressing production for the consumer market. But it is to be done at the expense of other branches, disrupting cooperation between enterprises as well as investment policy; ultimately, instead of increasing consumer goods production, it often contributes to its decline.

"Second, the development of a system that introduces detailed norms and regulations everywhere and demands that they be observed with total rigor. The hitch is, however, that a modern economy has become much too complicated to be managed by a vast number of detailed orders and instructions issued by a single central authority. The experience of history[35] teaches us that under certain circumstances, it may indeed be possible by means of commands and discipline to wring out high production growth rates in particular sectors (e.g., by priority allocations); however, high quality, so essential to our exports, cannot be forced."

"The methods in use at the moment are weak and ineffective," writes respondent No. 24, "because they only touch the surface. It is like treating only the symptoms of an illness without attacking its underlying causes. The method of preparing and making important economic decisions is the same as the one that led to the present difficulties. Furthermore, the system for translating economic policy into action programs for individual enterprises has undergone no change. We still have the system, which has been long and almost universally criticized, of administrative management of the economy. Despite the economic and financial ornaments with which that system has been adorned, it has in fact not lost its basically administrative character."

Respondent No. 36 attributes these tendencies to what he calls the "directorial mentality" of national economic managers:

"With very few exceptions, nearly all the managers in Poland's economy over the last thirty years have treated it as if it were one great factory of which they were the director. Their ambition, as I understand it, was and is not only to resemble but to actually play the role of good, concerned masters who appreciate the importance of detail and do not begrudge time spent personally overseeing their factory's operations. Such a mentality is manifested not only by people who, as in the early years, had very little organizational experience, but also by those who have taken courses in organization at colleges and universities, and those who seem to be well-acquainted with the modern literature on the art of management. One would have to look into the question more deeply to determine to what extent this 'directorial mentality' has been created by the system of management itself, and to what extent it is the need for self-fulfillment and personal vanity that is satisfied by this 'personal' wielding of power. It is enough to say that the managers of our economy lovingly and enthusiastically devote their time to details, yet they are usually unable to organize and carry out the Center's tasks. It is a case of constant amateurish and perpetual improvisation, lacking any routines for even the simplest recurrent tasks."

The present mess in planning development has reached scandalous proportions. "This is the one area in which a centralized system can demonstrate its worth, and it is precisely in this area that it has been most dramatically compromised," stresses the same respondent. "The coordination of energy and transport needs with production growth is one of the simplest planning tasks, yet the managers of our economy have failed even in this. After years of experience, investment planning should have become virtually a professional speciality of a socialist economy. However, it is precisely here that it has suffered its most bitter defeat, the consequences of which will be with us for a very long time to come."

Management experts have on many occasions drawn attention to the lack of procedures for planning and analyzing the achievement of nonquantifiable economic goals (social goals such as health, access to culture, etc.); the lack of procedures for coordinating material planning with budget planning; the fact that no data are collected and no studies made of investment processes to project future developments; and finally, that as a result there is no way really to coordinate the financial, material, and manpower requirements of any investment plan. "The recurrent collapse of investment plans in the third year of each five-year period," points out respondent No. 37, "stems from the fact that at the start of the five-year period, the decision-makers are convinced that this time they have based their calculations on valid premises. Each time the resource balance fails, unleashing a frenzy of corrective measures that freeze resources already invested and concentrate an excess of nonplanned productive energy in areas where, with good organization, only 50-60 percent of the original estimate would have been needed (the Katowice steel works is a good example)."[36]

A partial justification (if it can be taken as a justification of the people managing our economy) is the inadequate supply of information. However, "the concealment and distortion of information is an inherent feature of the system," as the same respondent points out. "The system does not reward, but on the contrary penalizes, truth. The free flow of information is obstructed by all the existing forces and mechanisms of our

economy. The central authorities believe that they have a
monopoly on all information, while in fact they have a monopoly only on that information which the source of the information has an interest in passing on. No one knows how much
there is of anything in our country, be it machine tools, land in
cultivation, construction equipment in working order, unused
factory floorspace, the amount of coal extracted, printing
machinery, etc. We do not have a complete list of licenses
purchased abroad (let alone an analysis of the cost-effectiveness
of such purchases); nor is there any such thing as even the most
basic promotional catalogue indicating who could produce what
in case a firm order were placed with this or that factory; nor
does anyone know exactly who produces what, since attempts
to publish information of this kind have proved to be contrary
to the interests of the producers themselves."

The system of financing enterprises distorts current production planning. First of all, production is not planned by the
producer himself but is built into the "plan maneuvers" that go
on over his head; second, he produces for the plan and not to
sell his product. Furthermore, "planning is excessively detailed
as regards economic units and limits chances to adjust production to the needs of the market," notes respondent No. 4, quoting a passage from an interview with the vice-manager of a grinding wheel factory: "I have to produce not only machine tools
but also indicators . . . to arrange my product mix so that it fits
all the directives imposed on me: directives concerning the total
sale value and the value in per capita terms of the work force,
the ratio between the average rise in wages and the gain in productivity, the share in export production, the cost factor, the
size of accumulation, and so on. Compared to all this activity,
the development of a new generation of tools seems child's
play."

Studies by Janusz Seksiak and Urszula Libur (*Economic
Equilibrium under Socialism*) have confirmed the observations
of organization specialists: the present system of financing enterprises "cranks up" prime costs. Not only does it not contribute
to lowering them, in many cases it rewards raising them. Prime
costs are multiplied by the system of central coordination, centralized allocations, and mechanically applied commands and
prohibitions. Steel from Silesian mills is transported to industrial sites at Zagłębie Staropolskie in central Poland;[37] similar
mechanisms are at work in consumer goods production—the
products generally pass through central warehouses, taking up

space and multiplying transportation costs. The same applies to shoes, which the central authorities allocate among the various retail shops irrespective of the demand for this or that kind of footwear in this or that locality. The same happens with books, as was shown in the "Report on Books" compiled by the basic party cell organization at the Warsaw branch of the Union of Polish Writers: books, which because they are in short supply can be guaranteed from the outset a certain sales volume and hence could be shipped directly to retail sales outlets, wander from the printer to central warehouses and then after repacking are sent to provincial warehouses and only then to bookshops.

It is even difficult to say what percentage of rail cargo is completely superfluous (experts estimate it at between 30 and 40 percent), since, for instance, construction enterprises have to haul in construction materials from a distance of at least 100 kilometers even if there are supplies nearby. This is so because of a decision forbidding railways to accept heavy loads for journeys of fewer than 100 kilometers.

Prime costs are also increased by the unfair employment structure. The system of financing enterprises and the elaborate planning and consultation procedures have created a massive bureaucracy. The classic example here is the system of purchasing, supply, and trade. In the warehouses and behind shop counters there are very few employees, but there are a great many sitting behind desks. The costs entailed in the purchasing, supply, and commercial sales system are staggeringly high in relation to the very low cost of human labor; but it is easy to understand why this is so when we consider the bureaucratic load that the ordinary employee of a wholesale department or retail shop bears.

The myth of the superiority of large industrial plants and the historical necessity of eliminating the small ones has led to a concentration (to be sure, often in terms of organization, not production) of industry that exceeds what we find in countries considerably more advanced than we are. A comparison with both Germanies shows that whereas in Poland enterprises employing fewer than 100 people constituted 11.3 percent of all enterprises and employed 0.7 percent of the work force, in the same period in the GDR these figures were 61.5 and 7.1 percent, and in the FRG they were 86 and 19.7 percent. These figures also reveal the underdevelopment of the service sector in our country—the negligible number of small artisan workshops, the underdevelopment of the commercial trade network, and the lack of subsidiary production in small workshops (so that as a result, we import the most ordinary items and accessories from, for example, Japan). The key industries, with their bureaucratic humps that paralyze small-scale production, at the same time block innovation.

The inefficiency of organization and the incompetence of economic management impact on all citizens as customers and consumers; for producers the effect is doubled. We can see in industry the exacerbation of such chronic ailments of Polish enterprise as erraticism—temporary halts or slowdowns in production alternating with frenzied activity to catch up with the plan—which results in increased overtime and work on Sundays and holidays. Many of these practices amount to exploitation of the work force. Retaliatory strikes are spreading. All this has a negative effect on productivity.

The phenomena we have described stem in part from the international situation; we were not the only ones to fail to foresee the dimensions and the duration of the economic recession in the West, from which we imported plant, technology, and certain raw materials to renovate our industrial base. This development has turned against us, and production line stoppages are now often the result of a lack of imported materials and spare parts. All this, as well as last year's winter,[38] which spelled disaster to the fuel and transport sectors, does not absolve anyone from responsibility for the mistakes made that we discussed earlier.

The picture we have painted of our system of economic management is a depressing one. It contains, however, a certain, albeit concealed, element of optimism: behind all the anachronistic and inefficient structures and mechanisms stand only entrenched routines and vested interests; no ideological arguments can defend them. On the contrary, critics can even levy doctrinal objections based on the defense of the fundamental principles of our political and social order.

The picture is different for the management of agricultural production. In Poland agriculture is weighed down by what is, from the point of view of ideological dogmas, the original sin of private ownership, which still holds about 75 percent of the arable land. Faced with these dogmas—all the respondents agree on this point—all arguments drawn from a realistic analysis of the facts pale into insignificance. The danger of a collapse in agricultural production and, as a result, in exports to hard-currency areas counts for nothing; reliable data about the efficiency of medium-sized farming compared to large farms count for nothing; and the dangers of social conflict, with its incalculable consequences, count for nothing as well. Despite pledges and verbal declarations by the authorities, in many provinces the policy of limiting private ownership in agriculture is still pursued. Previously it took the form of collectivization imposed administratively; now it involves a program of establishing state farms. This program was promoted by systematically limiting land that could be sold to individual peasants and restricting tenancy and, on the other hand, by investing resources in state farms[39] in dramatic disproportion to investment in industrial production intended to meet the needs of private farmers.

"I suspect," writes respondent No. 36, "that behind these ideological arguments lies the same 'directorial mentality' from economic management. They want to manage agriculture in the same way as industry, with the same methods, with the same sense of power. Ideologues take talk about cooperation seriously: the 'directors' of our economy use this concept as a smokescreen. Had they been genuinely concerned about cooperatives, they would have attempted to give purchasing agencies cooperative features, since the employees in this sector, who for all practical purposes are free from all supervision and checks, expropriate 10 to 15 percent of rural income; they would have tried to transform the 'Peasant Self-Help' agencies[40] into genuine cooperatives, which today they are not; they would have allowed self-managed farm equipment fleets to develop;[41] they would have supported dairy cooperatives instead of sinking their funds in faulty and poorly managed investment projects and undertakings; and they would have made room for the development of various forms of cooperative and intervillage projects (for instance, in construction). They didn't. In light of what has been said, their actual ideal is simply the same model of management cultivated in industry."

⎛Agricultural policy, then, consists of contradictory tendencies—an official policy that accepts the existence of private farming, and a second policy that combats it. The first gains ground each time the second has managed to cause yet another crisis in agriculture. However, that is all it does; it merely "gains ground," which means instituting ad hoc, makeshift measures to replenish livestock, for instance, or increase the amount of land under crops. Never does it go so far as restructuring and balancing long-term policy, which once again amounts to a program of industrial activity and construction for the foodstuffs sector, a program that is inadequate and structurally unsuited to the

needs of agriculture. This happens because, as one economist
put it, "agriculture as a sector of the nation's economy is an unloved child." But especially unloved is individual peasant farming, which in all areas displays greater efficiency than state
farms, cooperatives,[42] and farm equipment fleets. Given any pa-
rameters, even those in which large-scale farming can and should
have a clear advantage—e.g., crop production—its productivity is lower than that of individual farms: grain yields per hectare
of arable land on state farms are 20-25 percent lower than on
private farms, despite the fact that they are more highly mech-
anized and consume more chemical fertilizers, in other words,
despite higher investments and costs. Statistics on livestock raising put the state farms in an even worse light. Hog production
on state farms is six times more costly than on private farms.

The expropriation and cultivation by the state farms of
land from the State Land Fund is extremely costly: 100,000
zlotys per hectare, and in some regions even more. The thought-
less policy of forcing collectivization threatens us with no more
and no less than a food catastrophe. Meanwhile, although state
agriculture has in no way demonstrated its superiority, from
1971 through 1973 the state farms received ten times more land
from the State Land Fund than individual peasants. This happened despite the fact that agricultural economists, although
differing on various matters, are solidly in agreement that in the
future a sound agricultural sector must be based on viable and
resilient individual farms, following the model operating throughout Europe (with the exception of England and the Soviet
Union).

The demographic structure of our country also militates
against such a policy. The rural population is becoming older,
and the number of people willing to stay on the land is getting
smaller. The practice of trading in farms for old-age pensions,
despite all the errors in its implementation, is a sound one. The
problem is just who is to get the land. Recently the authorities
appeared to lean more decidedly toward the unanimous opinion
of the experts that potential energetic producers may appear
distrustful in view of the experience of the last thirty-five years.

For agriculture to grow, it must first be supplied with the
means of production, which up to now have been in permanent
short supply.

Gigantomania, which accords with our economic leaders'
notions of what constitutes progress, has been particularly destructive for Polish agriculture. Livestock farms with animal

holdings in numbers unheard of in other countries have sustained monumental losses. State farm combines have made an efficient and economically viable agriculture totally impossible and have led to bureaucratization and waste on a scale difficult even to measure.

In other words, state agriculture suffers from the same ailments as the rest of the state-run economy. The food-producing sector shows all the structural and mechanical defects we have already described.

To recapitulate, the present state of Polish agriculture is not the result of single, isolated mistakes or impulsive managerial decisions that go beyond the limits of sound risk. It is the result of structural defects that can distort the best plans and intentions and block any chance to avoid and correct mistakes.

The Functioning of the Mass Media

So far we have been describing the pillars on which our system of power presently rests—the representative bodies, the executive, the judiciary, and the economy. No treatment of the subject would be complete, however, without a look at the problem of the mass media. Traditional analyses of systems of government tend to ignore the mass media because their influence and social role were never as great as they are today; today they are a basic instrument of governance and at the same time a pillar of power on which the stability of many contemporary systems rests. The party controls the mass media as an instrument of its authority in three ways: first, through recommendations and directives regarding the main lines of propaganda policy; second, through personnel decisions on appointments to key positions and cadre policy; and third, through censorship and restrictions on the dissemination of information. However, the first and second means can only be applied to media that are directly under party control. In the case of the various Catholic publications[43] and the newspapers controlled by the United People's Party and the Democratic Alliance,[44] the principal instrument remains censorship and the restriction of dissemination. At the same time, the mass media, which are wholly under party control, and which on a number of occasions during Poland's postwar history served as an instrument of public control and a source of corrective information for the economy, have gradually come under the control of the administrative and

economic apparatus, which over the years have steadily broadened their influence on both the intent of promulgated directives and on censorship regulations. Moreover, the administrative and economic establishment has by various means systematically corrupted the journalistic profession. All these factors
combined have worked to gradually deprive most of the mass
media of their powers of persuasion. The public has come to regard them as unreliable, especially for matters of political significance. Now even factual information appears to be less than
factual, since no one believes in either people or methods of
presentation that themselves merit no trust. Furthermore, the
people in charge of the mass media in Poland fail to realize that
even their monopoly on information could prove to be quite
limited. Foreign media[45] and the upsurge of publishing activity
beyond the reaches of the censor[46] are sapping this illusory monopoly, and other word-of-mouth forms of communication are
emerging. All in all, it seems that this pillar of the system of political power suffers from the same ailments as all the others: inefficiency, ineffectiveness, inauthenticity, and the inability to
correct itself.

The Functioning of Social Policy

The description of the structures and mechanisms of our system
of power would not be complete if the problems of social policy in the 1970s were disregarded; its fate and its distortion during those years can be considered significant.

The team that took over the government of our country
after the events of December 1970 came to power with the
slogan of a new social policy. And indeed, particularly during
the first years of the regime, several of its undertakings met
with public approval. Popular language was enriched by such
phrases as "Gierek's bonus" or "Gierek's Saturday."[47] Then,
suddenly, these trends slowed and finally collapsed. There was
even pressure, mainly from managers and a part of the administration, to cancel or limit the gains that had been made on the
ground that they were too costly or "demoralizing."

This slowdown was compounded by other, perhaps even
more harmful processes. Social policy cannot be divorced from
the problems of equality, or rather inequality, in our society.
The last ten years have been characterized by a growing stratification of the Polish nation, the reasons for which are both eco-

nomic and political and often difficult to separate/ The seventies were a decade when incomes rose rapidly, albeit most rapidly in the highest income brackets, the end result being a widening of the income differential to a ratio of 1 : 20. Our political system, therefore lost a powerful argument in its favor vis-à-vis capitalist societies—the argument of egalitarianism, which in turn was one of the basic aims of socialist society. Income privileges acquire political overtones for the rest of society. It is well known that 80 percent of factory directors are members of the Polish United Workers' Party, and that 60 percent hold influential party positions at various levels; political inequality has been sanctioned by law in an amendment to the Polish Constitution.[48] The mere fact of belonging to the Polish United Workers' Party does not automatically yield benefits. Only members of the active political core of the party, its allied political groupings, and the administrative apparatus enjoy a privileged position in society. Their privileges extend to almost all spheres of life: access to status positions, real incomes, easier shopping, health, education, foreign travel, to say nothing of wielding power to a greater or lesser degree. What is more, during the 1970s these privileges were extended to relatively large groups in society: the decade also witnessed the inheritance of privilege. These groups, which do not share the concerns of the majority, are more interested in supplementing existing privileges and acquiring new ones than they are in improving any aspect of public life.

What is more, there is an increasing tendency to fill posts with "one's own people" from the younger generation. This is the case not only with leading positions in agriculture or the administrative apparatus, but with all kinds of posts in, e.g., publishing houses, institutions of learning, and scientific jobs. It is likely that this kind of inequality, i.e., an inequality rooted in politics, will spread in the next few years. It is a particularly important symptom of the crisis.

Somewhat paradoxically, there has been a sort of merger between these privileged groups and other milieus that enjoy a high standard of living, e.g., private initiative.[49] Some of these private proprietors, whose prosperity depends on the authorities, are willing to share their income with them. In some cases their traditional hostility to the communists has evaporated, probably because they are themselves the products of the present system, not capitalism, and they are able to operate in it. A certain style of life and a conspicuous mode of consumption are characteristic of both these groups.

As regards social policy in the classical sense of the word, regression in this area can be measured by the amount of money allotted to those sectors that convention has dubiously dubbed "unproductive," such as education, health, social welfare, recreation, and sports. In 1960 expenditures in these areas still amounted to about one third of all capital investments. Since then they have fallen to a current 19 percent. The waiting lists for housing have grown longer, as has the waiting time; in building new housing, despite the "economic maneuver" attempted, we are behind not only the other countries of the socialist camp but even a poor capitalist country like Greece. Health, culture, education, and recreational facilities will be discussed elsewhere.

So, as we see, social policy also displays the unmistakable symptoms of crisis. We feel that we have provided ample proof that the crisis in our system is indeed genuine. The extent to which this crisis threatens our future will be shown in later chapters.

CHAPTER 3

The State of Society
and Public Consciousness

In our description of society we will concentrate mainly on those disturbing issues that stood out in sharpest relief in the poll responses. They concern: the social structure, its hierarchical character, antiegalitarian tendencies, and the emergence of a system of privileges that conflicts with the sense of social justice so deeply rooted——thanks to socialist ideology——in our society. The respondents point out the emergence of new interest groups and of new divisions that have damaging social effects. Many vital questions have not been included among the issues considered in this incomplete study, partly because they were not dealt with specifically in the poll responses, and partly because they have not yet received the systematic attention of social science, although there certainly exists a genuine need to subject them to scientific analysis.

The axis around which any vision of contemporary Polish society revolves is the process of spreading social inequalities, the social consequences of blocking civic initiative, and a lack of prospects for ways out of this impasse.

We are well aware that many crucial elements are lacking for a complete description of society. Above all, it would be necessary to outline the existing social structure, the balance of class forces, and the relationships between the particular classes and strata. Then, against this background, we could proceed to an analysis of society and its various parts and the way they are linked together in the public mind.

However, there are sound reasons for saying——and we will discuss this later——that the state of public consciousness is just as real a fact as the existence of social classes. People's acts, opinions, and aspirations are equally produced by the content of consciousness.

* * *

Polish society emerged from World War II not only poor but also considerably transformed. There were substantial shifts in our borders that caused demographic displacements—not mentioned, by the way, in our history books. Respondent No. 26 writes: "The history of the Polish people begins with the period after the occupation, that is, a situation in which the very fabric of the nation was threatened with physical extinction. This period is of crucial significance; it represents a landmark in our collective destiny. This period, by virtue of the powers of endurance shown in the face of a collective threat, the rendering of mutual assistance in extreme situations, and the collective struggle and concern for fundamental values, produced, particularly among the younger generation, a profound response to the call for social justice and the conviction that a radical rebuilding of society was essential. At the same time, it created a basic sensitivity to the whole problem of independence as a result of the return to a situation of bondage."

The project of social reforms to which the new authorities addressed their appeal had two components, by no means identical, although they were always presented together in the light of the political reality referred to as People's Poland. Each of them drew on divergent notions of the "good society" and entailed different concepts of how to organize public life. Even today these two components form two different poles toward which gravitate the views of broad segments of the public, views concerning both "what is" as well as "what ought to be."

The differences that emerged correspond to "the differences between two types of social order," which Stanisław Ossowski[50] defined as a type governed by the principle of monocentric control and a type based on the principle of polycentric cooperation within the institutions of economic and social planning. In the authoritarian type hierarchic control of all facets of public life is favored, while in the cooperative form unrestricted communication is preferred. Ossowski therefore called this type "an order of compromises."

In the bitter struggle that took place just after the war, ideological and political tendencies predominated over strictly class factors. The agrarian reform and the nationalization of industry, planned economic development, and social progress through the democratization of education, science, and the arts were goals and values accepted by everyone.)

Therefore, despite the drama of those first years and, somewhat later, of the painful experiences of the Stalinist period, an enduring compromise between the authorities and society was——and still is——possible. The instances cited in the preceding chapters are ample testimony to this. We have in mind, in particular, the Catholic Church, to which a substantial portion of society has strong ties. These ties are not only related to world view. Of no less importance is tradition, particularly the role the Church has played in the history of our nation, especially over the past two centuries.[51] It has experienced genuine evolution. During particularly trying periods the Church was——and still is——the institution that has safeguarded and defended the historical and cultural, ethical and educational values of the Polish nation. It has also tried to assume the role of spokesman for the interests of different classes and professional groups.

(Following the war and the transformations in the system, a new society took shape, a society that accepted the model of a socialist state. The proposals it has made for putting the Republic in order remain within the framework of the system, the basic premises of which are not challenged. Studies by both sociologists and historians have confirmed the enduring nature of these views. Respondent No. 47 points out that "most of the criticism we hear so much about in Poland concerning the functioning of various institutions is made from the viewpoint of different standards within socialist ideology. The socialism that people see is compared to the socialism they want to see, and the discrepancy between reality and their standards is painful."

The Critical Consciousness of a New Society

More than one respondent noted that the critical consciousness of a new society receives its fullest expression in times of crisis. So it was in 1956 and again in 1970. Critical consciousness not only——and not merely——addressed itself to economic and social demands but also to injecting genuine life into the institutions that express the needs of both society as a whole and its groups. These proposals concerned effective operation of the Sejm and of the local councils and trade unions (in place of which workers'

councils and factory committees had spontaneously sprung up),
the expansion of various forms of self-management, establishment of a sound legal order, and creation of conditions for
genuine expression of public opinion. The term "facade," in
universal currency in 1956, sums up the point quite succinctly.
It was urgent to give genuine life to these institutions.

The activities of institutions and proposals for changing
them will be dealt with more extensively elsewhere in our discussion. At this point, as we said at the outset, we will discuss
them from the standpoint of how people assess these institutions,
how they experience them, and how they relate to them.

This is an extremely important and fundamental point.
Social consciousness is no less important than the objective
state of things. No less important than actual participation is
people's awareness that they share in collective governance,
collective decisions, and cooperation. The tendencies we sometimes see to analyze only the objective state of things while
disregarding people's consciousness are totally wrong and
unjustified. The possibility of taking active part in social life is
an important need in itself. Indeed, without it a person is
mutilated. A man feels merely an instrument of momentary ends.

Yet as Jan Szczepański[52] aptly wrote in 1964, "A socialist
society can function in accordance with its fundamental principles if it is able to create a type of human being who acts in
accordance with motives that become the guidelines for action,
and that develop the social institutions and structures of that
society" (*Changes in the Present Tense*, p. 275). Without the
requisite development of participation in the formulation of
goals and decisions and in their achievement and implementation,
the sense of responsibility, not only for the results of practical
actions but also for the conditions of life itself, evaporates. At
the same time, people become dissatisfied even with the achieved
level of gratification of needs. Many respondents took up this
problem.

In questionnaire No. 8 we read, "The mediating institutions
(the schools, trade unions, public organizations, etc.) that
replaced initiative groups have ceased to productively perform
their functions, since they are subject to such extensive checks
and controls that the overwhelming majority of people, consciously or unconsciously, have become immunized to their
influence and avoid having anything to do with them, preferring
instead to arrange their lives on an individual basis (sometimes
in small clique groups). The importance of private motives has

grown tremendously. On the other hand, social ties have become weaker, and the resultant signs of disorganization are multiplying." Respondent No. 7 made similar observations: "The greatest internal threat today is to be found in the weakening of social bonds, the decline in a sense of responsibility for the whole, and the total erosion of social solidarity."

Commenting on the atomization of society, respondent No. 1 writes: "People identify primarily with the smallest and largest of the basic groups in society——the family and the nation——demonstrating the total futility of reliance on more indirect social ties. Such a society is not capable of generating enough momentum to defend its principles or to avoid a harmful decision." Another respondent notes that "between the primary groups (family, friends) and the nation as a social totality there exists a kind of sociological void with regard to people's identification and emotional involvements," and that "institutions are often perceived as something distasteful, undesirable, dishonest, and at times even as simply threatening."

With many of the public institutions and organizations created to express the needs and interests of different groups of citizens regarded as inauthentic, formalized, and spurious, groups have emerged——and are still emerging——throughout postwar history that claim to express the needs and interests of society. Both workers' councils in 1956 and the factory committees at Wybrzeż[53] were symptoms of such spontaneous activity, until the councils were incorporated into the system of workers' self-management and the committees were dissolved. At the root of these initiatives lay the feeling among workers that the trade unions did not really represent them.

At various points in postwar history, sociological discussions have focused on the need to delimit more broadly the notion of self-government so that different social and professional groups can express their needs and interests.

Under the conditions of secrecy in public life and in the critical situation that has engulfed various areas of collective life in the past few years, groups purporting to express these needs and interests have sprung up. Some of them have set themselves the goal of defending the interests of workers and peasants by social and legal means; others are concerned with breaking the monopoly on information distorted by the mass media, with spreading knowledge, and finally, with publishing works that have been banned from the cultural mainstream, often because of their author rather than their content.

Some of these groups and circles call themselves opposi-
tional; others are so named by the official propaganda agencies.

From the viewpoint of society, what is most important is
that these groups have appeared whenever the symptoms of
crisis have become exacerbated, and the sense has grown more
acute that various demands for justice, information, culture,
and so forth are not being met.

At a time when demands for democratization are being
met, the crucial values these groups represent are expressed in
the activities of legalized institutions that discover and rectify
what is amiss in relations between the authorities and society.
They do this not in an atmosphere of tension but through
dialogue between the authorities and various authentic social
groups that articulate their own aspirations.

The Growth of Social Inequalities

Scholars and laymen alike speak of widening social distances
and mounting social inequalities. Especially instructive in this
respect is the material from the first plenary meeting of the
"Experience and the Future" group, which was devoted to social
policy. The discussion was dominated by criticism and proposals,
but the criticism entailed a diagnosis. "None of our ills equally
afflict the whole nation," asserted one panelist. "We are a socially
stratified nation, but we have no suitable tools to define the
boundaries of class and strata. These boundaries do exist, however, and make themselves known at every time of crisis."
Another panelist, suggesting that what we are currently witnessing is the birth of a new class system, stated that privileges are
inherited in our country. At Polish Sociological Society meetings
in March and May of this year there was much discussion about
the growth of inequality in earnings, incoherence and irration-
ality in the system of wages, and discrimination in the sharing
of power and the privileges attached to it.

These issues found strong reflection in the poll. Respondent
No. 9 put it in a nutshell: "Inequality and injustice are everywhere. There are hospitals that are so poorly supplied they do
not even have cotton, and our relatives die in the corridors; but
other hospitals are equipped with private rooms and full medical
care for each room. We pay fines for traffic violations, but some
people commit highway manslaughter while drunk and are let
off with impunity. In some places there are better shops and

superior vacation houses, with huge fenced-in grounds that ordinary people cannot enter. People see all this, and they know that high-ranking officials drive luxurious cars, although they have also heard stories about prime ministers riding buses. People cannot excuse the injustices associated with anyone these days in Poland who has any connections with power. It is not a question of money so much as a whole range of informal benefits that accrue from having a share in power. This state of affairs is totally at variance with the basic principles of our system, yet it is painfully common knowledge. Worst of all is the feeling of helplessness, the impossibility of changing the system that produced all this."

We will return frequently to the problems caused by these phenomena. At this point let us merely observe that most of the respondents who raised these issues noted that it is mainly the weaker groups in society who pay the price for this disharmony in our development. Respondent No. 47 had this to say: "Differences between individuals in our society are very pronounced, and income differences (although not them alone) are particularly regarded as severely dividing people and generating tensions and antagonisms between them."

There was almost total agreement that equality of opportunity is a universally accepted axiom in our society. "It is generally agreed that training, education, responsibility, and honest productive work should be rewarded proportionately; only a very small number of people believe in total equality of incomes." Thus social differences are provisionally accepted, without losing sight of the egalitarian ideal. What is not accepted is differentiation in which income and privileges are only loosely or dubiously related to a person's function in the social division of labor.

It is from this perspective that we should view the responses that dealt with problems of social differences and the conflicts they generate between society and the authorities and within society itself. It is against this background as well that we should view the formation——amply discussed in the responses——of an elite (with regard to advancement and career), inequalities of income and privileges between different groups, the problem of pressure groups and interest groups (usually covert) that want to maintain or increase their share in power and national income, and the situation of various professional groups in various walks of life and of different age groups.

Respondent No. 25, writing about the discrepancy between

egalitarian slogans and actual practice, says: "Egalitarianism is transformed into hierarchy, stratification, and inequality. Vertical and horizontal mobility has become immobility and ossification of structures; a person is assigned a workplace or residence often not where he chooses but where circumstances dictate." "One hears complaints about unfair appointments to leadership positions and administrative posts. But how, indeed, can it be otherwise if the ability to pursue a career depends on obedience rather than independence of mind, on readiness to shift positions quickly rather than firm convictions? To obtain a top job where decisions are made, one must know how to do one thing: carry out the orders of others, although they may contradict themselves from one day to the next." This problem is often raised in the poll. There is an almost universally shared belief in society that the road to promotion and successful careers is most open to the obedient; a kind of negative selection is operative from the outset.

Growing social differences led some of the respondents to take up the question of conflict of social interests. We will try to arrange the opinions of the respondents, starting with the most general (No. 10):

"Conflicts of group interests are indeed a major issue. It amounts to observing that: it is high time to introduce the category of special interest into analyses of socialist society; doing away with private ownership of the means of production by no means eliminates conflicts of group interests; in Poland there is a relatively large group of people who have a lot to lose and are capable of doing anything to preserve their privileges. The real reason for stagnation is that an economically privileged group holds a de facto monopoly on political action." Others feel that this diagnosis misses the point: "The situation has reversed itself. A share in power entails economic advantages; an almost feudal dependence on the authorities has been created."

Respondent No. 7 submits a question. "What is the basic conflict of interest in society?" His reply: "First of all we must find who benefits from the present situation. We could do this through an analysis of the state budget (which is kept secret) and of the contents of plans and plan revisions prompted by investment projects that exceed plans. In all these areas the hand of special interests is evident. The polarization of social conflict is a phenomenon not to be denied."

Respondent No. 21 pursues the same topic, saying: "There are certain contradictions or, in any event, differences of interests between, for example, the peasants and workers in heavy industry. I do not think that they are necessarily a source of conflict. On the other hand, if we regard the bureaucracy as a social group, we will find very clearly defined and conflict-generating differences between it and, for example, the creative intelligentsia. I am personally most interested in what might be called the socialist middle classes or a socialist petite bourgeoisie. They have an unquestionable influence on the party and government apparatuses, the greater part of which are manned by these middle classes. Do they have any interests in common with the working classes? Absolutely not. They grow richer and richer, but still not as rich as they would like. They are hampered by the remnants of socialist phraseology at the top (the apparatus that whetted appetites and introduced the ideal of 'prosperity,' which the middle classes understand to mean 'wealth,' nonetheless speaks the language of Marxism) and socialist ideology at the bottom. The differences of interests between the middle groups and others are certainly a source of conflicts, and in the future may even become more so, especially if opportunities for broad disclosure and discussion of conflict issues are limited."

Respondent No. 12 elaborates on this problem: "Social differences are growing. Part of society continues to live with lower than the social minimum income, while another segment, consisting of the privileged, has incomes several or even dozens of times the average." We will not go into detail here because social scientists have set this social minimum at different levels. ' According to Andrzej Tymowski's calculation in his book *The Social Minimum* (1973), the minimum necessary for an unmarried man in 1970 was 1,515 zlotys. In 1976, according to Lucyna Deniszczuk (*Standards of Subsistence Consumption*), it had risen to almost 2,000 zlotys as a result of imbalances in supply and demand. Respondent No. 25, dealing with the same problem, claims that a distinct social stratification had become a reality in the seventies. "Some can afford commercial prices,[54] while others—and there are many of them—cannot. It is worth looking more closely at the latter group. Those who cannot afford them comprise the whole of the working class—light industry, many of the lower-level office workers, many of those working in education and public health, not to mention old-age pensioners (especially those in rural areas). Many of these deprived people are often notoriously undernourished. There exists in Poland a very large group of people who live in poverty, quite often near the subsistence level." Respondent No. 8 puts the reasons for the current sharpening of conflicts in these terms:

"Rapid growth inevitably brought with it differences in income that were viewed with disapproval in our egalitarian society. They became intolerable in an atmosphere of stagnation and crisis, when for many social groups the standard of living had sunk even lower." Respondent No. 1 claims that "one reason for conflict is the fundamental opposition of interests between members of the establishment and other social groups who pay the price for their inefficiency. On top of this there are also conflicts between interest groups within the establishment who draw other segments of society into their sphere of influence (managerial groups, professional groups, regional groups, groups representing the different branches of industry)."

The activities of special interest and pressure groups (mostly covert) are touched on fragmentarily in the poll material. The responses generally point out the existence of a problem that is often the subject of private conversations, and whose extent we can only guess. At this point, we merely want to mention the problem, which we will discuss in more detail later.

Our survey focused on both the present and future. We were aware, however, that certain social and economic differences stemming from the workings of the old order reappeared immediately after the war and became entrenched with the passing of the years. Preferential treatment of some sectors at the expense of others, the rigid division between productive and nonproductive investment, and——following from this——differentiation of wages by industrial branch were all factors that immediately after the war forced people out of professions like teaching and local government, engendered a process of selection and counterselection in occupations, and produced a system of wages that bore no relation to knowledge or qualifications. Respondent No. 14 addresses this issue particularly forcefully: "The present wage system and wage practices have obliterated the hierarchy that existed. . . . Not only was the traditional relation between skilled intellectual and manual labor destroyed, but among the producers of material goods and services, understood in the broad sense, thoughtful work requiring initiative and a high level of skills was downgraded. Our school system, years behind, neglected in terms of capital investment, and practicing a negative selection[55] of qualified personnel, is in the throes of a profound crisis."

Many respondents underscored the demoralizing effect of various kinds of covert privileges deriving from institutional and personal connections. At the first meeting of the "Experience and the Future" group, one of the participants noted that "privilege linked to better material standards is (however) better than noneconomic or political privilege, privilege stemming from personal connections, or privilege that is hidden and that creates the keenest sense of injustice."

Better and Worse:
Egalitarianism and Hierarchy

Let us turn now from hypotheses and broad diagnoses——in which we have used some specific examples——to a more detailed description of the situation. Society, including the poll respondents, harbors some strong egalitarian ideas and finds these ideas confronted with elitist practices. It therefore would like to know what relationship could exist between the general slogans and the practices and prevailing standards of social differentiation. It contrasts official slogans to practices that lead to growing class divisions. Since social change is fundamentally influenced by politics, the emergence of an elite has mainly to do with holding a position in the political and economic apparatus. The relationship between the elite and society is therefore discussed in the responses, and the paths and rules for advancement and career are compared with the trumpeted slogans. Carrying the problem further, the relationship between workers and the intelligentsia and between the old and the young intelligentsia, as well as the situation of young people, is dealt with.

Most of the respondents had no doubt that the massive mobility of the postwar years gave the popular masses broad and significant opportunities for advancement. Their criticism and concern therefore have more to do with the entrenchment of criteria based on other factors than merit for advancement and the de facto classification of citizens into better and worse.

In the public mind the division runs mainly between party members and nonmembers; but it also exists between rich and poor, the well-connected and those without "contacts." In the opinion of many of the respondents, party membership is a necessary but not sufficient condition for a successful career. The entrenchment of undemocratic procedures in the party splits it between members of the ruling apparatus and a largely silent majority that experiences and suffers the same problems as the rest of society. Some respondents dwelled heavily on the fact that any democratization of the state was contingent on a democratization of the party and the other officially recognized political groupings collaborating with it, which should be allowed to fully express the interests of the segments of society they represent.

Then there is the division between believers and non-believers, often within the same family. Sociological studies and casual observations alike show that this rift generally does not produce any internal strains and that life together proceeds along the lines of mutual tolerance. However, the authorities interpret the principle of the secular state in a way that discriminates against believers. There is ample evidence of this in everyday life, from which the respondents draw examples.

Inheritance of position and privileges is a recurrent theme in the poll responses directed at growing social divisions. We referred earlier to this problem in another context. Respondent No. 25 gets to the heart of the matter: "The elite seeks not only to preserve its numerous, almost feudal privileges to the end of its days, but also, in keeping with the rules of the feudal order, to pass on these privileges to its descendants."

With regard to the formation of political, economic, and regional elites, respondent No. 27 had this to say concerning their status: "Because of their status they (or their parents) do not have to pay for the disorganization that surrounds us. The authorities give them access to the second economy[56] for goods, apartments, health care, and so on. Moreover, the more inefficient the national economy, the more trumps the authorities hold to gain supporters by handing out privileges. The same applies to information——the more barren the official sources, the more highly valued is 'confidential information.'"[57]

The new hierarchy in society creates problems with relations between the different classes, strata, and groups. The poll responses do not heavily stress the stratification taking place among different categories of workers, although the problem was touched on by those respondents who discussed the preferential treatment or handicaps suffered by workers in different branches of industry (for example, differences in the equipment of health care services and recreation facilities provided in different branches of industry, or the much-criticized system of providing meat to large industrial enterprises). Little space was devoted to the firmly entrenched division between local workers and those who have to commute; they are mainly peasant workers whose living conditions are especially harsh, and about whom one could validly say that they have more than their share of handicaps.

More attention was devoted to relations between workers and the administrative apparatus and to differences between the new and old intelligentsia. The problem of youth, its situation, and its opportunities in life were also dealt with in this context. These relations, like international conflicts, were treated only fragmentarily, in no more than general terms. The situation of workers in large, preferentially treated branches of industry is different from that in backward branches in which capital investment has lagged. Similarly, the situation of the peasant population has its own special features. Thirty percent of all rural households have only a half to two hectares of land. Peasant workers constitute a special category, as we have already said. The situation of old-age pensioners is also special. Some are well-off; others border on poverty. The price of this disharmonious development falls especially heavily on the shoulders of working women, who waste vast amounts of time standing in lines. Finally, there is the situation of young people, which varies depending on the wealth or place of residence of their parents. In the course of the past few years, distances between homes and schools——even elementary schools——have increased. According to some studies it ranges between four and thirteen kilometers. Equipment and teaching aids are in short supply, and it is difficult for pupils to get textbooks. Yet the Ministry of Culture is planning to cut the number of rural libraries from the current 6,500 to 3,000 by 1990. The problems of young people in rural areas——how to gain access to cultural goods, how to spend leisure time——were recurrent themes in the survey material that we can only mention here. The aspirations of rural youth are growing, yet opportunities to realize them are diminishing, as are chances to modernize agriculture and bring the achievements of civilization to the countryside.

The respondents deal with only a few of these problems. However, the observations they do make point out some internal tensions that can be, and often are, manipulated to antagonize groups whose interests should be reconcilable. The respondents point out certain sensitive points in relations between groups that merit attention.

Respondent No. 20 mentions the growing mutual hostility between workers and factory administrations. Two others discuss the antagonism between the old and new intelligentsia. On this matter No. 35 observes: "Although the small group of intellectuals of peasant origin has not lost touch with its roots, it is a disturbing fact that many intellectuals of working-class origin feel no ties with the class from which they come."

Many respondents called attention to growing elitism in education and noted that different social classes and groups enjoy varying degrees of access to education, in violation of a basic premise of the system and one of its declared principles. It was said, for instance, that the abandonment of educational ambitions is "turning society into a creature made up of two unequal parts——a small elite with access to education and a great mass deprived of any opportunity for personal growth." For example, only 9 percent of students in higher education are peasant youth. Against this background the educational reform[58] arouses many misgivings and serious reservations, which will be taken up in the next chapter.

Youth: Its Situation and Aspirations

While relatively little attention was paid in the poll material to the often dramatic situation of the aged, youth received proportionately more. Growing social and educational differences are systematically giving some members of the younger generation a better start in life than others. Furthermore, the fact that parents' positions can be handed down to the next generation testifies to growing class differences in society. Observing adult life, youth from the better-off strata are in no hurry to reach social maturity. Respondent No. 47 writes: "Ambition and lofty aspirations are relatively rare among youth, as rare even as a romantic life style. Young people want to be better off than their parents but seem to be more realistic in limiting their aspirations to existing possibilities. Generally speaking, they are basically no different from their parents as regards their own aspirations and life values."

Unequal opportunity in getting a start in life was also mentioned by one of the speakers at the first meeting of the "Experience and the Future" group: "The miserably low wages received by young people (especially those with higher education) have made it necessary for many of them to continue to rely on their parents for help, which has some very disadvantageous social consequences (for example, the lingering infantility repeatedly observed in persons who have long since reached adulthood). Moreover, this creates a situation in which even at the very start of life, young people's positions differ extensively depending on how well off their families are. Those whose families cannot help face an exceptionally difficult start in life, while others who continue to live at their families' expense can keep their earnings as pocket money."

The problem of the younger generation was best expressed by respondent No. 23, who emphasized the particularly difficult situation of newlyweds as well as the parlous state of the labor market: "A professional career depends increasingly on 'push,' that is, on personal drive and lack of scruples, on the ability to manipulate people and situations (ignoring the cost to others), on political flexibility, and on an unlimited readiness to offer favors and concessions to one's superiors and one's own colleagues. Moral laxity toward oneself is permissible as long as one does not permit it in others. In this situation the moral example of a good professional who pursues his calling in accordance with his professional ethics and his own notions of personal responsibility for work done is becoming increasingly private. Official, publicly proclaimed models and real cases are growing further apart. This gulf devalues the slogan of the socialist morality of labor."

Because of social differentiation and the conformist patterns necessary for career and advancement, the problem of youth and its partnership role in social and political life have assumed fundamental importance.

The possibilities afforded by the official political arena or by youth organizations are principally an invitation to the individual to accommodate himself to existing conditions. The invaluable asset of a creative but critical outlook aimed at improving the existing state of affairs in various areas by dint of personal participation is rarely invested. The lack of an affirmative and convincing model of the individual who identifies himself with the values of the system has a destructive effect. Apart from conformity, this lack creates negative attitudes and a total privatization of goals. Most of all, it wastes Poland's greatest resource——the large numbers of young educated people who have everything it takes to meet the cultural and technological challenge of the next century.

False Consciousness

The responses presented above for the most part demonstrate

that even ordinary, everyday knowledge and experience of reality often concur quite well with the picture painted by sociological studies, as well as with the careful reflections of the civic-minded observer, such as have found expression in the poll material. This might——and indeed does——lead us to conclusions that despite everything are optimistic, since people everywhere can distinguish black from white, appearances from reality. This means that they have not lost their critical capacity nor their sensitivity to social problems.

The matter is, however, more complicated. Appearances are also to a certain extent real (since they do persist and function). Second, we have to deal not only with the blocking of all channels conducive to a genuine public opinion, but, more importantly, with the manipulation of this opinion. The monopoly on false or spurious information, on indoctrination and the screening of facts, makes possible any number of different forms of manipulation, the consequences of which we know very little about. Many of the respondents call attention to the numerous effects of distorting public opinion. But we should be clear at the outset that it is not only the lack of sufficient information among the public that is the problem. "Total secrecy in the public domain," as one of the respondents put it, is only one side of the coin. The other is the inculcation of false consciousness and the manipulation of public consciousness, which often foster antagonism between social groups.

"The distortions practiced by the mass media amount to a deliberate effort to prevent the formation of public opinion," writes respondent No. 8. "As a result, public consciousness is to a large extent shaped by partial and incomplete information, which contributes to the formation of irrational attitudes."

At this point let us return to those responses which, though dealing with a variety of matters, nonetheless share a common theme. We refer to certain states of mind and attitudes displayed by Poles that superficially seem to be internally contradictory. What are they? Their disapproval of the existing situation and, at the same time, a sense of the impossibility of changing it. They way Poles "play" not only with the authorities but with themselves (but playing with the authorities is at bottom also playing with oneself, since so many people are themselves entangled with the authorities and structures of power). Privately they say one thing, in public another; yet few suffer a split personality as a result. Many are demonstratively believers, but their faith is often a separate thing, divorced from morality, public or private. Their goals become private, not in a sense that would be human and laudable, but in the sense that their private, personal goals run counter to those of other people. For in acknowledging the impossibility of attempting any action of any real public consequence, they feel they have absolved themselves and are henceforth free to indulge in apathy or even asocial conduct. This is the reason for the social inertia, the frequent feelings of frustration, the mutual hostility, and the exacerbation of pathological phenomena we are witnessing. People experience such situations yet are barely touched by sentiments of social solidarity, for in the end it is always "they" who are at fault. And thus, along with these understandable self-defensive attitudes, dangerous elements of false consciousness emerge, antagonizing others who are often in similar predicaments.

Alone and against Oneself

The passivity and apathy of the greater part of the public are dangerous for both the state and the authorities. "I believe," says No. 28, "that the dominant strain in public consciousness today is the sense of crisis in the economy and in social institutions, coupled with the conviction that any change is impossible and, at the same time, with the expectation, often assuming an absurd form, of impending catastrophe. The waning belief in honest work, the determination of individuals to enrich themselves at any price, to 'get what is coming to them,' is yet another problem. Then there is the paralysis of public initiative, although it is difficult to say whether it is due to bureaucratic inertia or to the fact that representatives of various social groups are inclined to justify their own incompetence and laziness by blaming the general mess."

Many respondents took up the problem of bureaucratization, which suffocates creative initiative and undermines social vitality. The feedback mechanism leading from mistake to information to correction is growing feebler and feebler. In such a situation, if any changes are made, they will originate in problems and tensions, at the price of needless loss. It is then easy to settle for partial, often marginal ends, losing sight of ultimate, proper goals.

"Polish society," says respondent No. 27, "seems to be experiencing a state of extreme exhaustion, the result primarily of economic stagnation in which prospects for advancement and prompt improvement in the material situation have become non-existent, and frustration is deep. . . . The lack of social energy has been noticeable for some time . . . motivation to undertake anything in the economy at any level has disappeared. Hostility between groups and classes is growing——partly as a result of a sense of the absurdity of the present polarization, partly out of a sense of guilt for not being able to do otherwise. One of the basic threats is the lack of any way to preserve one's sense of pride; this is even becoming a social phenomenon. The drama of the situation lies in the fact that society is at cross-purposes with itself. Often one's only interest is in stabilizing for at least a while some small area of reality one can call one's own, and in not giving up one's privileges and perquisites (one in every three men between the ages of 30 and 40 holds some position of responsibility). The conjunction of all these stabilizing tendencies is one of the basic mechanisms perpetuating this absurd situation. For it *is* absurd seen from the outside. Dissolved into fragments——to those in the driver's seat——it seems quite rational."

This is the reason for the frustration noted by many of the respondents. Author No. 1 writes: "A sense of frustration is created by a gap between one's critical attitude toward the reality in which one lives and the vital necessity of having constantly to adapt to its mechanisms and the rules of the game, from which there is no escape. This division of the self perverts the moral and civic consciousness of society, producing, as it were, an accumulation of negative symptoms."

"People drink and steal," we read in No. 9. "People give and take bribes. They make deals. They make a joke out of everything. Any topic will do. It's all dreadfully depressing, but I am convinced that we are not the only ones to blame. For one has to take into account the fact that when you get right down to it, society approves and accepts all these unsavory traits, since it would otherwise be impossible for them to have become so widespread. How low have we sunk if to lead a normal and honest life no longer seems to be the right thing to do, if to do so is seen as a sign of weakness?"

Favoritism, nepotism, corruption, violation of the basic rules of living together, alcoholism——these are but a few of the plagues on our lives. We will discuss some of them, e.g., alcoholism, in the next section. Here we will just cite a few figures. According to the Central Bureau of Statistics, in 1977 every Pole drank 8.2 liters of pure alcohol, i.e., 20 liters of vodka. According to the experts, in fact, taking into account illicitly distilled liquor and imported cognacs, he drank more than 10 liters. He could buy it almost anywhere. In Sweden there is only one liquor store for every 25,000 inhabitants——only 350 shops. In Poland there are thirty times as many. True, some antialcohol campaigners have worked out ambitious plans to combat the scourge, which one respondent called "the nation's gradual mass suicide." Yet at the same time, the government has an interest in maintaining liquor sales for the revenues they produce——in 1974 the price of vodka went up by 20.6 percent and wine by 41.4 percent. There are a number of factors that contribute to the scourge of alcoholism. One of these factors, but by no means the only one, is the blocking of all ways to satisfy social needs.

* * *

The diagnosis that has emerged from the poll material is a critical one. Social changes in Poland have always been and continue to be directly influenced by political factors; hence a considerable number of the proposals made on the basis of an assessment of the current state of affairs are proposals for changes in political structures and mechanisms. It is common knowledge that social results are increasingly remote from proclaimed political slogans, and that our chaotic development is spreading social differences, for which the weakest pay most dearly. The term "poor people" often occurs in our poll material; it may be sociologically imprecise, but it is very significant. The state of society depends on a great variety of political activities whose outcome is often unpredictable; hence spontaneous processes gain in momentum. They are also much more complex than in a capitalist society (because of the altered relationship between politics and economics). This, however, does not protect us, as history shows, from unexpected eruptions of crisis.

Only through a conscious effort by the whole of society across a broad front can we emerge from the present crisis. Without such an effort we will not be able to survive the economic crisis, carry out the necessary reforms, cope with competition from other nations, or meet the challenges of the epoch.

CHAPTER 4

Threats

A society never develops without disturbances. All kinds of threats intrude on it. They are normal. Moreover, they are a test of its vitality. This is especially so for a society experiencing radical transformation.

Polish society has had to face a variety of threats on many occasions. Often it has been able to overcome and eliminate them. But the current situation is more complicated and more difficult than any in the past. Two factors in particular cause concern. They are the pace and scope of both immediate and long-term threats and, as we have already said, the lack of any mechanisms capable of eliminating immediate dangers and protecting against long-term ones.

The current situation is particularly marked by the variety of threats. We face further weakening of the power and sovereignty of the state; a breakdown in our economy; increasing economic dependence on others; a further deterioration in living conditions and the intensification of internal conflicts that follows from it; the spreading weakness and ineffectiveness of political authority; and conflicts caused by inequalities of incomes and by exploitation. We face a dramatic drop in population growth; a worsening state of public health; further cultural and educational regression; and above all, a deepening moral and political crisis——and everything that such a crisis entails: the evaporation of trust, growing passivity and the disappearance of public initiative, and a general weakening of society's defenses.

When we talk about the lack of effective mechanisms capable of defending society against these threats, we mean that no one is doing anything to prod society to take effective countermeasures; that no conscious and organized effort is being made to build or rebuild institutions and social mechanisms that are essential if society is to meet the challenge successfully.

The Danger of Explosion

The immediate threat lies in the possibility of a further deterioration of the economic crisis as a result of mismanagement, growing balance-of-payment difficulties, and a drop in domestic production. The expected decline in living standards over the next two or three years may prove more than society is psychologically able to bear. The sacrifices that will have to be made will certainly not be spread evenly. Social tensions——especially among certain social groups——will therefore be particularly acute. In such a situation disturbances, such as a spreading wave of strikes, demonstrations, or even acts of violence against official institutions, could be sparked off by a quite trivial event or conflict.

"It is difficult to predict the consequences in any detail," writes respondent No. 6, "but it is possible to imagine their basic shape. Sooner or later there will be an explosion of the kind we have already experienced. It is a matter of secondary importance what specific event will trigger it. (In the event of a struggle for power, one cannot exclude the possibility of a deliberate provocation.) The social cost of such explosions is always high. But in this case it could exceed anything we have experienced since the war. Experience shows that any attempt to control the course of events by force would have little chance of success. It is particularly difficult, it seems, to make Polish society do something by intimidation."

This beleaguered state of affairs is being and will be dealt with by a party and administration cadres who have no genuine experience of politics and are totally unprepared for the task in similar social conditions.

"Experience shows that local disturbances can spread with surprising ease and cause the abrupt wilting of existing organizational structures——and even of the apparatus of power and repression" (No. 8).

Such eruptions need not be seen as entirely negative in their effects. In fact, for the last twenty years or so they have been the only effective regulator of a system that has failed to create any other mechanism for correcting mistakes and replacing personnel. This method, however, is very costly in social terms, and its basic political educative value to the nation must be assessed rather skeptically. It does teach effective action and how to defend personal dignity and interests, but it affords no experience in other ways to resolve conflicts. It does not contribute to strengthening political authority (which must also be based on trust) nor to broadening society's control over its affairs: for this, society has greater need of political and legal institutions than of a tradition of triumphant confrontation with its own power.

No. 8 continues: "We have seen on three separate occasions how a mass eruption of rage is followed almost immediately by retreat and concessions from the authorities (usually of a temporary or illusory nature). Only enormous mistakes or flagrant crimes can prompt bloody nationwide confrontations. Such a mistake or crime would be the inability of the authorities to make concessions and to maintain a dialogue with society. Only in such a case and under certain conditions will another variant emerge: pacification of the country by foreign intervention, a pacification more costly for our country and for those intervening than similar interventions in the past.

"It must be emphasized, however, that the second variant will occur——though it need not——only if the centers of power are totally paralyzed from within. Until now neither experience nor an analysis of the situation inclines us to believe that pressure on the part of the masses can become so strong that it would create an unacceptable political and military situation for the bloc of which we are a part. On the contrary, Polish society has shown considerable restraint in its political and economic demands on the authorities——just as it did between the two world wars. In both cases there was an awareness of what the total situation required."

"Yet the situation is very grave," writes respondent No. 13. "The social cost of the crisis could be much higher this time than in the 1950s, at the beginning of the 1970s, or even in 1976. Popular aspirations are growing, and the gap between them and the means available to satisfy them is widening. Obviously a successful economic maneuver would have been much easier to perform two or three years ago than now."

We must realize that in 1956 there were considerable reserves and room for political maneuver, and they were taken advantage of. Among other things we had a political leader with sufficient prestige.[59] It was possible to halt the collectivization of agriculture. The cause of worker self-management was taken up, and wages were raised. Some of the injustices of the Stalin period were atoned for. The Catholic Cardinal[60] was released from detention; certain temporary concessions were made to him, and his support was obtained; and it was shown that a greater degree of national sovereignty was possible. Economic reserves built up in the same way during the 1960s enabled the new leadership in 1971 to make promises that were partially kept during the economic boom of 1972 to 1974.

Today, generally speaking, the political and economic reserves that would permit a new bid to society are nonexistent or are far more difficult to mobilize.

The situation considerably worsened after 1976. Because no real change was forthcoming, social frustrations increased, causing a polarization of positions. In some people the desire to make one's fortune by any means——even illegal——took hold. The price was moral compromise, conformity, and outward acquiescence in everything the authorities did. There was a revival of the old tacit alliance or at least mutual tolerance for various groups grasping at privileges——those within and outside the ruling apparatus——an alliance often based on mutual corruption. Others were pushed into political opposition. Still others, convinced of their impotence, surrendered themselves to a sense of powerlessness and its attendant apathy, occasionally interrupted by acts of aggression against the nearest person in a line or in another social group, or outbursts of blind revolt.

In response No. 2 we have an account of the attitudes of the ruling apparatus toward the emergence of these problems. "Part of the apparatus favors: strengthening the leading role of the party along traditional lines; tightening social and political discipline——conceived mechanistically and imposed by administrative coercion. ... The representatives of these views do not realize how dangerous these tendencies could be for the country and for themselves given our present situation."

The same reply analyzes another view prevalent among the ruling political and economic groups that shape current policy. This view advocates "increasing the effectiveness of the system by means of constant adjustments and improvements, which would not affect any of its basic elements." This is the policy of economic maneuver, the basic principle and aim of which is survival.[61]

The Tactics of Maneuver

Both experience and the current symptoms suggest that the strategy of maneuver[62] will probably be continued.

The cornerstone of this policy is relative tactical flexibility combined with the extreme rigidity of the system. If the need arises, the authorities will make concessions to various social groups, often paying a very high price (usually out of the national purse). Such a concession is, for example, the practice of paying factory workers during stoppages. Another is granting permits to build churches and—*toutes proportions gardées*—the papal visit. Yet another is tolerating various opposition groups and periodicals.

We will probably see more concessions made to avoid serious tensions and social unrest. They will be interspersed with attempts at administrative, economic, or police pressure.

The economic maneuver will probably be carried out by the following means:

a. a further cutback in investments coupled with a switch in resources to the most needy sectors: energy, transportation, agriculture, and export production. There might be an increase in investment in housing construction;

b. a relocation of the labor force;

c. an attempt to reschedule debts or obtain new credits abroad;

d. an attempt to stabilize the money market by further price rises and the elimination of privileges based on unearned high pay and of the so-called "wage chimneys,"[63] which benefit about 10 percent of the population (through progressive taxation and elimination of social benefits). These methods are analyzed in replies Nos. 1, 4, 11, and 13.

An essential element of all such holding tactics is foreign aid. Help from Poland's allies will, no doubt, be essential; but most important will be assistance from the West. Until now, on the whole, the West has been willing to offer Poland limited support on less favorable terms than before. One can assume that the following factors play a part in this policy: the experience of trade with the Eastern bloc, which until now has met its obligations on time; the fact that Poland's existing debt is too large to allow the Poles to go bankrupt, hence the need for more aid; Poland's reserves of raw materials, skilled labor, and developed economic potential to some extent provide a long-term guarantee that obligations will be met and that cooperation will be effective; and our Western partners will probably make further help conditional on reforms in the system of economic management, on the assumption that such changes are to a limited extent possible, and in connection with their desire to maintain a certain degree of independence for Poland from the Soviet Union.

All the elements of this survival strategy will be associated with an appropriate modification of the means employed. On the whole, though, efforts will be made not to change the overall political climate and setup. An exception is possible only with regard to the Church. In order to obtain its support, or at least to neutralize it, further concessions may be made—not only tactical but also legal (for instance, the regulation of the Church's legal status).

The outline of a way out of the present political and economic crisis we have sketched is also fraught with great dangers for the country because it is as divorced from reality as the idea of a return to stern methods of government.

Any plan for resolving the crisis by economic means alone is, under today's circumstances, unrealistic because the deeper causes of the crisis are not economic. Without a reform of the system of management and a change in the social climate, it will be impossible to create any reserves; the "rigid factors" in the economy we will describe in more detail in Chapter 7 militate against any influx of extra means.

In this situation projects, for instance, to abolish privileges based on access to money or goods or to limit the incomes of certain social groups are unrealistic. Unjustified wage increases impose a burden on the money supply and cost us all dearly; but the authorities know that one must not upset the emotional and political equilibrium of the leading battalions of the working class—that is, the work force of the 150 largest enterprises— because that might bring them out onto the streets. This is because—given the deficits, the major shortages of energy, transportation, and hard currency, as well as the general disarray of the economy—plant stoppages and an erratic production process will continue to be the rule, and we will continue to pay the price. A considerable price. The same will apply to the meat supply and other scarce goods as well as to the distribution of the social welfare fund. Some industrial workers will continue to be bought off at the expense of the rest of society. As a straightforward political calculation this makes sense, for instead of trying to "buy" the majority of the population, one has only to apply a slightly different pay policy with regard to 7 to 15 percent of the work force (the key enterprises and the ruling apparatus). It is doubtful whether any future policy aimed at boosting exports will be able to undermine this principle, based as it is on the experiences of the last few years. At the same time, this practice in effect destroys any chance of controlling the money supply and easing pressure on the consumer market.

Equally ineffective will be any policy aimed at demolishing the "wage chimneys," taxing excessive incomes, or curtailing other privileges. The managements of priority investment projects will still have to pay very high wages, and will have to pay for export and anti-import production. We will also have to pay more to private farmers. The imposition of further taxes on truck farmers and artisans is dangerous because it could undermine production. In any case it is not really necessary, because the high incomes of these groups are diminished by the high cost of investment funds and luxury consumer goods. Apart from that, one has to remember that high-income party and managerial groups did not obtain a much higher standard of living during the 1970s in order to give it up without a fight.

At the same time, popular pressure on the wage fund will grow. The author of response No. 8 writes:

"Today motivations are changing, or rather are being expanded. This concerns, in particular, such needs as housing or cars. In the case of housing, shortages and price increases mean, in effect, that for many young people and many of the older, poorer people, an apartment has become completely unattainable, or something obtained only after many years of waiting.

"For a long time a car was a luxury item available only to the few; it was not the object of common desire. Now things have changed. If 20 to 30 percent of the fellows at work have a car, I am indignant if I do not. Both these factors will exert considerable pressure on wages."

There remains foreign aid. This year servicing and repayment of foreign debts will amount to about $4 billion, or the equivalent of 65 to 70 percent of the value of exports in convertible currency. Next year it is hoped to diminish the current debt burden by about 10 percent. It is difficult to say how realistic these plans are. The situation on the world markets will still be extremely difficult. There is no reason to think that we will find it any easier to export. At the same time, our heavily expanded metallurgical and chemical industries cannot operate without a supply of raw materials and semifinished products from the capitalist countries. So the only remedy is to draw on further credits similar to those obtained during the first quarter of 1979, with the difference that they will be more expensive and the prospects for recovery even more remote.

All this supports the thesis that it is impossible to resolve the present crisis by economic means. Attempts to do so will, as in the past, be little more than patchwork, while the cost of real repairs will have to be paid in full at some later date. The author of reply No. 34 shares this view: "Up to now government policies aimed at overcoming the situation have not promised success. The change in economic program and the celebrated 'economic maneuver' have not worked out. The results of successive economic plans, which have clearly missed their goals, show this. The avalanche of incidental directives and restrictions only spreads the chaos because it is not and cannot be internally coherent."

It is difficult to see how a system of economic management that during the last three years has only made the crisis worse could do anything except drive the economy right into the ground. Practices that have almost totally deranged our economy cannot set it straight; they can only continue their work.

The Social Consequences of a "Holding Tactic"

A social explosion or a series of conflicts could bring about a fundamental change in the situation and would require the application of certain political measures, for example, a dialogue between the authorities and the public on new grounds. But it might also be the case that under certain circumstances, a "holding tactic" could achieve some results, postponing an explosion for, say, two or three years. Respondent No. 13 has the following to say: "Going into the streets . . . it might happen . . . but I would say that is much less likely than some other kind of long-term threat. I have in mind stagnation of the economy and the persistence of the ills visible everywhere around us, a growing weariness with the 'mess,' and at the same time, an increasing acceptance, as it were, of all the negative phenomena. The state I fear I would call 'false accord'——both the authorities and society would tolerate each other while feeling neither respect nor trust toward each other."

This state of affairs has an adverse effect on public morale and contributes to a further weakening of the authority of the state. "This demoralization," writes the author of reply No. 28, "is particularly noticeable in the present crisis; this is so because of certain specific stabilizing factors. The acceptance of consumerism as an economic ideal without the means to achieve it has led many people to adopt the habit of feathering their own nests, which, given the inefficiency of economic mechanisms in our country, leads to theft of public property, corruption, every kind of conformism——all happily accepted if the payoff is adequate. Inflationary policy creates new psychological states. A person with no money is inclined to rebel. A person who has money but cannot find goods to buy with it is ready to scour the countryside with only that purpose in mind. In a paradoxical way these phenomena tend to stabilize the system; the crisis, having become a kind of prolonged gangrene slowly but surely killing the social organism, loses its explosive aspects and can change into a chronic, lingering condition. A situation also arises in which certain, even quite large, sections of the population come to have an interest in maintaining anarchy: part of the working class because it is able in this way to avoid too strict work discipline; part of the peasantry because the situation creates opportunities for speculative activity; part of the intelligentsia that sees chances to make a career or gain material rewards on the basis of conformity and favoritism. The disadvantages of economic anarchy are, for a certain group in society, balanced by the possibility of getting income on the side, by transactions based on favoritism, by the opportunity to devote more time to improving one's own affairs, and so on. The frustrations of the more active sections of our youth are relieved to some degree by so-called 'working holidays,' which let a person fill in the few years he or she has to wait for an apartment or a car (of course, we are talking about the student population and not young workers, whose situation is the most difficult). It also seems that this state of disorder has its advantages for the clergy, strengthening its social position and authority."

In answer No. 27 we read: "Apathy, sterility, boredom, and total stagnation in every quarter. In this light the sporadic explosions of aggression are acts of despair. The moral and intellectual crisis is as serious as the economic one. A gradual slide into the ranks of those countries that count for absolutely nothing in the world. Increasing enmity between different groups and classes, partly the result of an awareness of the absurdity of the present polarization . . . and also a feeling of guilt because one cannot play the game in any other way. One of the basic threats, in my opinion, is the social phenomenon of there being no chance to maintain one's dignity."

Enmity between different social groups will inevitably increase. "Rapid growth," writes the author of reply No. 8, "has inevitably produced differences in income, something looked at askance in our egalitarian society and quite unbearable at a time of stagnation or crisis, when the standard of living of certain social groups declines, while other people are able to arrange things quite well for themselves." "The so-called Polish paradoxes," stresses respondent No. 25, "derive from the fact that in Poland there are quite sizable social groups whose aim is lavish, not to say luxurious, consumption—which means that there are no goods too expensive to find a buyer, a fact that creates the impression of general prosperity and also further gears production and trade toward those same groups. At the same time, there are whole layers of society that live, if not below the social minimum, then at least just above it, in a state of considerable deprivation, poverty, and often on the borders of mere subsistence and outright destitution."

Respondent No. 7 adds: "The dissolution of social ties, combined with an increasing polarization of social forces, can only lead to internal conflicts whose scale one can neither foresee nor define."

This circumstance can sometimes create opportunities for the authorities to try to turn such tensions to their advantage. It will, however, be an illusory advantage. Eventually it might prove very dangerous. People's anger can easily turn away from the new petit bourgeois parvenus and against the authorities themselves. This is because the authorities, in their own and everyone else's view, are responsible for everything. Quite apart from the fact, of course, that among this group too one finds examples of extravagant consumption.

So even the intermittent adoption of a "holding" tactic, a tactic of muddling through, does not eliminate the threat of an explosion. It only postpones it, while all the while tension grows. Public consciousness crystallizes and is driven by inevitable reflex toward rebellion. This process is described by respondent No. 9:

"More and more frequently I observe that people are asking themselves more serious questions, that the sources of frustration lie deeper. Why is my work worth so little? Where does the money go that I earn? Why if it must be spent on something, do I not know what that is? Why can my most serious doubts not be voiced in any forum? Why do I have to be afraid to voice

them? Why must I so often do things to get a promotion or
improve my family's living standard that run against my conscience? Why and how has it become true that I am a swine?
When did I realize it, and when did I stop caring?"

In other words, the trigger to rebellion is no longer just the
activity of opposition elements but also simple, basic moral
reflection. Every church sermon about conscience, every book
that reminds the reader of human dignity, even every television
program dealing with the apparently abstract themes of honesty
and nobility must in the present state of affairs act as a catalyst
of protest.

* * *

So far we have discussed the immediate threats stemming
from political and economic sources. However, there is another
group of threats that stem mainly from mistakes made in social,
educational, and cultural policies in the broad sense.

We have in mind:

——the deteriorating health of the population;
——disturbing trends in national education;
——the state of cultural life.

Health

In this area, as in many others, information about the actual
state of national health is not available. Here we can therefore
do no more than call attention to a few points: the demographic
situation and that of the family, conditions in the hospitals, the
availability of medicine, the cost of treatment, alcoholism, and
the state of the environment.

Population growth in Poland stems largely from the poorest
families. The families of the professional classes and skilled
workers usually have one child, while one third of these families
have no children at all. There is a clear tendency to strive for a
higher standard of living, yet many families nonetheless find
themselves in very serious straits. One third of young couples
have no accommodations of their own, and the waiting lists for
apartments constantly grow.

Other problems that seriously impair family life are very
high numbers of abortions, frequent family conflicts leading to
the breakup of marriages, and the steadily growing number of

one-parent children——tens of thousands more each year.

As regards the number of hospital beds per capita, we have fallen to next to last place among the socialist countries. Even in Warsaw the number of hospital beds is barely half the European average. The state of the municipal and general hospitals is catastrophic; hospital wards are overcrowded, and cases of death among patients left in hospital corridors are not uncommon. Conditions created by chronic underinvestment in health services fully warrant the assertion that access to treatment, hospitals, good doctors, and medical equipment has become very difficult to obtain for the majority of the public. At the same time, the privileged few have special enclaves of luxury closed to people who do not belong to that group. A glaring example is the Ministry of Health clinic at Anin.

Free health care for the vast majority of the population was once considered an achievement of People's Poland. But unfortunately, today the situation is completely different. Irregularities and deficiencies in health care have meant that medical treatment now requires money, quite a bit of money, as well as connections and pull. They have led to a distressing situation——if one does not bribe the nursing staff, one does not get decent attention, and if one does not bribe the doctor, his care will be marginal. One now pays to get a bed in a hospital or an operation, to say nothing of medicine. Gradually the public is being divided into two categories: those who can afford proper medical care and those who cannot. If the situation does not improve substantially, the latter group will get even larger. If we were to compare incomes to the real costs of obtaining treatment by a specialist, we would probably find that at least half the public could not afford it today. This situation is alarming in the extreme.

The public health system was reorganized a few years ago; but because of underinvestment, low doctors' salaries, and inadequate production of medical equipment, the situation has not improved. It is difficult to predict the consequences of this. Suffice it to mention the growing number of infections in hospitals and, most alarming of all, the high rate of infant mortality (at the moment we are fifth in Europe), or the crying lack of even the simplest prosthetic devices for the handicapped (we have four and a half million invalids in Poland, two million of whom are of productive age). We should add that Polish industry regards production for the needs of the young unprofitable, unlike our neighbors (Czechoslovakia and the GDR), who give priority to these needs.

Neglect of the pharmaceutical industry has resulted in a complete breakdown in medical supplies. The Polish Sejm Commission on Health and Physical Education found that of 2,148 items on the Offical List of Medicines, 600 are in chronically short supply.[64] When some hospital pharmacies tried to produce a few of these medicines, it was found that in many cases profits on some drugs were as much as ten times the cost of production. This is in glaring contradiction to the principle of free health care. If the price of medicine is ten times the cost of production, then even if an insured patient must pay only 30 percent of that price, the profit made on the medicine he buys is still improbably large.

The population's health is affected to a considerable degree by the instability and chaotic state of the food market. In 1976, after the attempt to raise all food prices at a stroke had failed, these prices still soared as a result of covert but drastic increases.[65] The creation of "commercial" shops[66] has divided the public into two groups: those who can and those who cannot afford to buy high-priced meat and sausage, that is, those who are and those who are not so well nourished, depending on material conditions. The sorry state of the food market has created a situation in which ever greater numbers of the population get inadequate nutrition. In view of progressive inflation, this situation is bound to get worse. Considering that the greater part of the population growth in our country comes from families with the lowest standard of living, it is not far-fetched to say that this constitutes a real threat to the nation's health. It is worth pointing out that according to research done by health and epidemiological authorities, 25 percent of the food products on sale have characteristics that are to some degree harmful to health, to say nothing of the many food products that are commonly adulterated by producers. Consumers have essentially no way to defend themselves against these practices, while supervision from official quarters is totally ineffective.

In a situation of chronic, serious food shortages, the steady spread of alcoholism seems especially threatening. The facts of the matter are too well known to require further elaboration. The situation is all the more alarming in light of the futility of all the appeals and attempts made to combat this staggering phenomenon. We should, however, look into why people are drinking more, why alcohol is the only consumer product on sale virtually all day, and why we have thirty times as many liquor shops as Sweden. According to the experts (and common knowl-

edge), the spread of alcoholism is a sign that something is profoundly wrong in social life. Respondent No. 7 reminds us of
Engels' famous statement: "Alcoholism is to a great extent a
reaction to frustrations and the lack of prospects in life." There
is no need to point out that alcoholism is one of the most serious
threats to social existence.

* * *

When we discuss the biological threats that stem from prolongation of the current situation in our country, we cannot fail
to mention the steady deterioration in the environment in which
we live. The total neglect of environmental matters for many
years gave way in 1970 to a formal recognition of their importance. In practice, however, nothing, or in any event very little,
changed.

A few facts. According to the *Statistical Yearbook* for
1978, of the 90,600 wells from which people drew water in 1977,
only 5 percent had water fit for drinking, 25 percent were classi-
fied as safe, and 69.1 percent were rated bad. In 1975 bad water
was found in only 44.2 percent of the wells.

The water along the entire course of the Vistula River was
monitored, and at no point was it found fit for drinking (grade I
water); 16.8 percent of the samples were rated grade II (fit for
farm animals and for swimming); 54.4 percent were grade III
(fit for use only in industry and for farm irrigation); while 28.8
percent were so polluted that they were suited for none of these
purposes.

The situation in the Oder River is even worse: grade I——0
percent; grade II——2.4 percent; grade III——32.9 percent; and
water unfit for use——64.7 percent.

Of 803 towns, only 336 have sewage treatment facilities.
In 1977, 4.321 million cubic meters of communal and industrial
sewage in need of treatment was discharged into rivers, but only
2.554 million cubic meters had been treated.

Industrial enterprises emitted 3.439 million tons of gases
into the atmosphere but trapped only 667,000 tons. If one adds
to this that the majority of stack filters are almost always shut
down because of the energy shortage, it must be concluded that
Poland is one of the few countries in the world in which the
emission of industrial gases and particles into the air is not subject
to control.

* * *

To sum up, we feel that the biological threats we have discussed are quite serious. Each of them is dismissed by various authorities with the added suggestion that they are only temporary. In reality, however, they are permanent and even now have effects that, from the point of view of health, are beginning to put us clearly behind the rest of Europe. This, together with growing social inequalities in the domain of health, is, as we have said, endangering the biological future of the entire nation.

Education

One of the unquestionable achievements stemming from the postwar changes in Poland is education. It is common knowledge that during the first postwar years, both the state and society made an enormous effort to make education accessible to all young people, despite the destruction caused by the war and the lack of teachers and materials.

But we also know the troubles and flaws in our educational system. Much has been written about them. The *Report on the State of Education*[67] contains a full analysis of the situation in our school system, its needs, and its deficiencies, so there is no need to take up these many important matters now. In the last few years, however, some tendencies that date back to the beginning of the postwar era have become exacerbated. We would like to dwell a bit on them here because they could effectively obstruct the basic functions of our educational system. More importantly, as many respondents pointed out, they could weigh heavily on the future of our society.

They concern:

——the role of the educational system as a factor facilitating or obstructing social advancement;

——the intensification of antieducational attitudes.

Let us examine these points one at a time.

As regards social processes, the educational system is the most important factor in social advancement. The universality, availability, and accessibility of the system predetermine the scale of social mobility and indirectly set the pace for the progress of society as a whole. In this respect the situation has aroused considerable doubts since the very first years after the war. From the outset various selective barriers have operated between the rungs of the educational ladder; since the very beginning we have never had an effective system for equalizing educational opportunities for peasants, the working class, or people from small towns; and from the very beginning standards in primary and secondary schools have been very uneven. Children from the lower-quality schools did not have much chance to continue their schooling in secondary school or higher education. Soon after the war the decision was made to expand the whole system of vocational and trade schools, the practical effect of which was to close the door to any further education for pupils attending these institutions. This state of affairs, which has often been criticized, has done considerable damage, frequently irreparable. It is sufficient to look at the level of education of people born during the years of the demographic explosion to realize the scale of the problem: about 70 percent of young people born during those years have had a basic (complete or incomplete) or elementary vocational education.

In the last few years, however, the situation has deteriorated further. As the level of culture has advanced generally, the educational aspirations of Polish society have risen notably. The number of families in which the parents have completed secondary or higher education has increased, and hence they too would like to secure at least the same education for their children. At the same time, young people born during the years of the demographic explosion began to enter higher education in the late sixties, although the number of places available in these institutions, especially at the lyceum level, increased at a pace barely able to meet the most urgent needs of that group. The level of admissions remained static, overcrowding worsened, and the conditions of instruction deteriorated.

As a result competition for places in secondary and higher education sharpened. Because of growing material differences among the population, the material situation of pupils' parents began to play a role in this competition (e.g., the ability to pay for private tutors), along with their professional situation, status, and share in power—in a word, pull. Prospects for working-class, peasant, and small town and village young people appreciably diminished.

As the years passed and the divisions grew among the population, differences in opportunity steadily widened, so that today factors such as professional status and parental wealth play a far greater role in determining access to education. A recent study showed that today a child whose parents have a higher education has a 7.5 time greater chance of remaining within the ranks of the intelligentsia than the child of a farm worker has of entering them.

The educational authorities have at least made a series of attempts to alleviate this situation, establishing, for example, local comprehensive schools and initiating a campaign for further teachers' education. But the chronic lack of funds for investments, repair, and equipping schools and the lack of means to transport children to the comprehensive schools made these efforts largely fruitless.

It is therefore possible today to speak of the existence of educational privilege, the inheritance of status, and even the class nature of education. As a result a large percentage of gifted young people are denied the possibility of an education, in violation of the basic principles of justice and at a great loss to our country.

The processes we have described have been reinforced by the intensification of antieducational attitudes. These attitudes have in fact long existed to some degree, surfacing periodically in all sorts of decision-making circles. In practice they amounted to giving priority to vocational schooling at the expense of general education. Respondent No. 25 put this point as follows: "There has been a pattern in education that for some time has favored the idea of vocational training, understood narrowly as the acquisition of trade skills, over general education. The proportion of pupils completing seven years of school who go on to the lower level of vocational school, compared to the number of those going on to various types of higher secondary schools, has remained almost constant at 60 : 40. In the early days of industrialization, when people were streaming from the countryside in huge numbers to work on construction sites or in towns, this trend was to some extent understandable. But the pattern has proved to be a tenacious one, and for years now lower-level vocational schools, which provide a very poor and narrow education, have become a major obstacle to education progress in our society."

The same attitudes have also been apparent in the chronic underfunding of education and in low teachers' salaries. It seemed, however, that after the publication of the *Report on the State of Education* and the decision to introduce ten-year compulsory schooling, things would improve, that some heed would be paid to the principle of creating equal opportunity for youth coming from different backgrounds, and that, above all,

the reforms would substantially raise the level of general education of young workers. In fact the opposite happened. It is now
evident that despite the shared opinion of educators and, it
seems, of the educational authorities, the tendency is for the
existing differences to continue and for 60 percent of pupils
completing eight years of schooling to be sent to the basic
vocational schools. This amounts to total nullification of the
educational reform. For if we recall that it has been proposed to
bridge the gap between the ten-year school and higher education
by means of a two-year school in a selected area of specialization,
then we are faced with the prospect of a further deterioration
in what is already an unsatisfactory situation. Instead of two
points at which to choose——after the eighth year and after the
lyceum——there would be three: after the eighth year, when 60
percent of all youth will have gone on to vocational schools,
after the tenth year, and after the two-year school. If such an
idea were to become a reality, it could only be interpreted as a
conscious decision to exclude young people from the low-income
layers, working-class youth, and peasant youth from enjoying
the benefits that stem from the two-year extension of compulsory schooling.

It should be stressed that no eduational arguments could
be made in favor of such a policy decision. Given the level of
our country's development, we have too few people with a
secondary education and too few with higher education. Apart
from that it has by now become a cliché that the development
of education cannot be based entirely on the need for personnel.
Education has become a value in itself and a keystone in personal aspirations.

It is difficult to avoid the impression that making education
into a rare commodity inaccessible to the general public, and in
fact destined only for certain social strata, simply reveals fear of
an enlightened society and of an enlightened working class and
peasantry.

* * *

The list of problems facing our educational system is long:
——Low salaries and low professional prestige have meant
that a process of "negative selection" has long been at work in
the teaching profession. Teachers are burdened with a mass of
nonteaching activities, are often inadequately trained, and——as
research has shown——about 50 percent of them are in a state of

constant internal moral conflict caused by having to say one thing while they think another. As a result the moral authority of the teacher, his prestige as a pedagogue molding young people's characters and moral attitudes, has declined.

——School programs are overburdened, are often simply not good enough, and in some subjects, such as history or the Polish language, are full of gaps and distortions. This fundamentally undermines the school's authority in the eyes of the pupils.

——School has long since ceased to be a learning place; it no longer shapes the attitudes of youth, no longer teaches them to think for themselves, and no longer prepares them for genuine participation in political and cultural life.

——The state of higher education is particularly troubling. A paradoxical situation has emerged there. During the last few years there has been a significant decline in the number of candidates accepted for studies, so that today our institutions of higher learning have a clearly elitist character. At the same time, as a result of chronic underinvestment, these institutions must grapple with lack of space, facilities, and teaching staff and cannot do their jobs.

Each of these problems——and they do not exhaust the list of criticisms one could level at our educational system——has a negative effect on the educational level of our society. Each could be considered a source of threats to Polish culture.

It is our view, however, that the most serious threats to the future of our nation are the inability of the educational system to perform its basic social functions and the antieducational attitudes referred to above. Persistence of these tendencies would mean the abandonment of basic socialist values as well as the threat of deep and permanent social rifts and——in the longer term——the intellectual degradation of society, with all the consequences that entails.

Creativity and Culture

In assessing the dangers of the current situation in culture, one can draw a comparison with the threats in the field of education we have described: they are, after all, inextricably linked. Two areas in particular, however, must be distinguished in which the present situation and the way in which official policy is conducted are having an especially pernicious effect. We refer to cultural creativity and the dissemination of culture among broad segments of the public, which (especially the latter) are supposed to have been cornerstones of the legitimacy of the socialist system.

In the field of artistic activity of all kinds, our country has to its credit many achievements of the highest order, although they were often made in the teeth of officially imposed obstacles and in defiance of official tendencies. Nonetheless we have managed to create many outstanding works, especially in music, the theater, film, as well as in literature. However, in all these areas we find persistent obstacles that cast into doubt the possibility of further development.

A separate issue, to which we shall devote more space in the following chapters, is that of censorship, which impinges in equal measure on culture, learning, and education. Respondent No. 20 makes a typical comment:

"The thoughts and imaginations of our contemporaries are quite strongly affected by examples drawn from the history of those dearest to them. The fate of our older brothers, our fathers, and grandfathers aroused the most intense interest in us. The immense interest demonstrated by members of the younger generation in the series of very worthwhile publications that appeared to commemorate the sixtieth anniversary of the restoration of Polish independence[68] confirmed the truism that creative historical thought seeks the roots of today in the past. One must give its full due to the felicitous decision of the authorities to celebrate the sixtieth anniversary of the restoration of our statehood; the anniversary occasioned the publication of many significant books; there were a number of important films; the silence surrounding certain events and people was broken. It is true that this time, too, this sincerely desired initiative was partially smothered in opportunism and the phobias of certain forces about the Pilsudski era;[69] a number of brakes were applied, and a number of publications were stopped or their circulation drastically limited; films were consigned to languish on the shelf (e.g., a splendid television film about Grot-Rowecki).[70] However, despite all the inconsistencies, the sixtieth anniversary celebrations were undoubtedly an event worthy of note. The important point is that once again, the matter should not be thought of as being 'dealt with' and either hushed up or given a cavalier treatment for the momentary purposes of propaganda. The source of public consciousness in Poland today lies in the nineteenth century (particularly its second half) and in the first half of the twentieth century. Modern political thought emerged during this period; timetables were set and choices made that are often relevant to this day. That is why a young person seeking the roots of his ideological identity will turn to the decades immediately before him. If he is a student born around 1960, he will obviously be mainly interested in discovering the historical truth about the Polish People's Republic. What will he find out from academic textbooks, from the so-called works of contemporary history, from literature as a whole? What will he learn about the events of 1948, 1968, and 1970? He will read how the party, step by step, consistently led the nation to ever new achievements, how the principles and aims of socialism were consistently realized. Very soon, first in his imagination and then with the rest of his mind, he will turn away from these monotonous falsehoods. The period of World War II and the occupation is particularly falsified when it comes to Polish-Soviet relations."

Elsewhere in this same response we read: "There was a time, not so long ago, when even *Forefathers' Eve*[71] could not appear on the Polish stage. Today this national classic has its place in cultural policy, albeit a tightly circumscribed one. Despite many attempts it has never been possible to film either the *Faithful River* or *Sisyphus* or *The Charm of Life* or *Forest Echoes*.[72] Equally fruitless have been attempts to film contemporary historical novels such as Terlecki's *Conspiracy* or *Black Romance*, or J. J. Szczepański's *Island*. (In this last case the refusal was caused by the fact that the hero of the book is Aleksander Berezowski, the unsuccessful would-be murderer of a tsar.) This negative program of the Polish film industry was described by a film maker a couple of years ago, when he said that in a Polish film, a Russian uniform—even a tsarist one— has no place summoning up unfriendly associations."

According to our respondents the cultural policy being pursued today in Poland threatens Polish national identity.

It finds expression, for instance, in the harrassment and restrictions that every artist encounters when he dares to express a view of his own that differs from the officially sanctioned one. Such people are relentlessly persecuted, and many of them are condemned to being public "nonpersons." Above all, conformist attitudes are rewarded. As a result many of the most splendid works have disappeared from the cultural scene. The prolongation of such a state of affairs can have the direst consequences for culture and intellectual life.

In the dissemination of culture, as in education, People's Poland initially chalked up some notable successes. Alas, the same cannot be said today. The author of the passage above sees the regression in universal access to culture and its social consequences in this way:

"The sorry picture of housing project Poland—identical from the Carpathians to Pomerania, identical from the Oder to Podlasie—can be only partly explained by the industrial character of contemporary architecture. The identical forms of these projects also reflect a lack of local initiative and ideas. Throughout the whole of Poland identical shows are put on in Ruch cafes and night clubs, book clubs, or the local housing project reading rooms.[73] In their identically planned apartments model families live to the rhythm of work and leisure planned from above, with the television as the source of their emotions. This uniformity is nothing to be happy about. In it the energies and creative talents of society lie sleeping; people do not even suspect the existence in themselves of any creative life. Forced into mere subsistence, whose ideal has become consumerist stability, they lose their chance ever more irrevocably as the days and years pass. At the same time, the country, deprived of the creative energies of its people, loses its chance."

It is difficult not to mention the backsliding in the material basis for culture: supplies of paper for books are diminishing, as is the number of movie theaters; the number of libraries is shrinking, as are their means to expand their collections. Not long ago the minister of culture told a Sejm committee that even essential textbooks would not be published.

In the early days of People's Poland, reading became a mass need. Today worthwhile books are sold under the counter like luxury imports. Ample proof has been supplied by the findings of the Basic Party Cell in the Writers' Union; we do not have to go over the details again. We fail to satisfy the needs of the educated reading public or literate workers and peasants. Good children's literature has become almost unobtainable. There is a lack of textbooks, dictionaries, and technical books. Poland is slowly turning into a country with a shortage of the printed word; it is already close to last place in Europe. These are not temporary difficulties; they represent a condition that has been deteriorating for many years.

On the one hand, then, there are censorship restrictions, and on the other, material ones that result in chronic underinvestment and financial cutbacks in all areas of culture. They stem from a lack of appreciation of cultural needs. This state of affairs is reflected in both aspects of culture: in its creation and in its dissemination. For a time there was a clear tendency (derived from a profound misunderstanding of the basis of cultural needs) to replace both with television. It was, of course, misconceived, and today even this idea is foundering. Television is more and more firmly subordinated to the instrumental needs of propaganda, and the old ambitions are dying.

* * *

Among people who have a deciding voice in Polish affairs, both in the political apparatus and in higher and middle economic management, one often hears it said of culture: "We cannot afford such luxuries; their time will come later." The time, however, never comes. And we are not talking about luxuries but about one of the most important issues in Poland. In our country culture has always played an enormous role. It let our nation survive the partitions and in great measure helped it preserve its identity. This role was confirmed during the period of Nazi occupation. That is why the conscious curtailment, mutilation, and trivialization of national culture are contrary to the basic interests of the Polish people. Culture is not a luxury. It ranks among the most fundamental values we have talked about in this chapter.

The direct and long-term threats we have discussed have had——in the views of our respondents——a decisive influence on the moral state of society.

The Moral State of Society

The author of response No. 3 writes: "The professionally most active generation in our country is characterized by a state of lassitude and apathy. The old enthusiasm of the Union of Polish Youth[74] has been eroded. Frequent disappointments have taught people to be pragmatic. Most people in our country avoid the risk of any kind of innovation, which is first stifled in their own circles and then, anonymously, by representatives of the authorities at various levels.

"It is my profound conviction that the crisis we are experiencing is above all political. We have reached the point in the development of the forces of production, technology, and education at which the old political structures, with their inherent inertia, are beginning to paralyze us and to spawn enormous waste of resources and a system of negative incentives."

According to our respondents, the unsatisfactory moral state of our society——something on which everybody concurs, and which is, moreover, often commented on in our own mass media——is caused in the first instance by public awareness of the enormous squandering of our resources——especially human energy, good will, and talent. It is very difficult to convince people to work hard and to show a respect for public property if everywhere they see how great wealth is wasted by bad management and careless decisions; how corruption spreads everywhere while its agents are protected; how middle-ranking representatives of the power structure, and often high-ranking ones, derive great personal benefit from exercising their power and have at their disposal a variety of privileges they enjoy at the expense of the public (e.g., luxury residences built practically free). In this way the basic slogans of socialism are steadily abandoned: social justice, equality, universal access to education and culture, equality of opportunity, access to holidays and recreation for everyone, and so on. Working people are asked to sacrifice themselves, to tighten their belts, and to resign themselves to their fate.

Respondent No. 20 writes: "The authorities have destroyed in society the habit of criticism from below and of genuine initiative. Having created for themselves the role of unique and unrivaled decision-maker, the authorities have instilled in society the reflex of waiting for decisions to come from above. The most recent demonstration of this state of mind came during the 'catastrophic' winter just past.[75] This attitude, which sees the authorities as the sole wielder of power, is combined with, to put it mildly, a critical assessment of their activities and with contempt for inept and often dishonest representatives at various rungs of the political ladder. This extremely negative assessment of the leadership, coupled with the preconceived conviction that they alone make decisions, that everything is dictated from above, contributes to the formation of a disastrous complex of national impotence."

"Falling back into an attitude of ever greater passivity toward the goods and achievements of the community that the state should represent," continues respondent No. 20, "people concentrate all their efforts on their own private affairs. The interdependence of the development of society at large and personal interest becomes more and more illusory in the minds of the public. In general a citizen in our country is convinced that improvements in his own and his family's living conditions depend not on how industrial or agricultural production grows, but on how he manages to arrange things for himself, how effectively he is able to grease other people's palms in order to guarantee a supply of goods or good prospects for his child, and on his own moonlighting. This state of mind is, in a sense, useful to the people in power, as long as the standard for their actions continues to be maintaining their own positions and status. Such people can play on degenerate consumerist attitudes, whet appetites, ensnare subordinates in a system of rewarded dependency, and dispense favors (tax exemptions, extra rations, etc.). People, often without realizing it, trap themselves in the all-pervasive net of such arrangements. And even if they are not basically without character, at some point they lose the ability to say no, begin to prize the arrangements that assure them a certain level of daily existence, and cease to have an interest in altering existing conditions."

So with the passage of the years, slowly but surely, we began to lose those great traits of character that our society displayed during the occupation and the first years after the war, when our nation was being rebuilt; traits that briefly reappeared in 1959 and 1970 and were promptly shoved into the shadows as something unnecessary and suspect. That is why we again need those great traits of character which belong to the Polish working class, which were shaped in former years, and about which Maria Dąbrowska wrote:[76]

"If workers had no sense of professional morality, if they did not love and value their work and did not want to do it, if despite their justifiable displeasure with capitalist ways they did not do their work as well as they could, then they would not have developed the magnificent dignity that characterizes the working man and the strict sense of the importance of work that enabled working people to play an enormous role in the creation of modern democracy."

The lack of democracy, the lack of participation in decision-making, and the consequent disappearance of a sense of shared responsibility have led to a situation in which, after thirty-five years of building a socialist system, the character traits that developed under capitalism during real unemployment and in conditions of social injustice and acute class rifts are now evaporating and dying, giving rise to those irritating and sterile complaints by our journalists and our rulers about our society and our national weaknesses.

Such complaints will solve nothing. They have the same effect as the maneuvers and manipulations we have already mentioned. Let us conclude this chapter with a passage by respondent No. 10: "It is becoming more and more doubtful whether economic problems can be solved successfully without creating the political and social conditions necessary to restore even minimum confidence in those in power, a sense of decent work and the possibility of working for oneself, a sense of a balance between reward and merit, and so on. Even if these conditions are created, one should not expect in the foreseeable future an economic change that would provide our society with the profusion of material goods needed to satisfy aspirations patterned on the wealthiest capitalist countries. It is now apparent that socialism cannot provide unconditional guarantees of economic development rapid enough to 'overtake' the West."

Under these conditions the author of this passage believes it is of fundamental importance for our society, while accepting a reasonable level of material wealth, to adopt other values than consumption and property as worthy of prestige and satisfaction.

"The future of socialism in Poland," he writes, "depends on it. Our future is far from certain given the erosion of the socialist system of values we see at every turn."

Perhaps precisely this troubling moral state of society—which reveals itself in ever more unsatisfactory relations between individuals, dishonesty, indifference to matters of common concern, and the collapse of social ties—is the greatest threat we face.

CHAPTER 5

International Relations
and Poland's Sovereignty

This brings us to the most important and at the same time most difficult problems with which we have yet to deal: constructive proposals or ways to heal the Republic. It is the conviction of our respondents that the most important points at issue here are our national sovereignty, the existing state of international relations, and external conditions that impinge on us.

Respondent No. 17 writes: "The Poles are a people for whom the question of sovereignty is of paramount importance. One can, of course, say that for every nation sovereignty is the most important matter, and one would be right. But not every nation has, as we have had, the opportunity to discover how easy it is to lose one's independence and how difficult to regain it, and furthermore, that the loss of independence can raise the specter of extinction of one's very national identity or, quite simply, of biological annihilation. That is why every Pole has from childhood had engrained in his subconscious the conviction that independence is of paramount importance and that everything should and must be sacrificed and subordinated to it."

At the same time, public opinion in Poland, in the view of our respondents, sees a deep contradiction between the interests of Poland and the present configuration of international relations, between the interests of the outside world and our own national interests.

Respondent No. 4 writes: "Reform of the political system cannot tip the present balance of international forces in Europe and must take into account external conditions."

None of the participants in our study questioned this point of view.

This feeling of a discrepancy between the existing international order and the national aspirations of the Polish people causes deep resentment and anxiety; at certain crucial moments it can accumulate to form an explosive charge capable of laying waste to the whole of social life in our country, its institutions, and the established system of international equilibrium. That is why no one can treat it lightly. The emotions associated with this state of affairs long ago became a genuine social factor deeply affecting the atmosphere of life in the country; in politics they are, as the facts suggest, a real force——one of major importance.

Respondent No. 35 writes: "Very few nations on today's political map of the world have had experiences similar to ours. Very few nations carry about in their historical baggage so many scars, injustices, and anachronisms. They were and are the results of many years of national enslavement. The force of our national consciousness derives from the experience of those years: the years of struggle for survival, for the maintenance of our own national identity, and for the restoration of our own state."

Respondent No. 36 fills out the picture: "We were able to field the fourth largest army on the side of the allies. Upwards of a million Poles fought on all the European fronts during World War II, not counting the underground army. Unlike others, we fought from the first to the last moment, suffering proportionately the highest human and material losses. Despite this we proved to be the only large European nation not permitted to decide independently its own fate. We had been too badly ravaged and were too weak——and in politics it is the strong who set the conditions. Human memory, however, does not draw up the accounts of blood spilled in terms of a simple calculation of strength but in terms of the value of that blood itself. It is hard to forget that during the period in which the present European system was being born, the fate of entire nations was decided by the good or bad mood of individual statesmen, by a country's possession or lack of strong-willed and authoritative representatives——and not by an understanding of the needs and the opinions of millions of people."

Sovereignty and National Identity

Respondent No. 20 writes: "The awareness of limited national sovereignty . . . the doctrine expressed in the article of the Polish Constitution[77] that treats our alliance and friendship with the USSR as a guaranteed political duty of Poland, weighs painfully (more or less so depending on people and circumstances) on the civic attitudes of the Poles; it imposes a certain ceiling on their national aspirations and subordinates Polish society to a foreign state (even when that state is accepted as our genuine historical ally). This pressure varies in its intensity but is generally felt as a dull, dark, and ubiquitous factor paralyzing the will. The leadership of the party and state, or at least some of its representatives, seem not to perceive the inhibiting influence this complex of dependency has on people's nonmaterial civic motives. The patriotic pride of Poles is bolstered by examples of glory, achievements, and successes drawn from the past."

Since they fully understand the difficult, delicate, and complicated nature of this problem, the contributors to our study see not only the necessity but also, more appropriately, the possibility of change and improvement in this area. They understand——we stress this point again——that the present situation engenders tensions and feelings of revolt and frustration, is a threat to internal peace, and entails baleful political consequences, which in turn have a negative impact on every aspect of the state's activities and on the life of society. They understand that the significance of national sovereignty is so great for the Polish nation that any violation in this regard prompts a powerful and dangerous buildup of tension. They point out, however, that the task of altering this situation must begin with changes in the way this question is dealt with inside Poland; it must begin with acceptance of the principles of openness and probity, genuine discussion, and a determination not to conceal the truth.

However one sees the problem, one has to come to the conclusion that the methods used so far have not been successful.

Respondent No. 2 writes: "The profound changes that Polish society is undergoing, as well as the internal and external conditions in which it has to exist and develop, cause major disturbances in national identity. This appears, for instance, in a warped view of history and national traditions, as well as of the inherited values that shape our attitudes toward present and future tasks and goals. The lack of a real development of divergent strands of thought and of national consciousness (and philosophical outlook) is the result of a mechanistic restriction on discussion and creative activities whenever they appear to diverge from what happens to be the official line at the moment. Defensive reactions, often characterized by excessive emotionalism and negativism, can also be dangerous. To put the problem in the form of a paradox: the threats to the healthy development of national consciousness lie in servile and conformist surrender to simplistic phrases as well as in an emotional 'anti-Sovietism,' since national identity cannot base itself on contradiction, on negation. National identity is based on a whole heritage, not on selected siftings from the nation's past, accepted critically but honestly by the present generation of Poles. National identity is a sense of unity of purpose that transcends differences of view and attitude, differences that cannot always be reconciled or eliminated (their mechanistic elimination produces only a superficial unity)."

Finally, respondent No. 20: "A list of topics that it is strictly forbidden to discuss in print and the suppression of individual statements will not solve anything. The dislike, to put it mildly, for the Soviet Union has assumed, in broad segments of our society, an almost pathological character. How many times have we been shocked to see the hostile reaction of crowds to Soviet athletes at sporting events. Yet the decision-makers in our country, even when they recognize such phenomena, draw entirely wrong conclusions from them. They still think that they can talk the nation into having the right attitude and shape its consciousness by excising some trends and facts in history and by carefully retouching the past. In this way the schizophrenic character of our society is created, full of bitterness toward a country and nation with which we actually ought to be developing relations based on the principles of good neighborliness and friendly coexistence."

It boils down, then, to recognizing the principle of an honest and open discussion of all facts concerning both our history and contemporary politics. Release from this "schizophrenic state of mind" in Poland is an urgent social need. Although much has been said and continues to be said about the traditional romanticism of Polish attitudes, history has on many occasions proved that Poles have a natural tendency to base their politics on sound common sense. It was this common sense that enabled the Polish nobility in the sixteenth and seventeenth centuries to avoid the religious wars and at the end of the eighteenth century[78] to initiate reforms, which unfortunately came too late,[79] but which in a country better situated from a geographical point of view would have led to a flowering of society. It was this same sense of responsibility and good sense that after 1918 enabled our country to quickly form a unified whole from its three partitioned areas, and to integrate its population into a single society that during the period of occupation proved capable of maintaining a unified stance. This common sense, finally, has appeared on many occasions since World War II, particularly in 1956, when it alone saved our country from acts of revenge that could have led to civil war. Complaining about the state of our nation has become the favorite trick of some journalists who cannot suggest better ideas, but it has no basis in any sociological studies nor in history.

The respondents agreed that the common sense and sense of responsibility of the Polish people are still an important trump card which, however, can be played only if one talks to Poles in a serious and honest way, treating them as a proper partner and as masters of their own land.

In order to achieve a minimum of internal agreement, it is essential to create a climate of cooperation and trust and to accept the existence of certain historical facts that cannot be erased.

"Poland is a country," writes respondent No. 17, "which for a thousand years grew and developed in contact with Latin culture. Polish cultural and political traditions grow from European roots. In this way Poland's republican and freedom-loving tradition developed, a tradition that has characterized the Poles for centuries and that still marks the Polish mentality. Other traditions——the monarchic and despotic——are foreign to us. We are not making a value judgment. We are simply stating historical fact. Attempts to tear Poland away from that tradition, to sever the ties of a thousand years, are doomed to failure. They have caused and will continue to generate unrest and opposition that will preclude the peaceful and creative development of the nation and the state.

"Poland is different, and the Polish nation has its own unique traits. Some are its weakness, others constitute its strength. They must be treated together, with an awareness of the complicated social material with which we in Poland have to deal. All attempts to cut away some traditions and impose others, to liquidate some and spread others, must lead to ferment and disaffection."

It is worth recalling the eminent historian Tadeusz Manteuffl,[80] who made the following lapidary remark: "It is surely incontrovertible that just as a country whose economy is sick cannot develop, so a society that has turned away and cut itself off from its own history is condemned to a state of cultural atavism and stagnation." Because, as respondent No. 35 wrote:

"The awareness of a common past is one of the most powerful elements of social cohesion. It gives us our sense of identity. It distinguishes us from others."

Poland and the European Balance of Forces

During the course of our study, we have returned time and again to the assertion that it is in Poland's national interest to maintain internal peace. It is therefore evident that it is in our own vital interest for international peace to be preserved. No other country in Europe is as interested in international détente as Poland.

The international balance that has existed in Europe since 1945 serves to preserve peace in Europe. Of course, there have been frequent tensions; there are still many harmful barriers; the state of economic and cultural exchange is not fully satisfactory; and there are still limitations on the free movement of people and ideas and on the freedom to settle where one wants and to travel. Nonetheless peace has been maintained. That is why as a nation we are not interested in upsetting this balance. In this situation, recognizing geopolitical realities, Poland's place is in the Warsaw Pact; we think it is fair to say that there is no one in Poland who thinks we ought to change our international allegiances. In a divided Europe still affected by the memories of German expansion, in a situation in which not all significant political forces in the FRG have recognized Poland's western frontier as final and inviolable, no one can proclaim such a policy without laying himself open to a charge of irresponsibility.

Respondent No. 17 writes: "The German question weighs on the minds of Poles and must affect the nature of Polish politics. It cannot be left out of any deliberations on the future of our country. This does not mean that we should abandon our attempts to arrange our relations with our Western neighbors so that they will be better than in the past and to shape them in the spirit of peace and mutual respect and understanding. In the future such a mutual process should lead to a healing of the wounds of the past and to a situation in which no one will exploit the Polish-German problem as a useful tool for political manipulation, intimidation, and the pursuit of their own aims. A precondition for such a relationship, however, must be universal acceptance of Poland's western frontier as a fundamental and inviolable prop of European peace."

Respondent No. 37 adds: "The hope of some FRG circles for a return to solving the problems of Central Europe by Bismarckian methods runs counter to the aims of European peace and stability. It is true that the main guarantor of Poland's western frontier is the Soviet Union, but the permanence of this frontier does not depend entirely on the USSR. A nation of 35 million people cannot be a 'displaced people'; everyone in Europe must understand that questioning Poland's western frontiers threatens peace and prompts violent and dangerous reactions on the part of the Poles. On this question the Polish nation is completely united."

Nor are there differences of opinion among the contributors to our study on this score.

Poland and the USSR

Because of its geographical location, Poland is a country on whose territory various interests and aims cross paths and where influences from different sides meet. This fact also constitutes part of the reality that must be taken into account when formulating national policy.

On the one hand we have the powerful influence of the Soviet Union, with which our country is linked in a political, economic, and military alliance——an influence that has been one of the enduring results of World War II. The Soviet Union's interest in what happens in Poland cannot surprise anyone and is rooted in the objective political interests of that country.

Taught by the experience of history, which furnishes us with a number of examples of invasions of Russia from the west through Polish territory, the Soviet Union believes that that territory plays a fundamental role in its own defense. Moreover, the kind of system that prevails on Polish territory has for the Soviet Union not only strategic but an economic significance. It is also important for internal reasons.

It is evident that as regards the maintenance of equilibrium and peace in Europe, the interests of Poland and the Soviet Union and the other partners in the Warsaw Pact coincide. None of the participants in our study casts doubt on this assertion. It is also clear that any serious attempt to upset the prevailing balance of power in Europe, wherever it might occur, would face strong opposition from the Soviet Union. However, this problem has less obvious aspects that are interpreted by the contributors to this study in various ways. Above all there is the question of whether the Poles can have a genuine international policy of their own and affirm their sovereignty without upsetting the status quo or anyone else's genuine interests, while remaining true to the principles discussed above. There is another question that goes even further: whether Poland's internal decay and the crisis in Polish sovereignty are not in fact advantageous to its neighbors because, as respondent No. 28 writes, "The fear that might exist regarding Poland among our neighbors is only the fear of an explosive situation. However, a state of rot threatens no one."

In this remark we hear an echo of Poland's tragic experiences in the eighteenth century. However, today the situation is different. Then Poland was divided between the three partitioning powers and had ceased to exist as a separate political entity. Today Poland does exist. It is a united country of 35 million inhabitants; among the countries of the socialist alliance it ranks second in economic potential. To bet on the disintegration of Poland would be very shortsighted. It is in the objective interest of the Soviet Union, as understood by most of the participants in this study, that Poland be not only an effective but a genuine ally. Constant anxiety regarding the further course of events in Poland cannot be in anyone's interest.

The same applies in the economic domain. The efficiency and productiveness of Poland's economy not only do not conflict with the economic interests of our eastern neighbors but coincide with them. There is evidence for this not only from the period since 1945 but also from that around the turn of the century. Economic cooperation between the two countries can be extremely profitable for both sides. A precondition, however, is the existence of mutual trust and genuine partnership.

Finally, to quote respondent No. 37: "It does not appear that the USSR's interests in the ideological sphere could be satisfied by a state of affairs in our country in which the political order was constantly being torn apart by deep contradictions, tensions, and crises. This is a dangerous situation that cannot benefit anyone."

Poland and the West

On the other hand, we have the very powerful, though less direct, influence of the West. Having formally recognized the status quo, the West is, however, interested in maintaining some lack of stability and some tension which, however, does not cross the threshold of danger. In other words, it is interested in conditions that create maximum trouble for the Soviet Union with minimum risk and without the need for the West to be directly involved.

One might therefore assume that the West would be interested in a permanent state of crisis and tension in Poland and in preventing a lasting restoration of effective government and public institutions as well as economic health. Although such arguments are heard in the West, there is no lack of contrary voices as well. The latter come on the whole from the most sober and responsible politicians and journalists. They say that the paramount interest of the Western countries is also to maintain equilibrium in Europe and international détente, and that an improvement in the political and social situation in Poland will undoubtedly contribute to this.

This line of argument is supported by the rapid growth in recent years of economic ties between Poland (and other Eastern European socialist countries) and the economies of the West, particularly Western Europe. All the contributors to our study feel that the development of economic cooperation with the West is a beneficial process. There is no lack, however, of responsible voices pointing out that the policies of the present Polish leadership have immeasurably increased the country's dependence on both the East and the West. Economic cooperation is a good thing, but the same cannot be said for the excessive indebtedness of our country, based as it often is on a lack of foresight or even simple negligence. We discuss these questions more fully in other parts of our study; at this stage we will only say that the irresponsible and unproductive assumption of debts by our country undermines its sovereignty in a very troubling way.

One of our contributors (No. 37) pointed out a paradoxical result of such a situation: "Our hard-currency debt has grown to such an extent that our present creditors must be concerned about the creditworthiness of their debtor, perhaps even more so than he is himself. . . . A country with a disintegrating economy, shaken by internal discord, and disorganized by the passive resistance of the public cannot pay its debts."

Wittily put. However, most of the respondents expressed anxiety about developments in this area.

To sum up this section, let us quote respondent No. 17: "Poland cannot afford to cut its ties to either side. The ties to the East cannot and must not be broken. The same applies to our bonds with the West. The first split would upset the European balance of power and would have catastrophic political consequences. The second would contradict the whole of Polish cultural tradition and Polish history; it would strike at Poland's national identity, leading to serious social upheaval. It would also be harmful to Poland's economy. We therefore have to maintain a specifically Polish form of equilibrium that distinguishes us from some of our political partners but in no way threatens them."

How to Strengthen Sovereignty

What does the word "sovereignty" mean under the present circumstances, and what is its scope? Respondent No. 2 writes: "Sovereignty in effect means that a society independently and alone defines what is in its national interests and ways to further them; it verifies the results and on that basis maintains or changes the hierarchy of the various elements that together form what is called the national interest. Both the ruling apparatus and all independent formal and informal social institutions, circles, and trends, representing the diversity and richness of the nation's vitality, should participate in this process without external dictate. The focal point of thought and action should be the Polish nation and it alone. This does not mean that national sovereignty and self-determination in matters related to the national interest are exercised in isolation from external factors, from the international situation, or from tendencies that are apparent in the contemporary world. Obviously, the sovereign decisions made by society are sometimes made under the pressure of external factors. It is, however, important that external pressure not become the decisive mode of decision-making, overriding all others, and that recognition of these pressures be based on a sovereign assessment of common interests or on a sovereign decision to yield priority. Under the present circumstances it is a truism to say that there is a universal tendency for the sovereignty of the state, and consequently the sovereignty of the nation, to be restricted. The central problem, however, is how great that restriction should be and how it is put into effect."

So, sovereignty is essential for the national interest to prevail. Yet at the same time, the concept of national interest is a relative one, and different people, circles, and strata of society understand the word differently. Many respondents feel——and in this they are seconded by large segments of the public——that there is no justification for the idea that a single group and a single school of thought should determine what the national interest is and what it is not, how it is to be carried out, and what is considered inimical to it. There are, however, certain superior postulates, held in common by all who feel themselves to be Poles, that could be the basis of a reconciliation of different positions. To deny these postulates would be tantamount to suicide or national betrayal. They are:

a. a determination to safeguard the biological existence of the nation;

b. the desire to preserve national identity;

c. the desire to maintain social peace; in other words, to avoid civil war or a condition like it.

The fourth postulate, on which it is much more difficult to find agreement, is:

d. the desire to ensure optimum development in all spheres of life, in particular a rise in the standard of living and the development of culture.

* * *

The most important condition for realizing the basic national interest thus understood is reaching a minimum agreement on guidelines for joint action by everyone or the vast majority of groups and forces in society. If this minimum does not exist, there will be either civil war, a state of emergency, or a state of coercion in which no effective and creative action is possible. In other words, a state of more or less open, permanent conflict.

Someone could say that apart from the fourth postulate, all the points are obvious and not controversial. That is not so. The results of our survey and the material we present in this study provide alarming evidence that at present there is no agreement in society on any of these four points, or rather, there is no agreement on guidelines and methods for implementing them.

The creation of mechanisms that would enable society to unite divergent views on the national interest is a matter of prime importance; indeed, it is the main subject of our study. To achieve this, however, it is necessary to examine frankly, realistically, and without emotionalism the problem of national sovereignty and ways to consolidate it.

Although it may be generally accepted that the political alliance with the Soviet Union and broad cooperation with it are essential and important, there is still a sense of uneasiness among the public regarding the way this alliance and cooperation are maintained and exercised. The opinions of the broad public, their beliefs and common conceptions, must be treated as a social fact that cannot be stricken from the books, as it were, merely by means of a value judgment or a pejorative adjective. It has never been possible to consign these beliefs and general conceptions to some sort of subconsciousness.

Respondent No. 3 writes: "Our relations with the Soviet Union have an enormous importance both for today and for tomorrow. According to official information there are no difficult problems in this area. In the mind of the public, however, these relations are not based on partnership and are the source of many of our difficulties. Unfortunately, it must be said that treating all important aspects of these relations (also in history) as a taboo subject causes indifference or negative frustration."

Society wants to know the objective nature of these relations. It highly values its own dignity and sovereignty and expects both sides to rid themselves of those traits that do not accord with the principle of mutual advantage and friendship. Let us be frank: given the lack of information and the excess of pompous propaganda, certain negative views and complexes are difficult to combat, although one has to make a constant effort to overcome them.

Respondent No. 17 writes: "It is the common view that a genuine and lasting improvement in our internal affairs is not possible without a new set of relations with the Soviet Union based to a greater extent than now on the principle of equality. It is evident that any honest leadership that has at heart the good of the country and cares about its future must aim at such a change. It is a question of ensuring that the increase in self-government by the public, which is seen as an essential precondition for progress, is matched by increasing self-government on the part of the state. It is a question of ensuring that essential decisions concerning public and economic life are made inside the country, that they put the interests of Poland first, and that they not be made and kept in secret. We must not find ourselves in a situation in which the Politburo calls in its official communiqué on the party and the state, as well as on citizens, to honor agreements made during talks in Moscow but does not tell anyone what was agreed on."

In terms of its size and potential Poland is the second most important socialist country in Europe. In the estimation of Polish public opinion, this fact is not adequately reflected in the nature of our relationship with the Soviet Union.

Respondent No. 37 writes: "Poles realize that maintaining the alliance with the Soviet Union is beneficial to them, but they want it to be based on their own decisions and not decisions made for them. Friendship is better served by truth than by half-truths and distortions; it is better served by mutual respect than ostentatious servility." Respondent No. 20 draws attention to an important aspect of this problem: "A precondition for society trusting the party leadership is that the leadership be seen as acting as a free agent, and that there be no doubt about whether it is serving other aims apart from the sovereign interests of our country and the Polish people. Political inspiration and power in our country should reside in Warsaw and nowhere else."

The world is changing. The nationalistic and patriotic feelings that have surfaced in every part of the globe are one of the most powerful, and perhaps the greatest, force motivating the popular masses and shaping the character of world politics. No one should underestimate these feelings because such neglect must lead to catastrophe. World politics are also changing. The center of political gravity has begun to shift to new regions. Events around the Pacific and in the Far East are of enormous importance. There is a chance for Europe to become an area of lasting peace, where the present state of armed readiness and confrontation gradually disappear. In such a Europe Poland's role must become more important; this is the essential prerequisite for a permanent settlement of these questions. Poland's geographical position, which for many years was the cause of our national tragedy, could acquire for us a totally new and advantageous significance. We must be capable of realizing this and adapting our actions to such a contingency.

All balances of power, all structures of international relations, all strategic concepts are historical phenomena and are not lasting. Only the basic interests of nations endure. The contributors to our study have very clear views on the nature of our national interest.

We Poles can be valuable and trustworthy partners only when we are treated as partners. Then we repay friendship with friendship.

CHAPTER 6

Political Changes, Reforms, and Guarantees

From the responses to our questionnaire emerges a set of principles on which politics in our country should be based—principles that could guarantee the effectiveness of politics and hence public acceptance. We have arranged them in seven points:

1. *Power but not impotence*

Power in Poland should not strive for impotence because in our country, at least, this would lead to its own disintegration.

2. *Participation*

Participation——or negotiation——and not arbitrariness. In Poland the unilateral imposition of laws on society, even in the case of democratic reforms, is less effective than negotiation and compromise.

3. *An awareness of national heritage*

This involves a knowledge of and respect for the distinctiveness of Polish traditions and their incorporation in political, social, and cultural usages.

4. *Republicanism and the rule of law*

This point refers to the old Polish principle *non rex sed lex regnat* (not the king, but the law rules); the monarchical-despotic and the feudal tradition and arbitrariness in the application of law are profoundly foreign in Poland. That is why not verbal declarations but well thought-out and logical institutional-legal guarantees can shape our prospects for a genuine implementation of jointly accepted principles.

5. *Respect for the values of socialism*

This concerns respect for all those values which Polish public opinion associates with the idea of socialism; they should not be treated by the authorities as a troublesome burden on the system of economic management or the system of government; they should not be the handmaidens of authority but the authentic and genuine aims of the system. Equality of opportunity, equality before the law, the principle of reward for work (and not on the basis of private connections), the right to work, the right to social help, equal and universal access to culture, the growth of self-management, the defense of popular initiative, the right to express one's own opinions and to criticize the authorities——these are the values which in Poland are associated with the concept of socialism and are accepted by society.

6. *Assessment of people on the basis of their work*

Objective and empirically verifiable criteria, such as the results of people's labor, are in practice more useful than assessments based on personal acquaintances, personal attitudes, or membership in a political group or some organization. They have a better effect on social morale since they accept the principle of equality of opportunity as one of the fundamental values of socialism ("socialism for everyone").

7. *Openness of political life*

The principle of openness guarantees all the previous principles; adherence to it best serves the authorities and protects them from errors and their consequences.

The participants in our investigation believe that these seven principles on which political activity in Poland should be based do not belong to the realm of unattainable dreams. All these principles have been enunciated by the authorities themselves during the past thirty-five years. Every time an attempt was made to carry them out in practice, they bore successful fruit.

The Preconditions for Reform

The only thing that can be negotiated among the various participants in social life, that can elicit an agreement from all of them, is some form of compromise. But this always leaves us with an urgent question: does a given compromise protect the most basic interests of each of the parties to it, and will it therefore lead to a constructive consensus; or does the agreement only postpone a decisive clash, and hence the eruption of conflict, until later?

The proposed principles are meant to ground a philosophy of wielding power by the ruling groups in Poland on something that might be called a "package of safeguards" for the system. In other words, the authorities are guaranteed a certain basic security (majorities in the central and local legislative bodies, a controlling influence over appointments to leading posts in government, to top-level positions in the economy, and to the higher courts, influence over planning and supervisory agencies, and its own press). On the other hand, these proposals aim at satisfying the most urgently felt social needs, which might be described as "the craving for respect" (the craving for partnership), "the craving for the rule of law," "the craving for democracy," and "the craving for guarantees." This last need implies the need to provide society as well with a sense of security not so much against inevitable mistakes as against the inability to correct them, or against the threat of social paralysis that perpetuates errors.

There is a third precondition that shapes the course of the proposed changes. One of our respondents called the present system of government a "two-wheeler system," i.e., one that cannot react automatically to any wobbles and regain its balance because it lacks devices to make such a reaction. The only historically tested treatment in this case is the well-known "division of power," in other words, the total sharing of the prerogatives of the various institutions of power and arranging their mutual relations so that each of them has enough freedom to perform its constitutional tasks, while any mistakes made can be counteracted by other institutions. In other words, one premise for the proposed reform is to endeavor to assure the systems of power the effectiveness they need.

The Political Need for Reform

At the same time, it must be stressed that among the several hundred experts—economists, sociologists, specialists in organization and management, lawyers, specialists in social policy—

who during the last few months have taken part in and contributed to the work and the discussions going on in various institutions and organizations, such as the Poland 2000 Committee,[81] the Committee for the Sciences of Organization and Management of the Polish Academy of Sciences, the Polish Society of Economists, and the Polish Sociological Society, *not a single one of them* declared himself in favor of a policy that for the next two or three years provided solely for the application of economic instruments (distribution of national income, investment structure, employment, wages). This means that not one of the nearly 400 experts considered by the authorities and by public opinion as specialists of the highest order could envision such a policy being successful. On the contrary, it seems rather that such a policy would merely further the present disintegration and paralysis.

At the first plenary meeting of the "Experience and the Future" group, a specialist in social policy described the current political and economic needs as follows:

"The most important task today must be to halt negative processes and restore proportion to development. However, this must necessarily take several years, and no authorities, of whatever kind, could manage such a policy without the far-ranging cooperation, patience, and understanding of society. That is why the question of dialogue and participation is so relevant. It is our greatest noncapital reserve, one that with a great deal of effort we may be able to mobilize."

"Society must believe," wrote a journalist specializing in problems of organization and management and a member of the party, "that it will be treated seriously. If it does not believe this, then nothing will change. There is no place today for any attempt to manipulate—give a little here, take a little there. Without a society ready and willing to cooperate there is no chance of reviving the economy and the state."

A statement by a specialist in social policy at the meeting of the Poland 2000 Committee struck an almost identical note: "It seems to me that, generally speaking, society will not change its attitude unless it becomes convinced that a fundamental change is in the making in the attitude of those who are responsible for the fate of the country, those who are running the state."

And finally, at the same meeting, a sociologist had this to say: "Just to say we made a mistake is not enough—people simply no longer believe in words. Profound changes are necessary, changes, one should almost say, in the system itself."

Such opinions were voiced in various forms, various words by all the respondents.

This underscores the need for credible guarantees like the political and constitutional reforms we propose below, which in their turn are essential for the success of any reforms and corrective measures undertaken in the economic domain.

* * *

While our survey produced a wide variety of materials describing the present state of our society, its proposals for reforms and guarantees were modest.[82] The materials demonstrate that the respondents favored the ideals of social justice, genuine equality before the law, democracy, and open government, and that repairing the system requires not only legal guarantees but also those applicable to the political process itself.

The specific proposals for reforms and guarantees, given the diversity of the survey respondents, cannot be expected to agree as broadly as the diagnostic statements, especially since we were unable to discuss this aspect of our work at a plenary meeting.

We will therefore present a number of propositions and possible solutions in the hope that they will serve as points of departure for further discussion.

The Division of Power

The first point concerns a systematic separation of the party (and likewise of the professional apparatus of other political and social organizations) from the administrative apparatus, from the economic apparatus, and from the judiciary. This is not a new proposal; it has appeared and has been reiterated many times in resolutions and desiderata of the party leadership and the current regime. The assumption by the party apparatus (and that of other organizations) of the day-to-day running of the state, the economy, and the legal system (or even its involvement in it) not only causes the confusion that stems from dual authority but also burdens the party with responsibility for processes over which it can have no effective control (because it has no executive apparatus under its direct jurisdiction) nor exercise supervision because there is no clear delimitation of powers.

When the everyday, practical administration of the state and the nation's economy are especially susceptible, by the nature of things, to mistakes in making and executing decisions, the party apparatus becomes in effect a kind of "whipping boy," attracting all the criticism and odium of a dissatisfied society.

Both the theory of constitutional law and the recommendations of experts in organization and management indicate that the appropriate way for a ruling party to perform its functions is to define goals and the legislative regulation of social life *through the activities of representative bodies.* It should perform its control, supervisory, evaluative, and corrective functions in the same way.

The principle that the party should guide the life of the state exclusively through those of its members who hold seats in representative bodies and who have the support of their party apparatus, in other words, that the party should exercise control exclusively by constitutional means, regulated by law——this principle should be made the cornerstone of the contemporary order in Poland if that order is to be freed from the evils of disorganization, duality of rule, and lack of accountability.

The constitutional prerogatives of representative bodies ought, in the light of what we have said, to be broadened substantially (we will discuss this in more detail below). However, the principle that only representative bodies should be empowered to make decisions that are binding on all citizens ought to be expressly reflected in the Constitution.

To establish a clear separation of the prerogatives of the various institutions of power, the Constitution should forbid the accumulation in the same hands of leadership positions in the party, political and social organizations, and even——as some of our respondents say——representative bodies, the state administration, the economy, and the judiciary. This return to the old Polish principle of *incompatibility*, which precludes the holding of legislative, legal, or religious posts simultaneously with posts in the state administration, is of more than merely historical significance. Without such a separation the possibility of controlling, supervising, and assessing the workings of the administrative apparatus, the economy, or the judiciary becomes a fiction; indeed, the experience of the modern states that have instituted a separation between administrative posts and elected offices fully confirms the aptness of such a solution.

Any social consensus in Poland based on an awareness of the reality of Poland's situation would entail the Polish United

Workers' Party's obtaining a majority in the state and provincial representative bodies through negotiations with other political groups and associations of nonparty citizens. However, there would have to be a thorough discussion of how the electoral system could be organized to invest elections with as personal a character as possible. Lawyers participating in our group have suggested that a system of primary elections should be developed and instituted. Such a system would provide the public with a means to express its sympathies, so that the party, the other political groups, and professional circles represented in the Sejm could determine which of their candidates enjoyed the greatest support and popularity. Another proposition provides for a competition and for seats to be allocated on the basis of an agreement reached by consulative commissions mediating among the different political groups and professional organizations (with the exception of a group of seats reserved for public personalities of national or provincial stature, whose candidacies would likewise be advanced by commissions mediating among the political groups and professional organizations). The remaining seats would be filled by the electorate from a list of several candidates nominated for a predetermined number of seats allocated to each political group or professional organization. For example, two party candidates would vie for a seat allocated to their party, or two workers, say, would contest a seat allocated to the workers in a particular province. Such a scheme would make it possible to do away with the present annoying and immensely unpopular mechanical act of dropping a ballot in a ballot box and replace it with an institution somewhat resembling genuine elections, with the element of choice they suggest. Furthermore, it would ensure the authorities their "controlling share" yet force political and professional organizations nominating candidates to choose people capable of gaining the good will of the electorate. Finally, it would force those candidates who were elected to perform well enough to successfully challenge rivals for their seats in future elections.

A logical consequence of the proposed division of the institutions of power should be, in the opinion of some of our respondents, the establishment of direct elections for the head of government and the heads of provinces and local administrations. This solution, as our respondents point out, is unknown in our social and political traditions, although it is quite rational in a time when executives are much more important and must bear much more responsibility than in the past. Such a practice

would, moreover, duly enhance the social status of their positions and at the same time enable the public to make genuine
choices among the candidates nominated by consultative electoral
commissions, who then would have to make an honest effort to
gain genuine public approval.

There remains the question of the appropriate term in
office for various posts. Theories of administration suggest that
the holding of high-ranking or executive office in the government or at the provincial level ought to be limited to six years,
with no chance for reelection. Administrative experience suggests
that at the local level, a two-year term of office is appropriate
(with a chance for reelection). In the case of Sejm members and
provincial councilors, the traditional four-year term of office
with half the members up for reelection every two years is
reasonable, while local council members would have a two-year
term, with half the seats up for election each year (the same with
the possibility of running for reelection). More frequent elections would allow for a more frequent assessment of the mood
and opinions of the public, which, by showing its preference for
some candidates over others, would find a genuine outlet for
expressing those moods and opinions. Many of the respondents
call on the party and political groups in Poland to make rotation
a statutory rule for leading posts; they feel this principle is a
key element in any system of guarantees.

Broadening the Prerogatives of Representative Bodies

The second point is a logical complement of the first: it is
broadening the constitutional and practical prerogatives of representative bodies. The theory of the socialist state has from its
very inception assigned a paramount role to these bodies in the
system of power. Yet this principle has still not found adequate
reflection in institutional forms. The system of interpellation and
the possibility of setting up special Sejm committees (in practice,
unused) are not sufficient for exercising total supervision and
control over executive bodies. Representative bodies also lack a
special auxiliary apparatus for compiling statistical information
and reports and for carrying out supervisory activities.

Therefore legal experts and management specialists who
took part in the "Experience and the Future" study have proposed that representative bodies and their committees (not just
the special committees commonly referred to as investigative)
be constitutionally invested with the power to summon anyone

employed in executive offices or any citizen to obtain any information or explanations necessary under the burden of penal sanction for nonappearance, refusal to answer, or giving false information.

This would also entail empowering representative bodies to remove any official of the executive apparatus from his post by means of a duly and legally established procedure for nonperformance of his duties. The lack of such prerogatives, we should point out, is what has driven the ruling party, by virtue of the intrinsic impossibility of exercising leadership effectively, to take over directly the functions of the administrative and economic apparatus.

The sovereignty of representative bodies, in the view of some of our respondents, should be reinforced in a number of other ways as well. For instance, the Supreme Chamber of Control, the Planning Commission, and the Central Bureau of Statistics should be taken completely, both practically and constitutionally, from under the control of the government and the administrative and economic apparatus and placed under the representative bodies. There is no need to explain at great length the view that not only the planning of economic development but also the accounting, auditing, reporting, and monitoring and supervisory activities of the state should be functions of the highest organs of power, namely, the representative bodies and the leaders of political life serving in them (apart, of course, from offices that the government and its administrative apparatus must have at its disposal to perform such activities). At issue here is more than just a formal enhancement of the stature of representative bodies; we must henceforth preclude situations in which the leaders of political life have no staff of their own independent of administrative officials and managers of the economy, i.e., situations in which they are themselves the unwitting objects of manipulation and covert pressures. Even if the Central Bureau of Statistics and the Planning Commission were to remain under the executive, it would be necessary to ensure that the Sejm and other representative bodies are provided with an adequate and competent auxiliary apparatus to help them in matters of planning and statistics.

Regulation of the Mass Media

The third point relates to the functioning of the mass media. It is both possible and constitutionally appropriate to define the role and place of the press, radio, and television in the system of power and public order in Poland. The mass media satisfy the public need for information and culture. Equally they can serve as an outlet for public opinion on the activities of the administrative and economic apparatus, and they can act as a public watchdog, as has occurred during periods of democratization and increased political agitation. In the view of the leaders of our political life and our representative bodies, they can, as in those earlier periods, serve as a key source of information about the state of the economy and the nation and how they are functioning during times of turbulence.

For the mass media to play such a role, the influence of the administrative and economic apparatus on what is published in the press and broadcast on radio and television and on appointments to posts in the mass media must be eliminated. If the administrative and economic apparatus wants to cultivate its image in the mass media, it should do so only by performing its functions properly.

This would mean a fundamental curtailment of the powers of censorship and placing it on a legal basis. If censorship is to exist as a legal institution in a state founded on the rule of law, the scope of its powers must be statutorily defined, not determined by executive decisions. Its activities must be accountable before the courts, not subject to the very state executive bodies the press, radio, and television are attempting to open to public control and evaluation. Matters subject to preventive censorship can and must be clearly defined. Censorship may be used to safeguard such values as the constitutional foundations of our state and social order, the fundamental political alliances of our country, the constitiutionally defined rights and duties of citizens, and military secrets. Censorship may be used to strike down any form of propagation of discrimination or animosity on the basis of differences in outlook, creed, nationality, or race and to block the dissemination of material of a sadistic, violent, or pornographic nature.[83]

Furthermore, anyone who suffers financial loss or moral injury as a result of journalistic or editorial activity that cannot be justified in terms of the public interest must be guaranteed the right to sue for redress.

Democratization means guaranteeing creative, professional, autonomous, and religious groups the chance to express their views in their own press. Without such a guarantee it is difficult to expect any political changes in our country to enjoy credibility.

The survey responses point out that it is incumbent on the party, which controls the newspapers of the RSW—"Prasa-Książka-Ruch" concern,[84] to restore to the mass media the role they have played more than once in the history of the past thirty-five years—to provide a forum for dialogue between the political leaders and the public, to act as monitors of the activities of our administration and economy, and to serve as a source of information about these activities. The lack of this element in our system of power and social order paralyzes that system—as the experiences of past years have shown—in a much more drastic way than the worst administrative or economic blunders.

The Law, Its Rule, and Safeguarding Civil Rights

The fourth point in the proposed reforms concerns the legal system. A properly functioning state is inconceivable without a legal order: in the view of our respondents, a broad range of measures is necessary to restore its consistency.

First, it is necessary to legally guarantee control and checks over the constitutionality of the law and over government legislation, the scope of which has increased alarmingly. No matter which bodies perform this task, it is in the interests of the authorities themselves that they do so correctly and efficiently. As regards the economy, a legal order is a *sine qua non* for its proper functioning. It is no coincidence that feudalism, with its arbitrariness in the realm of law, fell under the pressure of the first industrial revolution, which required laws that were clear, equal for all, and purposeful.

The second problem concerns institutional guarantees for safeguarding civil rights vis-à-vis the administration. An administrative tribunal, for the restoration of which Polish specialists in administration have long been calling, should adjudicate matters of legality and the legal basis of administrative acts. It would be a special branch of the judiciary, separate from the rest of the judicial system. Such a tribunal is considered by scholars to be a fundamental condition for the stability of any system of power, inasmuch as when the administration is itself accountable before the law for its conduct, citizens lose their sense of defenselessness, and thus one of the reasons for public dissatisfaction disappears (public opposition is born not of administrative errors in themselves but of the lack of means to oppose them, correct them, and eliminate them). In setting up such a tribunal, due regard ought to be given to means for ensuring that an administrative court system is created to deal with matters effectively and promptly, e.g., by empowering it to suspend under certain circumstances a decision that might be contrary to law and to enforce provisional safeguards. The experience of countries with a long history of administrative courts shows how an administration is able to neutralize the effectiveness of such courts.

Furthermore, citizens should be guaranteed access to all administrative files and documents, and the observance of this rule should be ensured. Especially now, at the dawn of the era of the computer and the spread of various data banks, the citizen must be guaranteed some security with regard to the information gathered about him by administrative bodies of whatever kind.

Our respondents also felt it would be expedient to establish a special office with a function akin to that of the tribune of the people in Republican Rome or the ombudsman in Scandinavia. The powers of such an office, which we might call a "tribune of law" or, following ancient Polish tradition, a "guardian of the law," would have to be broader than those of an ombudsman. They should also include the power to suspend enforcement of any administrative decision if in the judgment of the officer there was reason to believe it contrary to the law, and in particular, if some decision contrary to the law threatened irreversible damage or loss to any person, either physical or legal. Careful analyses indicate that the only administrative decisions that preclude the right to suspend them are decisions having to do with military matters, emergency laws in cases of public danger or natural disasters, or acts safeguarding life and health. In all other cases the suspension of administrative action until a matter has been cleared up harms no one. It is to be hoped that an administration conscious of the prerogatives of such a "tribune of law" will draft its decisions more scrupulously. A "tribune of law" who is aware that an unjustified intervention will be censured by an administrative court, will——at least we hope——intervene only when there are good reasons for doing so.

Putting the legal system in order and establishing effective supervision and control over administrative actions will, first of all, ensure a smoothly and efficiently functioning state machinery; it will ensure a law that is rational, a law that is enforced, and a law that is equal for all citizens; and finally, it will ensure citizens' respect for the state that rules by that law.

Of course, there must also be guarantees that the law will be enforced. In the light of the negative experiences of recent years, as well as the centuries' old traditions of the Polish state since the times of the First Republic, there are good practical reasons, in the opinion of some of our respondents, for assuring the independence of the judiciary by removing the courts from the control of the government and the executive bodies of the state and making them a separate pillar of state authority and, furthermore, for adopting the principle of lifetime tenure[85] for judges and ensuring the judiciary appropriately high salaries. A judge who is sure that he will retain his post until retirement if he does not violate the norms and rules of his profession, a judge who is paid a salary on a par with that of the highest-ranking employees in the administration, has a better chance to achieve a reputation for integrity than a judge who is poor and unsure of his position. It is right to expect judges, as well as other professionals, to heed their professional honor, but it is also necessary to ensure conditions that favor the upholding of that honor.

Superficially it seems easy to exercise power under conditions of chaos and lack of norms, under conditions of privilege, and under conditions in which court verdicts can be manipulated. However, this apparent ease in the long run leads to social paralysis and frustration and, ultimately, to the dissolution of power and authority itself.

Rules for Advancement

The sixth point concerns the adoption of the rule that all posts in the administration, the judiciary, and the economy should be filled on the basis of the qualifications and competence of the candidate. No one can be discriminated against in getting proper work or advancing his career because of his beliefs, outlook, or other reasons. Observing this rule will instill a feeling of equality of opportunity among the public, a feeling of equal rights, and consequently, a sense of partnership vis-à-vis the leaders of political life, without which any change for the better is difficult to envisage. In turn, our political leaders, who retain their "controlling share" in power, need not feel their authority threatened if personnel decisions are made on the basis of the competence and qualifications of candidates for any position. For, as practice has shown, one can only count on a job being done properly if it is done by people who are competent and qualified to do it.

The choice of inferior candidates who render superficial loyalty not only frustrates those passed over but also humiliates future employees, which does not stimulate their desire to work. Setting goals, finding the best people to achieve them, supervising them, and drawing the appropriate conclusions based on evaluations of their performance are the proper political prerogatives for wielding power.

Respect for Self-Government and Autonomy

The respondents again and again stress the importance of various kinds of self-governing institutions in the social life of our country. Such institutions should not only reinforce a sense of partnership among the citizenry vis-à-vis the authorities, they should also perform a genuine opinion-shaping function, especially in the case of professional, cultural, and creative associations. At issue here are both the "craving for democracy" and the demand for efficiency of the system.

The principle that all autonomous and self-governing bodies and organizations should have full freedom to choose their leaders as they deem best is contained in the provisions of the law on associations. Bringing this law up to date and making it uniform and unambiguous will brook no delay because, since 1932, the year the law on associations was promulgated, it has undergone frequent and often chaotic modifications. In the future the right of autonomous and self-governing bodies and organizations to choose their own leaders without interference must undoubtedly be respected more than just formally. Practices that block this law also obstruct the activities of such organizations, which thereby lose their sense of identity. Nevertheless the point here is more than merely the manipulation of elections or the exerting of pressure; it has to do with counteracting such phenomena as the usually totally superfluous proliferation of hierarchical structures in self-governing and autonomous organizations, the subordination of such organizations to the administrative apparatus in terms of both personnel and formal structure, and the expansion of the bureaucratic apparatus, which prevails over the principle of self-government and autonomy. It is also a question of restoring autonomy to those institutions of public life (higher education, for example) able to perform their functions much better autonomously than within the framework of a bureaucratic and administrative structure. We can control the statutory formulation of the objectives of an organization, or examine whether it adheres to its statutes scrupulously (especially through the intermediacy of the committees of representative bodies); but it is in the interests of the authorities themselves for self-governing and autonomous bodies and organizations to function authentically and to find satisfaction in the effectiveness of their activities, assuming, of course, that their slate is clean. After all, they often take on tasks that no administrative apparatus will assume. To take an extreme example, in the past charitable organizations of a religious type would nominate candidates capable of incredible self-sacrifice and irreplaceable when it came to working in institutions for the mentally retarded or the incurably ill or caring for the disabled and the aged——all those incapable of looking after themselves. But we need only look at the results of the activities of the Czechoslovak "Brontosaurus" youth movement for environmental conservation or the consumer protection movements in the Western countries to realize how much social benefit can accrue from unfettered public initiative. On the other hand, the idea of "getting involved in everything," as experience has shown, simply does not work in practice. Public passivity toward it has, as we have seen, had catastrophic consequences for the authorities themselves.

In particular, autonomous youth groups (from political to sports organizations) should be given the means to develop in a genuine and spontaneous way, for without this it is impossible to instill in our future citizens a spirit of cooperation and shared responsibility.

Guarantees

In addition to constitutional and structural reforms, the survey respondents and participants in discussions in other institutions and organizations are convinced that it is necessary for the main classes of Polish society, as well as for society as a whole, to receive specific guarantees capable of inspiring a sense that changes instituted will last.

* * *

For the working class such a guarantee would be the transformation of the trade unions into organizations embracing wage

earners and at the same time excluding employers from membership. The function of trade unions should also be changed—in
a stable economy of a moderately developed country there is no
need to expect the trade unions to perform the function of
mobilizing the masses and stimulating them to productive work.[86]
Such a function can and ought to be performed more effectively
by a properly devised system of wages, an economic system
based on legal co-ownership of the means of production, and a
system of joint participation in management, about which we
will have more to say in the next chapter. On the other hand,
the trade unions should above all attend to their basic mission,
which is to represent employees in their dealings with employers, defend employee interests, etc. To these ends the principles
on which negotiations between employers and employees must
be based, principles on which a genuine workers' representation
can emerge, and principles guiding the intervention of trade
unions in defense of workers' interests should be worked out
with a minimum of delay. Once these practices become entrenched, the trade unions should be more likely to participate
on their own initiative in repairing our economy. As one of our
respondents put it: "Polish workers have frequently demonstrated that they are better able to look after their place of work
than their employers; treated as partners, they behave like
partners."[87]

Guarantees are also essential for the Polish countryside, for
the Polish peasant class. The first of these guarantees would be
full and genuine political representation. It is to be expected,
say our respondents, that people who are active in the United
Peasants' Party[88] will have to be able to have an open and frank
discussion with their members and their potential supporters in
the Polish countryside if they are to acquire, or reacquire, a
mandate based on full and genuine political representation. The
experience of the last few years shows that the peasant movement wants and expects just that.

The second guarantee would be to invest the self-governing
institutions[89] in the countryside with some authenticity. The
proposal of respondent No. 10 to "give the words content"
surely has no better application than in this case. Not only the
feelings of public opinion but also the economic interests of our
country demand radical debureaucratization of the structures of
rural self-government. The transformation of the "Peasants' Self-
Help" cooperatives,[90] which today represent an extension of
the state administration into genuine cooperatives, onto a volun-

tary basis; the transformation of the farm machinery fleets into genuinely self-governing bodies; and finally, the transformation into cooperative ventures of the various state agencies engaged in purchasing farm produce will not only give the Polish peasant the status of a genuine farmer but will permit the elimination of an expensive bureaucratic apparatus, which now employs more than 100,000 people. It will also eliminate the need for the present ineffective supervision now exercised by the higher levels of the bureaucracy. These people will contribute incomparably more to the nation's economy working directly at shop counters, in local workshops, or in wholesale trade.

The third guarantee would be to ensure genuine elections for the local authorities in rural areas. According to most leading theorists of administration around the world, and on the basis of experience itself, no local self-governing body can stand up to the central authorities or pose a threat to them in any way. State policy toward the countryside need not be represented by the heads of local administrations; it can be implemented through many other, more effective instruments. The existence of elected bodies in the countryside will, however, open the way to public initiative in the economy, culture, and the development of a civilized infrastructure. But such an initiative is contingent on meeting one basic requirement or, rather, precondition—rebuilding trust and faith in the significance of human action.

The fourth guarantee would entail formulating principles for a long-term policy toward the countryside, buttressed by appropriate legislation. These principles would amount to an agreement between the state, representing society as a whole, and the Polish peasant class. The laws embodying these principles would acquire the requisite weight with the establishment of, say, a "tribune of law" empowered to suspend any administrative decision inconsistent with this legislation. Without such procedures these principles would lack credibility because thus far the application of state policy on the countryside has confirmed in our peasantry their conviction that all legislation and all promises unsupported by appropriate guarantees are illusory.

* * *

Stable political principles—and therefore also political guarantees of a similar nature—are also required by small family private enterprises working in industry, the crafts, and trade. In social terms artisans and small private traders in Poland have acquired the same rights as other working people: the right to health insurance, old-age pensions, etc. This thoroughly justifiable policy (justifiable if only because the energy expended by a Polish artisan or salesman would in other circumstances be considered excessive) does not in itself suffice to create a feeling of security and guaranteed rights, without which this social class will not play its due and proper role in the Polish economy and society. Here, too, some form of long-term social contract is needed, i.e., certain principles to guide state policy, buttressed by guarantees and legislation.

* * *

There is no need to add that——not only in the opinion of our respondents——the question of cooperative ventures needs to be treated in a realistic way. Specious cooperatives, weighed down by bureaucracy and turned into a complex of hierarchic offices, cannot perform the economic, social, or cultural functions expected of them, for they leave no room for human initiative. There is therefore a need to change not only the official regulations but also the present practices of the cooperative movement. A vital and genuine cooperative movement in no way threatens the activities of state enterprises; on the contrary, it naturally complements them in all spheres of the economy where the personal resources of those involved are sufficient for appropriate investment to take place and for an enterprise's current needs for operating capital to be met. Furthermore, as regards the cooperative movement's importance for social integration, it cannot be overestimated.

* * *

Guarantees of just treatment by the judicial system and in state policy are also needed by the religious and by the Catholic Church, which ministers to the religious needs of the majority of them. Just like nonbelievers, they have the right to expect that the state will honor the principle of secularism. A secular state does not differentiate between the attitudes of its citizens regarding religious matters. In these matters it is "in absentia." It does not spread propaganda either for or against religion, nor does it restrict the freedom to demonstrate religious beliefs or opinions, as long as such demonstrations do not offend the feelings or the dignity of people who hold other beliefs and do not violate the principles of tolerance. In view of this the state should not block religious practice, limit the right of citizens to build places of worship, or obstruct religious life as it is expressed in the denominational press and other publications. Believers still constitute a majority in Polish society; the state has more than once had occasion to be grateful for the good will of the Church in maintaining internal peace. Removing every form of discrimination can only have a beneficial effect on the atmosphere of social life in our country and open the way toward making the slogan "socialism for everyone" a reality. On the other hand, the changes the Church has undergone both in Poland and in the world at large mean that despite its doctrinal differences with Marxism, there is reason to hope that eliminating every kind of discrimination against it and against believers will not prompt the Church's return to a policy of discriminating against people holding other beliefs.[91]

* * *

In its consideration of solutions bearing on the political system, the "Experience and the Future" report indicated one more specific need of Polish society as a whole. Polish society is seeking guarantees that, as one of the respondents put it, "good work will receive the acknowledgment due it." All groups of people or social bodies that properly perform their statutory tasks must be certain that their achievements and their accumulated experience will not be reduced to nothing from one day to the next by arbitrary personal decisions, reorganizations, or even dissolutions. Such practices, which affect the editorial boards of newspapers, construction projects, or even enterprises and undertakings, cause something more than disintegration— they engender demoralization and social paralysis. These practices can be totally prevented only by guarantees with a systemwide character, such as institutions set up with the prerogatives of a "tribune of law." They must be considered essential because, to date, all promises and declarations have proved illusory, and the arbitrariness of the bureaucracy has yet to encounter equally powerful resistance. In this situation it is hard to count on public confidence in any promise or declaration not backed up by appropriate guarantees.

* * *

Our respondents agree that adopting the reforms and the

guarantees described above would pave the way to an understanding between the authorities and society. It is the fruit of many months of discussion in all sorts of professional circles concerned with the problems of political authority in Poland. While we do not claim that this program is the final word on the subject, it appears to us to form a rather coherent edifice. We hope that the reader will come away with the same impression.

CHAPTER 7

Conclusions Concerning
the Economy and Social Policy

Our poll material, even when supplemented and enriched by materials from other discussions and analytic studies done by the organizations and institutions mentioned before, differ greatly, as is understandable, in the degree of detail in which they explore questions of the economy, social policy, and culture. However, all, *without exception*, agree on the need for profound reform. Furthermore, although the general lines of these reforms are sketched out quite unambiguously, it would be difficult to speak of a compact, coherent, detailed program for reform or even of a coherent package of proposals. We have therefore attempted to present below the most important ideas and suggestions, which could then be taken, as it were, as a point of departure for future discussion.

As regards the economy, several respondents discussed what respondent No. 24 described as "rigid factors, that is, those elements in the existing economic situation in Poland which, even with a leadership of genius, a perfect system of management, and extremely favorable external circumstances, would submit only very slowly and very reluctantly to change." The respondents agree on what these factors are:

1. *Frozen investments*. This problem concerns not only unfinished factories but also those which lack raw materials for production, either (as is most often the case) imported from abroad or procured domestically.

2. *Foreign trade*. The conference held in January at the Hotel Victoria with representatives of Western, mainly American, banks and the prospect of a further $500 million loan enabled Poland officially to continue the repayment of its debts and the interest on them. Our foreign debt will rise, and we have not yet managed to square our current foreign trade balance. It

must be remembered that the cost of imported grain and food-stuffs in 1978 came to more than $1 billion, and that in the case of both such supplies and the credits to pay for them, no country can replace the United States. Any disturbance in our relations with the United States means a catastrophe for the country.

3. *Food production.* The Polish countryside, despite many and different disincentives, responds relatively vigorously to positive incentives. But even if we pursue an "ideal" agricultural policy, improvements in agricultural production can only come slowly, given the enormous shortage of equipment, fertilizers, and materials for individual private farmers——something that cannot quickly be fixed. We can expect a great leap forward in the production of grain and fodder over the next three or four years because, according to expert estimates, several million hectares of arable land and meadow are poorly managed, neglected, or not used at all. However, even three or four years is an optimistic assessment. Given this situation, our country will remain, as it has been since 1974, a net importer of food.

4. *Raw materials, especially energy.* Since 1978 Poland has become a net importer of fuel, despite its huge exports of coal (40 million tons per year, of which 12 million tons go to the Soviet Union). Given the rising price of liquid fuels, this situation can only be rectified when the cost of acquiring imported oil balances the cost of obtaining liquid fuels from coal (thanks to the development of new and more productive technology in this area, in which both Poland and the United States have an interest). Such a project will take at least five or six years. The situation with electrical energy will not stabilize earlier than in four to five years' time, since even a correctly pursued energy policy (a program of eonomy measures involving the modernization of transmission lines and technical facilities) will in any case encounter obstacles to further development in the form of an inability to increase the productivity of the coal industry (inadequate manpower, delays in the implementation of automation).

The public must be acquainted with these factors so that it knows what to expect from our economy, and so that any revival of public initiative does not cause new frustrations resulting from a feeling of yet another failure.

Differences among the respondents regarding the nature of the most essential reforms were relatively small, and those that did exist had to do mainly with the pace at which any reform program should be implemented. Some of them are worth pointing out. Respondent No. 13 suggests: "There must be an extensive preliminary discussion, a broad understanding must be reached among top-level and rank-and-file personnel, and finally, the authorities must be ready for calm, measured, but thorough implementation of a coherent program. I think that this would require two, perhaps three years from the moment that real work started, which of course does not preclude the possibility of certain limited changes being made somewhat earlier."

This point of view is seconded by respondent No. 7, who proposes a strategy that he himself calls "piecemeal."

Other economists and management experts suggest, on the other hand, a strategy that might be described as "thorough discussion, speedy implementation." They recommend that even as discussions are going on, those anomalies for which the remedy is clear can be taken care of right away. The differences between these two points of view was put succinctly by respondent No. 36:

"All the experience of management science indicates that the reorganization of any institution or enterprise is something like a fire. Thus management experts since Taylor and Adamiecki[92] have said that reorganization needs to be well prepared but carried out as fast as possible. Otherwise the activity of institutions and enterprises, and even more so of the state, becomes provisional, and the rules of the game become vague, which only increases the existing defects and introduces new ones . . . compromising the very idea of reorganization."

This view is shared by most of the other respondents who expressed themselves on this subject. Respondent No. 35 observes: "In order to change relations between the authorities and the citizenry, given that economic reforms cannot be carried out in a day, it seems to me most essential now to spark a general and open discussion on the economy.[93] The public expects to be told the truth about the state of the economy and to be told it in a straightforward and credible way. Starting a discussion on the ways to achieve an economic recovery, while certainly a political matter, will remove from economic problems the odium associated with politics and will turn them into what they are in fact——a problem of organization, a problem of jointly finding the best way forward in all respects, technical, organizational, and economic."

All our respondents share this way of looking at economic questions. The remedy for today's ills cannot, in their opinion, lie in the acquisition of further managerial functions by political institutions because, as experience to date shows, this would actually only extend the present state of chaos. Respondent No. 34 describes the hoped for relations among the highest organs of power in this way: "The leading circles at the political center would move from a position of direct administration to one of party leadership with an absolute majority in parliament. This position means that leading circles at the political center could still decide about all the general matters concerning the country, but that they would not assume responsibility for them. They would not, on the other hand, deal with details that are beyond the prerogatives of parliament. The political center would be able to influence the government only through parliament, and in no other way. Of course, there are a number of possible variations on this solution."

The situation described above would allow the political leadership of the country to maintain its guiding and guardian role without responsibility for the routine workings of the economy and for all its day-to-day problems and difficulties. In the same way the party apparatus would not have to play the part of a "fire brigade" or the role of "commandos filling breaches in the system." Clarity with regard to competence and clarity with regard to responsibility——these are the main characteristics of a system of government capable of correcting itself in economic matters without thereby causing recurrent periods of political tension.

This is, indeed, a very profound reform because it contradicts accepted habits and traditions of rule. Such a reform implies a change in the method of wielding power and instilling greater awareness in the citizens about equality of rights and opportunity (since the economy and the leading positions in it today offer the most room for expansion to be filled by people of talent), while guaranteeing greater security for the authorities (since the system would not have to treat the unavoidable and numerous defects in the economy as a political taboo).

Respondent No. 37 adds: "Discussion is necessary not only as a pledge of good faith on the part of managers of the economy. It is also necessary because, since no genuine scholarly discussion takes place in economic circles, we have thus far not been able to sort out and explain many common concepts that have been and still often are the bases of fundamental decisions of a political nature."

In the view of another respondent, a wide-ranging public discussion on the economy would yield a further advantage by giving the public a basic education in economics supported by a sense of involvement in and control over the course of discussion. Among all possible topics of such a discussion, one in particular demands participation by all citizens: the kind of society and economy we as a country would like to bring into being during the next fifteen years. Fifteen years is not a very long time. It means that the public must make certain choices and define social preferences in such a way that at any given moment, the realization of a jointly held vision of progress would be subject to analysis and evaluation. One could then also count on the involvement of all society in realizing these aims, an involvement that is so indispensable for success.

The topics that, in the light of the poll material and material from other discussions, call for a public exchange of views are the following:

1. *Problems having to do with the development and the application of the theory of political economy.* In the view of our respondents there have been no decisions of the most basic nature, for instance, regarding the question of the extent to which the economic policy of a socialist country should be defined by economic growth. With economic growth as a standard, a whole range of ambitions emerges that rules out any other basis for assessing progress; this is, in a sense, to be expected, however, since our economists have never codified a list of goals to guide management. Without such a list of goals, furthermore, it is impossible to determine what areas of expenditure should be assessed in terms of profit and what areas cannot be assessed in terms of economic indicators (with the exception of cost studies). It has also been left unclear to what extent concepts of political economy and concepts of a general nature can be treated as the basis for practical decisions in economic policy. The everyday experience of our economy has demonstrated many times over how harmful it has been to base practical decisions on truths which, though scientific, are too abstract and generalized. Our respondents point out the inadequate development of the methods and techniques of planning, which has had a particularly disastrous effect on planning growth. Other questions that require broad and thorough discussion concern market equilibrium, money, wages, prices, and employment. For instance, as we well know, the problem of market imbalances and inflation in our economy can certainly not be analyzed with the traditional instruments. The excess of demand over supply that has marked the entire postwar period affects the market in a way that is either completely contrary to theory or is to a

large degree tangential to all expectations. In fact, it has never been possible to achieve a balanced market. There are many such intellectual gaps in almost any area one would care to mention: "The traditional means for limiting inflation by lowering employment and reducing the overall wage fund can be effective where there is a sound employment structure, where there are no labor reserves in the service sector," points out respondent No. 36. "However, if, as in Poland, employment in small-scale manufacturing services and retail trade is grotesquely low, it is possible that an adjustment in the employment structure by reducing the work force in industry would not result in a decrease in the overall number of people employed, and individual wages in industry would rise. The anti-inflationary effect is the same, but the social consequences are diametrically the opposite," concludes this respondent.

In the light of the survey material, it would therefore seem to be useful to work out a questionnaire to be addressed to professional economists and organization and management experts concerning the unresolved, yet to be clarified theoretical problems of our economy, since the economy and hence society as a whole must pay a price for these intellectual lacunae. This point was raised at the first meeting of the "Experience and the Future" group, a number of times at meetings of the Polish Society of Economists, and again at the May meeting of the Polish Society of Sociologists.

2. *Problems bearing on the state of the economy and opportunities for growth.* Experience has shown that closed discussions limited to committees of experts generally let certain opinions dominate at the expense of others. Unless this manner of arriving at decisions concerning the development of the economy is changed, our economy will have to bear the brunt of a further series of mistakes. Our respondents mentioned many sectors and branches of industry whose present state and future prospects are assessed in terms that are at total variance with reality as a result of the crisis in the information system. They also point out the urgent need for different groups of experts to prepare parallel reports about the current state and future prospects of the various branches of the economy.

3. *The needs of organizational structures.* According to our respondents, the situation is somewhat better with regard to the organizational structures of our economy. Studies by the Organizational and Management Committee of the Polish Academy of Sciences and a group of experts from the Polish Society of

Economists have yielded some useful results in this area.

As regards organizational structures——and this is worth noting——the prevailing opinion is that all intermediate organizational levels between the center of economic decision-making and those in charge at the production level should be reduced to the necessary minimum, and that the decision-making center should be represented at the state enterprise level by an institution more like a supervisory board than a ministry. It is pointed out that a supervisory board representing the interests of society as a whole vis-á-vis the directors of enterprises, since by its very nature it specializes in analyzing and assessing a particular economic organization, will act more effectively than the present economic ministries, none of which are able to say at a moment's notice how any particular enterprise under them is actually faring.

According to experts at the Institute of Organization, Management, and Economics of the Construction Industry, the implementation of investment policy requires separate organizational structures. They suggest we might profit from the experience of Czechoslovakia, where the entire investment program is administered by a special office set up for that purpose (but having no executive powers of its own), or from that of the German Democratic Republic, where housing construction is under local authorities (at the provincial level) who employ the services of a proxy investor to coordinate construction of an entire housing project. Quite apart from this, the suggestions by this group of experts stress the desirability of reform in the organization of the construction industry.

4. *The mechanisms of management.* The analyses and discussions concerning the mechanisms of management are at a much less advanced level. It is pointed out that in order to switch to monetary yardsticks for measuring the management of the economy, the whole problem of money, including its theoretical aspects, must be sorted out. Another problem requiring practical solution is the question of the legal and economic aspects of ownership in a state economy. Respondent No. 36 stressed that worker participation in management cannot rest exclusively on incentives of an ideological or moral kind.

"One ought rather to create within the state sector forms of co-ownership of the means of production: the state, as the representative of all society and holding an appropriate number of seats on an enterprise supervisory board, would hold 'shares' along with the workers, who would own the remaining 'shares,' would have their own representatives on the supervisory board, and would receive dividends from earnings (both directly and by increasing the size of the enterprise capital). Such a system, by creating an economic basis for participation in management, has, as the experience of enterprises around the world that have instituted such an arrangement teaches us, had a positive influence both on the efficiency of management and on workers' motivation."

Of course, this is only one of the possible ways to bring about genuine employee participation in management and to raise a firm's efficiency.

5. *Problems bearing on present economic policy and the current vision of growth.* Even a superficial discussion of all these problems would require a separate book. We have merely tried to present some of the most essential proposals and trains of thought. However, we think it is worthwhile now to dwell at somewhat greater length on a few problems of the country's present economic policy that have yet to be cleared up.

Respondent No. 13 stressed the need to control inflation and alleviate, or if possible eliminate, the disproportions in the material balances between the different sectors of the economy (energy, transportation, etc.), and finally, the need to restrict imports. However, quite a few economists and persons involved practically in economic matters understand control of inflation to mean a reduction in employment and not a change in its structure. There is also a tendency to skirt the question of what one might call "closing the taps of inflation," which leads to ideas calling for further "sacrifices" on the part of society. In the opinion of respondent No. 37, the only sacrifices that one ought to expect from the public are an acceptance of the principle that the economy will pay only for work that has actually been done, and furthermore, that ancillary sources of income, i.e., speculation, corruption, abuse of one's position, etc., must be eliminated. The public expects price stabilization. The idea that market equilibrium can be restored by a further rise in prices has already been shown to be worthless (in 1976, while budgeted earnings from industry rose by 33.7 billion zlotys, i.e., by 7.8 percent, budgeted expenditure on industry rose by 82.4 billion zlotys, i.e., by 114.9 percent) because employees automatically respond to price rises with demands for wage hikes to which, given the shortage of manpower, enterprises have to accede. "The public expects that as the workings of our economy are restored to good order, the lowering of prime costs and the rise in supplies will increase the purchasing power of people's disposable income. Society is willing to do its share to see that this happens," writes respondent No. 37. This view accords with what we know about the state of public opinion in our country. In turn, the reduction in hard-currency outlays must, considering the size of our debt, also be thoroughly examined, because the importation of consumer goods will counteract a growth in inflation in an economy that is concentrating on the production of goods for export (the only input that production for export contributes to the internal market is the wages paid for its manufacture; it therefore increases demand yet does not put on the market anything that might counterbalance this rise in demand). What is more, the intense expansion of exports so necessary today must inevitably lead to an excess of demand on the domestic market even were the production of goods for the domestic market to reach maximum efficiency. The straightforward conclusion from this is that the inflationary gap cannot be plugged by the production of goods alone, but also requires that services grow; in other words, there must be a fresh division of national income.

There remains one last issue of contention about which, however, our respondents are of one mind: the cost of reform.

All those who addressed the matter agreed that the Polish economy cannot afford a further postponement of basic reforms (of course, preceded by thorough analysis and preparation). These reforms should aim first and foremost at abolishing waste and chaos and at eliminating the ever growing losses to which our economy is subject. All the solutions discussed in various circles take this same premise as their starting point: "The question is not one of reserves for reforms but of reforms to create reserves," as one of the respondents put it. It must be further borne in mind that any moratorium on the foreign debt or any help from the International Monetary Fund is out of the question if the parties to the discussions on these issues do not obtain tangible guarantees that the funds obtained in this way will be utilized effectively. We cannot expect somebody to be ready to sink money into our country without the prospect of getting it back, especially at times when money can be expected to become more expensive on the international market. There is, of course, a paradoxical situation that is familiar to economic practice and that works to our advantage: because of the size of our debt, our creditors are just as interested as we are in restoring our economy to working order. Nonetheless, no one is going to finance a "bottomless well," as one Western commentator described our economy. A credible program of economic reform would entail, from the point of view of our partners, genuine, extrafinancial guarantees of its economic viability, as several respondents point out. Our resources and potentials are known: there must be a guarantee that they will be put to good use.

6. *Problems of social policy.* In the light of the survey material, we might also attempt to formulate a set of constructive proposals of both a general and particular nature regarding social policy.

First, we would like to propose that we accept, as a general premise for analysis and decision-making in social policy, the fact that ours is a stratified society. While showing particular concern for the fate of those whose living conditions are especially severe, i.e., many of our peasants and rank-and-file industrial workers, it must be recognized that the working class is seriously handicapped in certain fundamental aspects of its social position.

It is proposed that the overriding aim of social policy, an aim taking precedence above all others, must be to minimize and ultimately to eliminate class differences and social inequalities. This proposal also refers to inequalities stemming from other factors, such as sex, the differences between town and country or between physical and mental labor, or regional divisions. A program must also be worked out to halt the growing antiegalitarian tendencies in our society.

In wage and income policy the following matters are particularly important:

——minimum wages and pensions must be scaled to some standard minimum;

——wage policy should try to reduce the gap between the lowest and the highest wages;

——family policy should be adopted as the basis for social policy, in consideration of the fact that disproportions in incomes and living standards are particularly dependent on family conditions and family size;

——equal pay for men and women. The present discrimination against women in terms of wages recalls the similar phenomenon in certain capitalist countries;

——wage policy should provide for rises in the lowest wages and pensions at a pace equivalent to the rise in the cost of living. This principle has been adopted not only in capitalist countries but in some socialist countries as well, e.g., Yugoslavia;[94]

——a program must be developed to fight poverty and to

establish the magnitude of this phenomenon.

Another task of social policy would be to increase expenditures on the nonproductive sectors (education, health, social security, recreation facilities, science, sports).

There are two further aspects to the material existence of the population that should be noted: housing and the social infrastructure. Housing is social problem no. 1. The problem of urban and suburban transportation also requires solution. Workers in state industry should be able to get to and from work conveniently. The question of individual transportation can wait.

Poland has a very poorly developed social infrastructure. We build huge new housing projects without shops, drug stores, and various service facilities, which depresses the standard of living, causes massive waste of time, and further saps the strength of society.

Our labor legislation requires sorting out and improvement: regulation of working hours, better job safety and health conditions, elimination of night work, first for women and eventually for men as well (except in factories requiring round-the-clock work). It should be added that depriving some workers of a weekly day off and the almost universal practice of extending working hours cast doubts on the permanence of the social gains of the working class.

In view of the stamp of secrecy placed on accident statistics, it is very difficult to assess the state of work safety. This secrecy is, however, itself telling proof that the situation is not the best, as is borne out, for example, by confidential data concerning fatal and serious accidents and by the large number of people who apply for their pensions before retirement age in certain branches of industry.

Family policy ought to be as solicitous of the material well-being of the family as of its moral status, which requires better preparation for family life, safeguarding the stability of the family, and efforts to control the mass spread of abortion.

Alcoholism is increasing at an alarming rate in Poland. The creation of "drunken budgets" was a feature of Russia under the tsars. Drunkenness among the public can be likened to a slow, collective national suicide. A large-scale public program aimed at reducing alcoholism and eliminating the unfortunate social consequences of this scourge must be initiated.

* * *

This truncated presentation of opinions from our survey

respondents on questions concerning the economy and social policy could only deal with the most basic issues. Many of our respondents recommended continuing an open discussion. Our treatment of the results of our study bypassed one important element in the responses——what can and ought to be done by various circles, groups, or strata among the public to break out of the present impasse. We have not gone into this subject because at this juncture, both our respondents and the authors felt that it was far more important first to outline a possible common point of departure for achieving a general social consensus. It is clear that success or failure in this undertaking will depend on the future conduct of every citizen in the country.

Conclusion

By its very nature and the nature of the contributions to it, this report cannot contain a full, systematic description of the situation in our country, and it cannot deal exhaustively with the question of the long-awaited reforms. It is a compendium and an attempt to synthesize a variety of often subjective views that reflect different experiences and different standpoints concerning matters our respondents feel deeply about and believe to be highly significant.

Certain important matters have not been highlighted in separate chapters and developed to the extent they merit. This is especially so in the case of public morality, culture, social and professional ethics, and problems of the family. These problems cause great concern and demand a separate exhaustive investigation in a different form than this particular study, which is intended in the first instance as an analysis of the specific structures and mechanisms of our collective life. But most of our respondents have expressed unease about these matters and have contributed valuable reflections on them.

Apart from the constantly recurring themes, all the contributions to our study share one characteristic that is worth stressing: an uncompromising severity in their criticism of current methods of exercising power and an obstinate desire to reach an agreement and to initiate a dialogue with those in power. This is based on the conviction that such an agreement, despite all accepted practice, cannot be based on tactical maneuvers and half-truths; that it can only bear fruit when it is reached in an atmosphere of candor, even at the price of a sharp exchange of views.

Among the deficiencies our society must endure, the most

important is not the lack of meat or other goods but the lack of clarity and candor, the lack of trust in the words of our leaders, in official declarations, in information carried in the press or on television. Whenever a note of candor has sounded in the words of our leaders, whenever society has been trusted, whenever our difficulties, our mistakes, and ways to rectify them have been discussed openly, the social climate and people's attitudes have changed radically, and new energies and initiatives have been released.

Alas, these moments were too brief to yield permanent fruit. They were followed by long periods when the rulers separated themselves from society by a barrier of ritual gestures and words that sounded ever more hollow to the ruled. When, inevitably, the signs of crisis became more apparent, civic attitudes vanished, a greedy individual egotism began to reign supreme, as did passivity in social activity, bringing in its wake the threat of a dissolution of social ties.

Today we are again reaching the nadir of crisis, a crisis perhaps more profound than those of the past because the process of civilization imposes on the system of social cooperation ever harder and ever more complex tasks. In order to perform them successfully, we have to restore an authentic social life, we have to free ourselves of the delusions that have seized politics and the economy. One such a delusion is powerful and centralized authority, since the excess of matters it has to deal with condemns it to impotence or arbitrariness. Planning is a fiction if the factories that are built have no energy and raw materials. How often in our country sham work receives a sham reward. How often important matters are not tackled and roll on "in a way no one wanted but too many allowed."

This picture is not the result of bitterness. It corresponds to the experience of millions of people——mute and helpless witnesses to waste, incompetence, and lack of responsibility. Perhaps the signs of the deepening crisis are not so clearly visible from the point of view of the authorities, particularly at their highest level. That is one more argument for discussing them with brutal frankness. Such an attitude is the result of a feeling of civic responsibility; it has given birth to our questionnaire and this study. In any event, our study is not the only voice of warning. From all kinds of sources similar voices demand the adoption of radical and far-reaching reforms capable of cleansing the social atmosphere and dragging the country out of its present slough of impotence.

It is understandable that there can be differences of opinion about the scale, the depth, and the ways in which these essential reforms should be carried out. However, in our conditions, which do not favor collective reflection, thinking about the restoration of our Republic appears to us to be dangerously fragmented and to oscillate between dreams of an ideal order and a petty realism of half-hearted or sham reforms. One of the fundamental purposes of this study is to set our thinking about reform on the hard ground of our concrete historical situation and the conditions it imposes on us. That is why the proposals contained in this text are open to accusations on the one hand that they are minimal and on the other that they are excessively bold.

This is because, in the opinion of our respondents, when it comes to politics, only clearly perceiving what is possible makes it possible to do what is necessary.

The picture of an alienated leadership and a discouraged and apathetic society may appear extremely depressing; and our proposals for overcoming the crisis of confidence and for stubbornly rebuilding, in however limited and conditional a way, understanding between the authorities and society may be seen by many Poles as just as utopian, just as out of touch with reality, as the building of an ideal society.

In fact it is an extremely difficult task, and there are no guarantees that it will prove possible to do it. But it is by no means utopian. The essence of a utopia——and its attraction—— lies in the fact that it is easy, that it does not take into account the resistance of reality, and that it can move freely in worlds it creates by itself. It is limited only by the mind and the imagination of its creator. We, however, have dealt with real difficulties that exist in the attitudes and the habits of people, as well as with established organizational structures. But overcoming them is possible if a sufficiently large number of people decisively reject the humiliating and paralyzing conviction that a fundamental change is at once essential and impossible.

In the past our nation has often displayed in the face of difficulties and dangers an admirable vitality, determination, and self-sacrifice. This gives us hope that this time, too, we will be able to emerge victorious from the trials the future brings. It will demand great effort on the part of our most powerful minds and of millions of conscious people capable of demanding their civil rights with moderation and discretion.

Even the greatest difficulties do not endanger the existence of a nation while that nation retains the will to overcome them and the basic sense of a common fate shaped by collective effort.

The disappearance of that will and that feeling indicates the profundity of the present crisis. In order to overcome it we will need to act in a concerted and complementary way in both the material and institutional realms of life, as well as in the area of personal awareness. It will therefore demand the mobilization of various, even contradictory social forces. The difficulty of the task is not an argument against attempting it when there is nothing else to do except, perhaps, believe in a miracle or passively await catastrophe.

Which Way Out?

Introductory Remarks

In November 1978 a group of people representing various professions and viewpoints established the discussion group "Experience and the Future" under the auspices of the Collegium of the Society for the Free Diffusion of Knowledge. At its first (and, as it turned out, last) plenary session, it managed to bring together a hundred or so representatives of various scholarly disciplines, writers and journalists, and theater and film personalities, united by a common concern for the problems of the Republic and an awareness of the seriousness of the situation in which the country found itself.

Unfortunately, the group was prevented by the authorities from performing its normal activities, although its sole purpose was to encourage free discussion of the most vital issues bearing on our nation and state. In view of the scale and scope of the crisis that was to some degree affecting all areas of our social life, it was decided to continue the activities of the group in accordance with the wishes of its members. It was decided to work by correspondence, without giving up efforts to resume plenary meetings in accordance with the group's original intentions.

A questionnaire was sent to "Experience and the Future" participants that dealt with the most important problems of our country and state. The results were worked up by the Service Unit, together with other persons who declared their willingness to help, and published as "A Report on the State of the Republic and Ways to Rectify It" (see pages 3-150). This text, which was aimed at the public, was presented in late May 1979 to "Experience and the Future" members, to representatives of the highest political and state authorities, and to the moral authorities of Polish society.

Based on responses representing a wide range of viewpoints, the "Report" provided a diagnosis of the situation in which the country found itself, as well as a list of various proposals for reforms that could alleviate the effects of the crisis and create conditions conducive to instituting fundamental changes. It was meant neither as a petition nor a political program, as it repeatedly stressed. The overriding intent of the "Report" was to launch a discussion of the most crucial issues facing our nation and state as seen in different circles, to stimulate reflection, and to help transform general criticism into a driving force for necessary change.

The "Report" was received with considerable interest, extending far beyond "Experience and the Future." It was, and still is, being reproduced and disseminated without our active participation. The impact it has had is testimony to the state of mind of the Polish public, especially those circles that are aware of the existing state of affairs.

The Service Unit has received, and continues to receive, numerous responses touching on various problems dealt with in the "Report." All point out the need to continue this important discussion. We should stress that although the "Report" did not manage to achieve the response hoped for among official circles, it did (judging from evidence brought to our attention) provoke a lively interest in various circles within the power apparatus.

In December 1979, in view of the fact that the situation in the country had not improved and that the persistent difficulties and their consequences had merely deepened the apathy, dissaffection, and dissatisfaction of society, the Service Unit, taking its cue from the manifest concern of the public and the suggestions made by the participants in the first survey, decided to send out another questionnaire, this time entitled: WHICH WAY OUT?

This questionnaire concerned measures to be taken in the nearest future by the state authorities and by social institutions and circles to achieve a state of social consensus, initiate partnership relations between society and the authorities, and halt the process of decay in the economy and the state.

The responses to this new questionnaire arrived in December of 1979 and January of 1980. Despite the short period for responding—only one month—the questionnaire yielded a rich harvest that required more time to cull than we had anticipated.

We should like to express our profound thanks to all those who responded for their participation and contribution to the work that became for us a collective effort.

Between the time the survey was sent out and the editorial work on the responses was completed, certain changes in the leadership had taken place. Some public statements made at the Party Congress and the inaugural address of the new premier demonstrate that the state authorities were aware of the crisis in which the country found itself.[1] However, it turned out that those authorities and the party leadership were concerned almost exclusively with the economic situation, and any changes had to do with it alone. Without questioning the importance of these changes, it should nevertheless be stated that in the opinion of the respondents to both surveys, the country's current crisis is above all social and political; the success of any economic reforms is contingent in the first place on changes in the way power is exercised and politics are conducted. In view of this, it is safe to say that most of the problems and concerns expressed by the respondents remain timely, indeed, are now more so than ever before.

*   *   *

In this second survey we addressed a broader circle of people than just the "Experience and the Future" discussion group. We were concerned with obtaining the opinion of representatives of various areas of scholarship as well as of those strata (and age groups) that had been less well represented in the first survey.

The accumulated material is diverse and variegated. Despite the fact that the questions touched on only the most essential areas, many respondents accompanied their responses with an analysis of the present situation, and their proposals often went beyond mere stopgap measures. Hence this study also contains elements of diagnosis that refer to changes that have taken place since the first "Report" was compiled and presented.

The Service Unit got 141 responses, i.e., about three times as many as for the preceeding "Report." These responses came from prominent representatives of all sorts of professions, including sixty-five scholars, among them thirty-nine university professors. The following disciplines were represented: biology, construction, economics, philosophy, finance, physics, foreign trade, history, information theory, logic, mathematics, pedagogy, law, agriculture, sociology, the fine arts, technology, and management. There were also writers and journalists, film makers, and representatives of other areas of artistic creativity, directors of large industrial plants, organizers of economic life, representatives of various specialized areas of the technical intelligentsia, persons active in political and social life, practicing lawyers, architects, urban planners, and Catholic activists.

Fifty-one of the respondents were members of the Polish United Workers' Party and an equal number were from the other two parties.

The respondents included believers as well as nonbelievers.

The majority of the respondents considered the situation of the country to be extremely alarming and, moreover, steadily deteriorating.

Almost all agreed that reforms were necessary, yet at the same time, they expressed their skepticism about any real chances for them to be successful. The present survey, conducted among a much broader and more representative sample, confirmed the diagnosis made in the "Report."

Some of the respondents went further in their skepticism, declaring their disbelief in any chance for public negotiations. There were even a few odd cases of people who refused to participate in the survey on the grounds that they saw no point in what we were doing. However, the vast majority of those whom we addressed responded positively, and many even expressed their wholehearted support for our efforts.

Almost all the responses underscored, as their first premise, the need to expose *the full truth about the country's present situation.* "We need an 'hour of truth,'" writes one of the respondents, "during which complete, unfalsified information about the state of the Republic and about the factors that have led to it is made available to the public. An hour of truth would mean the right of society to ask whatever questions it had in mind and insist on honest answers. An hour of truth should take place on both a macro and micro scale." Another respondent formulated the same idea as follows: "The truth about the state of the nation must be publicly stated, not because society does not know it, at least in its general contours, but because it is a necessary—would that it were sufficient!—condition for the credibility of any further statements on the matter."

Many of the respondents seem to make special use of terms that indicate their taking for granted a difference between the social order and the political system. The political system is not considered the unique and ultimate expression of the fundamental features of the social order. For example, the uncontrolled omnipotence of the central authorities of the party apparatus is not counted among the features of the basic social and political order, while it is numbered among the negative manifestations of the political system. The organization of the system of information and misinformation and the arbitrariness of the censor are also not considered features of the social order but rather attributes of the system. The usurpation of the arena of public life, which has been transformed into a kind of theater where only designated actors appear with prepared texts, is also, in the eyes of the respondents, a feature of the system and not of the social order. One of the respondents writes: "There is a tragic discrepancy between declarations heralding the country's future and the vacuity and pointlessness of programs for achieving it. Everything is reduced to ritualistic ceremony, as dull for the celebrants and participants as it is for society at large."

We could mention many such issues and problems, but we feel it is most important to stress that in the views of the respondents, a major change in the features of the political system (from authoritarianism to democracy) would make it more compatible with their notions of the social order.

"The current economic and political crisis is unique in the history of postwar Poland, not only with regard to the collapse of our growth rate and our enormous debt, which has made further growth impossible, but also because the last decade has demonstrated the total inability of the present system of institutions to deal with economic and political problems in a rational way and to work out a long-term strategy of development," observes one of the respondents. Another notes: "The economic crisis situation in which Poland found itself in the second half of the seventies made graphically evident the rapidly dwindling ability of the system to ensure the proper functioning of the state machinery and hence its development toward realizing socialist principles."

The concentration of the leadership's efforts on combating economic difficulties was, however, no substitute for measures that would stimulate the citizenry to activity. One of the respondents writes: "The belief that accelerated economic growth in some way automatically resolves superstructural issues along with the problems of government (quite apart from the fact that it was simply wrong) also evokes objections for the simple reason that the system of economic management has been unable to cope with the tasks imposed by such growth." The respondents also point out the existence of a very numerous and influential group that, in catering to its own interests, gives shape to and determines how that system will function. "A way out of the current crisis and a way to ensure the country's harmonious and stable development," writes one of the respondents, "are impossible without a fundamental change in the existing style of governing the state. Indeed, a false style of government is the source and the cause of the current crisis. There is no doubt that the cause-and-effect relations underlying certain social phenomena are so obvious that it is impossible to remove the effects without removing the causes provoking them."

But how can this be done? How can we ensure that an obsolete and ineffective system of functioning of the state, the activities of its institutions, the management of the economy, and the organization of public life do not impede the creative activity of society and do not block development?

In the opinion of almost all the respondents, the first condition for the molding of a social consensus, a condition that will decisively influence the further course of events, is a change in the principles and methods of wielding power. Almost everyone agreed that in the difficult situation in which the country currently finds itself, it is necessary to seek the broadest possible consensus among different social groups and different segment of opinions. Such a consensus is necessary and possible on pragmatic grounds alone.

We could well say that in a country in Poland's geographic position, we would consider the desire to resolve conflicts through negotiation, that is, by presenting rational arguments and taking into account different interests, fundamental, even though initially it might be received with hostility by the two sides. The readiness to negotiate need not reflect opportunism or weakness: it can also reflect the attitude of people who are confident in their cause and are conscious of the social potential they represent.

CHAPTER 1

A Diagnosis
of the Situation—
Sources of Tension

The poll was not meant to describe the current state of affairs; nevertheless, direct statements in it about the present situation have enabled us to formulate a diagnosis pinpointing those spheres of social life in which the tensions most keenly felt by the public have appeared. The elimination or substantial relaxing of such tensions is crucial if we are to find a path toward social consensus and stave off those destructive and conflict-filled tendencies that are threatening the future of our country.

Here is a catalogue of the tensions mentioned by the respondents, listed in order of the frequency with which they occur in the poll material.

1. *Tensions stemming from the sense that the system is malfunctioning.* Vagueness of power and responsibility; the absence of checks and control; an atrophied sense of responsibility; layer on layer of ever more bureaucratic structures looking exclusively toward narrow self-interest; sham goals, sham institutions, sham actions; arbitrariness and authoritarianism on the part of leadership groups; demoralization of subordinates; distortion and suppression of information—all this combines to give a citizen the sense that the social mechanism is functioning improperly. As one of the respondents put it pointedly: "Even supposing we were a feudal state ruled by an oligarchy, we would still not be acting the way an oligarchy should." Or in someone else's words: "The public is oppressed by a feeling of disarray in our country." "The public perhaps sees the situation as being more dramatic than it is in reality; but for the atmosphere of political life, that feeling has the status of a fact more important than its basis in reality," to quote yet another typical response.

2. Tensions stemming from what the respondents defined in late 1979 as the *"lack of credibility of the leadership."* We

159

have a situation in which neither the apparat nor the public believes the declarations or the information coming from those within the leadership. Almost all the respondents call attention to the, in their view alarming, erosion of the leadership's authority. Considering that a loss of credibility is much more dangerous for the authorities than a decline in popularity, any future leadership must, in the view of the respondents, give serious consideration to the public sentiment described above.

3. In the same vein, tensions flowing from *the lack of credibility of the mass media*. In comparison with the situation described in the "Report," this problem has clearly become even graver in the past few months, as shown by the publication of many critical articles in our cultural and political press.[2] In the view of some of the respondents, the situation has reached virtually neurotic dimensions. "You can't believe even the bad news because you suspect that it is just another form of manipulation." Similar opinions expressed in different terms are repeated in many of the responses: "If people whom the public regards as figures of probity and rectitude ever return to the pages of the press and television screens, they must take care that they do not bring on themselves the odium of public mistrust and suspicion." "The mass media have for all practical purposes ceased to be an instrument of even current communication between the authorities and the public, not to speak of other functions." These passages sum up the views of almost all the respondents, who stressed that the authorities had lost all genuine contact with intellectual circles capable of influencing public opinion. They refer to and recall, for example, the views of J. Szczepański,[3] who a few months ago at a Sejm committee meeting observed: "The publication by a censor who defected to the West of our rules of censorship produced a shock in scholarly circles and a feeling of shame with regard to such a system of control over publications."[4]

4. It is common knowledge—fully supported by the poll —that *the question of state sovereignty* is a pregnant and urgent issue in the public mind. These tensions, according to the respondents, are intensified by the "lack of reliable information on economic conditions within the USSR" and the "servile," "almost obtuse style of propaganda, which offends Polish national pride." They are further deepened by the "lack of honest explanations of various facts from the past." We shall come back to this matter in more detail later in our discussion.

5. Next in order of frequency in the poll responses are

those tensions flowing from the whole range of economic problems. The growing feeling of economic destabilization, the disintegration of the system of economic management (according to the terse description of one of the respondents, "The government has shifted to manual controls"), a feeling of mismanagement of the economy, as well as the egotism of many "interest groups" at the departmental, branch, and local levels, the lack of confidence in and flight from the currency, the lack of any hope of rectifying the situation—all this combines into what the respondents identified as "a crisis of expectations,"[5] a crisis probably made much more acute by the continuing troubles besetting daily life and the current state of the economy. "Society does not know the whole picture but, forced to rely on its own fragmented experiences, creates its own dramatized image of our economy. The awareness of not knowing the whole truth serves to deepen the atmosphere of uncertainty, mistrust, and apathy both among the public as well as in the 'ruling apparatus.'"

As a result, a "spiral of hopelessness" is created, as one of the respondents put it: no confidence in tomorrow or the currency paralyzes the initiative of everyone functioning in the economy, as a result of which output falls; with the decline in production the feeling of crisis within the ruling apparatus deepens and spreads to the public, as does the lack of confidence in tomorrow, which in turn causes production to decline further, and so on.

6. The respondents mention *relations between the authorities and private farmers* as a separate area of tensions.[6] They note the feeling—and indeed the fact—of instability in agricultural policy, particularly in land policy. They speak of arbitrariness in interpreting this policy, not only at the provincial [*wojewoda*] level but even—and perhaps above all—at the local [*gmin*] level. It is precisely at these points that administrative arbitrariness is most widespread: the peasants are almost defenseless against the many forms of negligence, obstruction, and abuse on the part of various branches of the bureaucracy, whose employees appropriate a large portion of agricultural profits. The disappearance of any semblance of agricultural self-management, bureaucratization of every nominal "social" institution, their hollowness, and finally, shortages in the supply of fuel, investment funds, implements, fertilizer, and so on create a set of factors that, according to the respondents, together cause grave tensions with disastrous and pervasive consequences.

7. *Tensions stemming from everyday problems in the food supply* are singled out in the poll as a separate social problem. The respondents indicate two points of "extreme irritation." First, the meat shortage and, as a result of the introduction of commercial prices,[7] the drastic reduction in meat consumption among the less well paid layers of society. The children of large families have been hardest hit. The second point has to do with difficulties in providing infants and small children with adequate nourishment, difficulties that stem from prices, unavailability, and the contamination of many nutritional items needed by small children to grow. In both cases, according to the respondents, the problems of food supply intensify the growing stratification of society as well as the existence of a "second market."[8]

8. In many of the responses an area that particularly inflamed social frustration was the issue—taken in the most general sense—of *inequality*. It bears on various realms of social life whose ills can be reduced to this important common denominator. The responses mention, among other things, such phenomena as the emergence of "elite property" (as a separate category of "group" ownership in relation to private, cooperative, or state ownership), nepotism, privileges deriving from membership in the ruling strata and groups, inequality of opportunities for advancement and careers, inequality before the law, lack of citizens' protection from various forms of arbitrary administrative conduct, lack of any genuine means to safeguard workers' rights (especially in job safety), lack of effective means to protect the interests of society against pressures by various interest groups.

9. Some of the respondents took up *the problem of youth*. Several called tensions in this area "simply explosive." They noted the "crisis of youth organizations," "the official excision of youth problems from any genuine discussion," the "two currents of youth life, official and unofficial, that oppose one another and permit no contact," "the demoralizing influence of recruiting members by offering them privileges and material advantages" and the negative selection of youth workers,[9] and finally, the "morally and intellectually most worthy youth are forced by the logic of a system of fictions into a position of apathy and mistrust of even the watchwords of socialism." A crisis that concerned mainly university young people has now extended to pupils from the upper grades of secondary schools and has also affected young workers, albeit in a different and less obvious way.

In addition to immediate stresses, the respondents mentioned areas of tension of a more long-range nature. Since a good deal of space was devoted to these matters in the "Report on the State of the Republic and Ways to Rectify It," below we shall merely list them in the order of the frequency with which they appeared in the poll. They are:

——*Housing problems* ("The persistent housing crisis, which now is without counterpart in any other country of Europe").

——*The socioeconomic disadvantage of the most poorly paid segments of the population.*

——*The crisis in health services* ("the health services are going through an organizational, economic, and moral crisis, with disastrous consequences for the health of the nation").

——*The disadvantage of broad segments of society as regards access to culture* ("in no other area has the departure from the ideals of socialism emerged in such a statistically demonstrable manner").

——Increasingly frequent *breaches of the fundamental principles of the rule of law*, intensifying the sense of emergency among the populace.

Some of the other sources of social tension and frustration mentioned are:

——*Alcoholism*, or indeed, the policy of de facto acceptance of the spread of this plague.

——*The crisis situation in education* (the educational system continues to lag far behind the educational aspirations of society; the obstacles and barriers in the system and the negative consequences of poorly prepared reforms promote further social stratification and exacerbate social inequalities).

——The unregulated *relationship between the state and believers* (the devout continue to feel handicapped in public life).

Among the most alarming tensions of an objective sort, which cause social frustration and uneasiness and deepen the sense of a "crisis of expectations," the respondents point out:

——*The energy and transportation crisis.*

——The growing *foreign debt*.

——The burden on the economy of *armaments expenditures*.

——The increasing *pollution of the natural environment* (including contamination of food unbeknownst to the consumer).

Both those respondents who believe that the source of the impasse lies in the play of the objective interests of different strata and groups in our society, and those who think it stems principally from factors of a psychological nature, have more or less similarly outlined variants for possible future actions by the

authorities. Such actions could take the form of "a do-nothing
option," the manipulation of economic factors, or a "hard-line
course."

1. The *"no change" variant* (i.e., not disturbing the status
quo) was described in the "Report." In this variant the negative
changes described above would gradually accumulate and could
at any point avalanche, threatening to break out into open social conflict.

2. The *"economic"* variant is based exclusively on the manipulation of economic resources. In view of the steady depre-
ciation of our currency, as well as the absence of a credible program for rebuilding the economy and reforming management,
economic incentives will also not be able to achieve what is required of them, just as the command economy has thus far been
ineffective. The ultimate result will be the same as the first
variant.

3. The *"hard-line"* alternative is an attempt to suppress all
critical voices by compulsion and by restricting every critical
voice coming from influential circles, including elimination of
the press that operates outside censorship and hamstringing the
authentic instruments of public opinion. In a situation where
neither criticism nor the existence of independent circles, including an opposition, is the source of the negative developments taking place, this variant cannot resolve any real problem;
in fact it could even accelerate the buildup of a general mood of
protest and opposition, leading to an ultimate outcome quite
like the preceding variants.

Open social conflict, the prospects for which are noted by
the respondents, need not, in their opinion, take the form familiar to us from the years 1956, 1970, and 1976.[10] There are now
other sources of conflict unknown at that time, other reasons
for tension that now, under new conditions having no precedent
in the past, could engender new phenomena equally without
precedent. The gradual breakdown of market equilibrium threatens to intensify the state of uncertainty and apprehension, and
to set off waves of panic buying.[11] All this will lead to a further
decline in labor productivity and organizational anarchy.

None of these options makes any allowance for society's
participation in dealing with our mounting problems. However,
there exists a variant in which the public and the authorities
would cooperate as partners. Although at the moment there unfortunately appears to be little likelihood of this happening, it is
nonetheless the only alternative auguring any hope; and there-

fore we shall return to it in the following pages. Sooner or later it will become inevitable.

A factor in favor of a prognosis of this sort is the general levelheadedness of Polish society and its traditional dislike of extremes—the "common sense" that shows up in the most trying situations. However, the respondents foresee that all three variants described above will yield only negative results with regard to the attitudes of those elements that still are seeking every opportunity to negotiate and reach a social consensus.

The "areas of tension" we have presented here (quite briefly considering the nature of the survey) and certain alternative modes of conduct open to the authorities show that there can be no single answer to the question: *which way out*?

From the views of the respondents it is clear that only a whole package of solutions applied in different areas, at different times, and in different stages on the way toward fashioning a social consensus can guarantee the success of the entire process. We will propose some solutions in the next chapter.

CHAPTER 2

Which Way Out: Ends and Means

We would like to present here the set of political, social, economic, legal, and other goals, means, and practical measures that together represent the way *to escape the crisis* recommended by the participants in the poll. A group of 150 people representing different professions, fields of specialization, schools of thought, and philosophical outlooks exhibited a great degree of agreement in their responses about the steps that had to be taken to genuinely set the situation in the country aright.

From the poll responses we can extract the following main goals of proposed actions:

1. The forging of the requisite trust between the political leadership and the public, primarily by the leadership's assuring the credibility and restoring the integrity of the information media;

2. Stimulation and restoration of social life——within the confines of the existing social and economic system——by altering the methods of exercising power and by economic reform;

3. Obtaining the support of the general public for a program of changes and the creation of a climate and the mechanisms needed to promote initiative in different social groups;

4. Ensuring the durability of changes, particularly determining and implementing guidelines to regulate the major areas of political and economic activity;

5. The creation of a system that helps avoid or resolve social conflicts.

None of these objectives can be achieved in isolation; each depends on the others.

This chapter consists of two parts: the first presents a program, implicit in the poll responses, of political actions that must be undertaken to restore public life to good health and to invigorate society. They are steps that the respondents deemed indispensable for obtaining the trust and support of society, altering the mood, and freeing initiative, that is, for all those things on which the implementation of the measures discussed in the second part will also depend.

The second section presents measures aimed at economic reform, overcoming the economic crisis, and placing the existence of the nation on sound foundations that will promote harmonious development without the tensions threatening us today.

I

Confidence and credibility as primary conditions. The first precondition that must be met so that any change for the better can begin is that the authorities acquire at least a minimum of credibility and confidence among the population. Without them nothing can be achieved. As one of the respondents wrote: "Sustaining a compromise over a prolonged period is conceivable only if the government and its helmsmen enjoy the confidence of the overwhelming majority of the populace. Initially they must be made aware that they do not now enjoy this trust. To keep it they must bear in mind how easy it is to lose it." This view is repeated in almost all the questionnaires.

In the opinion of the overwhelming majority of the respondents, to achieve this objective it is necessary—as we noted at the outset—to begin by providing answers to society's questions about the real state of the country and the economy, how things got this way, and who is responsible and to what degree. The point is not to satisfy society's need for retribution for wrongs suffered; if answers to these questions and a genuine discussion of them are not attempted, it will be impossible to achieve credibility, to say nothing of trust. Any changes made will be perceived by society as an attempt at manipulation.

Foreign affairs—Poland in the international balance of power. Many of the respondents deem it impossible to separate the country's social and economic problems from the world situation and from our place in it.

Participants in the poll who addressed the problem generally recognized that in the foreseeable future, Poland will continue to be a part of the existing political, economic, and military structures, the existing system of alliances: the Warsaw Pact and the Council for Mutual Economic Assistance. Many, however, also pointed out that the state of Polish-Soviet relations is cause for vital concern among the public, including a deep sense of the unequal nature of these relations. Some—like the respondents in the earlier survey—note Poland's specific position among the bloc nations, particularly the deep historical and cultural ties linking Poland to the West, as well as the extensive economic relations that have evolved, especially in the last ten years. Recent international events have also elicited public concern lest, considering the country's unequal relations with its strongest ally, it be drawn without any prior consultation or approval into events which, given its general conditions, could have catastrophic consequences.[12]

The aspiration to maintain a policy of openness, stimulated by international détente, is, we think, not only a desire of the respondents to the survey, where the point recurs several times, but equally a reflection of the attitude of the whole society. This attitude stems not only from our cultural ties and traditions, but also from the feeling, deeply rooted in the hearts and minds of the citizenry, that they have the right to freedom of movement. Important economic considerations also favor such a policy: Poland is dependent on Western raw materials, spare parts, and food, as well as Western credit, and it will remain so for a long time to come. The breaking off or even weakening of relations with the West would threaten the country, quite simply, with economic paralysis.

Some of the respondents point out the tremendous burden of armament expenditures on our society: according to statistics from the Stockholm Peace Research Institute, our armaments budget is the eighth largest in the world. The view of the respondents is that we cannot afford such a huge share in the global commitments and enterprises of our allies.

Without a clearly and unambiguously defined policy in these matters, it is difficult even to think of securing the confidence and support of the public; not only, say the respondents, is clarity of policy necessary, but it is also necessary to foster in people a sense that stability is being safeguarded.

The respondents point out the objective need to improve the way our alliance system functions and to upgrade bilateral relations between Poland and the USSR; but they are equally concerned with changing the way the Polish party and government leadership view this alliance and these relations.

Nothing is so harmful to relations with the USSR in the eyes of the public as the cringing servility that has been demonstrated at every turn, the wheedling tone of our propaganda (de-scribed by many of the respondents as out-and-out toadying), and finally, the falsification of history——not only the history of recent years and the twentieth century but even that of the re-mote past.

Some of the respondents pointed out that in the eyes of the public, Polish-Soviet relations have very often been used by Polish leading circles as a smokescreen manipulated to relieve them of responsibility for their own actions.[13] On the other hand, a kind of social psychosis has developed that attributes every deficiency and shortcoming in public and economic life to the direct interference of the Soviet Union. In such a situation it is obviously impossible to gain the full trust and support of the public as long as it cannot be shown that all the basic deci-sions which affect national existence are made within the coun-try itself, and dignity is maintained in relations with our allies.

It will be impossible for the authorities to gain credibility in their foreign and domestic policy without a thoroughgoing change in the way the press, radio, and television conduct their affairs, basing their work on complete, accurate information, and not on vacuous, ritualistic phrases and the "propaganda of success," which, as one of the respondents noted, has been trans-formed into a "propaganda of social irritation."[14]

One guarantee of such a change would be extensive reduc-tion and regulation of the legally prescribed duties and powers of the censor.[15] First, we should determine what should be kept under censorship (e.g., areas constituting exceptions, such as military secrets or certain technological secrets); then we should establish a system regulating censorship blacklisting, provide permanent supervision and control of censorship under a body set up specifically for that purpose, set up ways to appeal cen-sorship decisions, and finally, remove scientific publications wholly from censorship.

The principle here must be openness, and acts of censor-ship must be only exceptionally applied. Censorship must al-ways concern things, never people.

A program of social change. The next steps, closely con-nected, however, with the preceding ones (and moreover coin-ciding with them in time as well), are aimed at convincing the public to accept the program and at mobilizing hitherto unuti-lized forces, enabling further measures, including those requiring patience and sacrifice, to be undertaken.

Such measures have to do, for instance, with:

a. the workers,

b. the countryside,

c. the party,

d. religious believers,

e. leadership cadres.

The working class and its families have become the largest social group in the country. Its significant, if uneven, educational, material, and cultural progress, its importance in the production process——all these things have determined that without it today no major social, political, and above all, economic reform is possible.

However, the forms of collective life acceptable to the working class do not provide it any real opportunities to participate in the governmental, administrative, or economic processes of the country. Furthermore, it does not have institutional opportunities to express and defend its professional, social, and economic interests. It is therefore necessary to reorganize and reform the trade unions in order to give the working class a say in those matters that are basic to it. The trade unions must become genuinely representative of the workers, building from the ground up, freely and in the ways the workers want (including structurally). The trade unions and their role therefore require legal definition. The skeleton law of 1949 has long since become inadequate.[16] Until now the activities of the trade unions, as well as the workers' self-management boards,[17] were actually guided by political decisions and declarations and not by law. The establishment of norms for the role of the trade unions and the clear definition of their rights do not threaten the political position of the party and the authorities; rather, such actions would enable them to considerably improve relations with the working class. This would equally facilitate the next steps in the economic reform, in that free, objective, and genuine negotiations on working conditions and wages would, on the one hand, make the factory work force into true partners conscious of their rights and obligations and, on the other hand, would help put the problems of efficiency, output, labor discipline, quality, and so forth, on a sound and healthy basis. The experience of the developed countries teaches us that the worker should be treated as a partner in the productive process, and that, indeed, enterprises have a vested interest in seeing that this happens. The denial of this right to the worker is both a social and an economic anachronism and can in no way be justified.

Credible and properly functioning trade unions would have

an important role to play in settling disputes. In contrast to technocratic and bureaucratic fears and inclinations, real and effective action on the part of the trade unions would be less costly than current day-to-day tensions and the need to "buy peace" from this or that factory work force, which is done at the expense of breaking rules, and which results in even deeper demoralization. Attempts by the police to intimidate the work force lead to similar disastrous results.

In the opinion of some of the respondents, viable and genuine trade unions should have their own representation in the Sejm. It is worth mentioning that in the German Democratic Republic, the trade unions have their own representation in the Volkskammer.

The interests of the working class demand greater participation in public life, the expansion of industrial democracy, the development of various forms of self-management, and full participation in social control. The respondents called special attention to the need to thoroughly discuss the roles, tasks, and methods of operation of the workers' self-management boards, and then to implement the results of this discussion (in the second part of this chapter we will present some suggestions by the respondents concerning how to create the legal and economic foundations for workers' participation in administration and supervision).

The countryside. The proclamation of an unambiguous and stable agricultural policy is absolutely indispensable; this policy should be based on realities and reject the imposition of doctrinal principles, for which society pays quite dearly, and which destroy the confidence of the farmers in the state (we shall go into this in more detail in the second section of this chapter).[18] The farmers thus should not be treated exclusively as producers of food but should be made full-fledged participants in social and cultural life by creating in the countryside the requisite cultural infrastructure. It is also necessary to rethink the way the current law for old-age pensioners works in practice;[19] its purpose should be primarily to insure old and solitary people and to protect their trades from disappearance when they have no successors.

Every level of state power and the economic administration should be placed under the categorical obligation to support and defend every self-governing farmers' organization, cooperative association, and farmers' collective, as well as the supply and sale of goods, decisions about which should be in the hands of the peasants and not those of the officials. Work on plans for economic reform should consider handing over to the peasants those numerous offices of economic administration whose operations in the current structure entail the tremendous expense of paying officials and inspectors; in the opinion of some of the respondents, government departments should restrict their activities to the wholesale level and not run shops, purchasing centers, collection points, and so on. It has similarly been suggested that the leaders of local communities be selected exclusively by elections, and moreover genuine, not sham ones.

The party. Many of the respondents observed that the success of reforms depends on the attitude of the party toward them. Some——especially those who themselves are party members——state that no economic or political reforms are possible without reform within the party, which must include:

——democratization of relations within the party;

——creation of mechanisms to formulate alternative general programs.

Democratization, say the respondents, should be based above all on openness in internal party life and the transfer of power, today exercised almost exclusively by an apparatus of officials, to collective bodies constituted by election (party committees). In the same vein there is a need for a broad discussion within the party, embracing every organizational level, on the party's operations and the way it exercises power.

Many of the respondents felt that an especially important condition for a transformation in the party was the possibility of forging alternative programs ("The goal would be the same, but ways of attaining it would be different. One team in power, on the field, another in the stands," as one respondent put it). The participants in the poll point out that in a one-party system, this is practically the only way to avoid a party bureaucracy and, at the same time, the only possible mechanism to maintain control over the ruling team.

The first condition for the democratization of intraparty life and to permit the formulation of alternative programs is, say the respondents, the introduction of a statute limiting terms in office for the top leadership levels of the party apparatus. Every response that took up the problem of the party made this point.

Many also dwelled on the question of "the leading role of the party." Most of the respondents to the first "Experience and the Future" poll accepted the nature of the existing political system as a fact stemming from the overall geopolitical situation, but they advocated a change in its operation. The suggestions indicated a multitude of possible alternate choices among those that would work against the postulate of repressing society. The quest continues in the same vein in the present poll, although the belief appears to be less strong that the alternatives most desired can be implemented.

The respondents realize that the "leading role of the party" does not derive from the majority of the society's having adopted the ideology of the Polish United Workers' Party as its own. In an effort to rationalize this situation, some of the respondents suggested that the "leading role of the party" might be construed as deriving from what could be called "controlled trusteeship." The party—because of the objective situation—has been "entrusted" with its role as the chief organizational link in the effort to develop the country governmentally, socially, and culturally, although the party cannot be the sole designer, executor, and judge of that effort. It exercises a kind of *fiduciary leadership* here and, furthermore, must be held accountable according to much broader criteria than have previously been applied. A situation in which a small minority accumulates in its hands every prerogative concerning governance of the country's affairs leads to mounting apathy among the "silent majority" and the paralysis of public life.

Under present circumstances, in which the idea of a "state of all the people"[20] has been proclaimed by official circles, it is incumbent on the party to pay careful attention to the multitude of attitudes and views existing among the public, and to set the machinery of democracy in motion over the broadest possible front in order to bring about social cooperation and collaboration. As many of the respondents pointed out, the internal party structure is an anachronism, one suited perhaps to seizing and holding power, but not to current conditions.

In arguing for their suggestions concerning the functioning and internal situation of the party, the nonparty respondents stressed that in a one-party system, the *entire society* has the right and must be interested in these issues and therefore in everything concerning the way power is exercised. Therefore the principles guiding the party's conduct with regard to the apparatus and state institutions must be clearly and unambiguously defined.

Relations between the authorities and believers. Many respondents feel that steps must be taken to free practicing Catholics from the sense that they have been stripped of some of their rights as citizens because of their religious convictions. A number of social groups in Poland, especially the nonparty majority of the population, feel they are subject to some discrimination; however, inequality with religious implications is even more serious, since there exists a general sentiment that religious faith should not divide people politically. One step that would help to substantially relieve the tensions associated with these problems would be to enforce the rule that the holding of a post in the administration, the economy, or the judicial system must be based on qualifications, competence, and an evaluation of past performance, rather than on organizational membership, personal acquaintances, or attitude toward religion. On the other hand, it is necessary to eliminate or curtail all sources of tension with regard to religious life. This includes, for example, permission to build new churches wherever people want; allowing the Church and denominational organizations to conduct cultural and educational activities without obstacles; the free development of the Catholic press (and that of other faiths) without the current discrimination (e.g., in obtaining paper and printing facilities); giving the Church access within agreed limits to the mass media; strictly observing the principle of separation of church and state; allowing Catholic charitable organizations (including youth organizations of this kind) to carry out their activities; allowing nuns to work in social welfare institutions, hospitals, homes for the aged, etc.; and finally, allowing the clergy to perform their rites in hospitals, prisons, and the army, as they did in the forties. This would not contradict the secularity of the state nor violate the principle of separation between church and state.

Some of the respondents noted that every one of the points mentioned had been respected from 1945 to 1948.[21] It was only later, during the period of "errors and distortions," that things tightened up.[22] Now, however, such a situation has no justification, since, indeed, it contradicts the officially proclaimed principle of a "national state." The principles of a secular state and separation between church and state should logically imply the neutrality of the authorities in matters of personal philosophy, belief, and convictions. One's personal philosophy, whether religious or not, should be treated as a matter of individual choice and should have no effect on one's status in social and political life. Just as there can be no return to a clerical state, so the doctrine of state atheism as a basis for qualifying for political status is alien to Polish traditions. Some respondents noted that the party must also deal with the question of participation by believers, whose membership would be based exclusively on their adherence to the party program, as well as formal recognition of pluralism in philosophical outlook (indeed, some communist parties have already adopted this principle).

Leading cadres and cadre policy. In this section we will propose various projects aimed at putting the enormous potentials of our technical and humanistic intelligentsia, its talents, and its enthusiasm to effective use. The respondents generally agreed on:

——the need to abolish, or at the very least severely restrict and revise, the rules for the *"nomenklatura,"*[23] since it is based on neither professional knowledge, responsibility, initiative, vocational skills, leadership talent, nor finally, moral qualities, but rather on criteria having nothing in common with any of these. To make matters worse, these criteria are secret (for example, the managerial personnel of economic organizations cannot be held accountable for the results of operations if they are not entitled to fill posts under their command as they see fit);

——promotion in every area must be based on merit, in accordance with performance;

——individual performance at all levels must be assessed on the basis of the criteria noted above, and people who do not do their jobs, are lazy, and place personal advantage ahead of the responsibilities of their jobs must accept the consequences;

——the "personnel merry-go-round," which enables a person listed on the *"nomenklatura"* to be appointed to a post conferring equivalent or even higher status after having bungled his previous job, is harmful and inadmissible;

——consistent application of the principle that all citizens have an equal right to work at any position for which they prove professionally and morally qualified; it follows from this that the percentage of nonparty persons at all levels must be increased, since there are no substantive reasons justifying such a preponderance of party members. Moreover, the current situation constitutes a breach of the pledge made to society in the early seventies.

Cadre policy is a complicated matter, and it can be put in order only within the framework of the entire set of changes proposed here. The respondents note, however, the need for as swift as possible a public declaration of intent with regard to these matters. Such a declaration should contain criticism of the methods used to date and the assurance that they will be changed, as well as an indication of the direction such changes are to take in accordance with the points mentioned above. The declaration should also include changes in the erroneous policy previously followed with regard to intellectual and professional circles.

A System of Guarantees and Guidelines for Exercising Power

The very presentation of a program and the mere initiation of measures to implement it should serve as an initial guarantee that substantial changes are in the offing. More specific guarantees that these changes will be of an enduring nature are necessary, both to gain the public's confidence and to overcome the inevitable resistance to such a program. This would also entail the introduction of new principles concerning:

——the establishment and functioning of representative bodies;

——the functioning of the law;

——the elimination of inequality before the law as well as inequitable privileges.

The respondents agreed that no effort to mend the state can be efficacious or lasting unless the highest representative bodies acquire *credibility*, and unless changes are made in the principles and means whereby the highest authorities of the state operate. Numerous and varied solutions have been proposed, with the respondents often differing in their evaluation of the feasibility of the changes deemed necessary. Most of the respondents favored the most realistic solutions considering all the conditions under which our country exists.

One of the respondents presented a minimum list of expectations in this regard: "It seems necessary to introduce the elements of genuine elections to the Sejm, the people's councils, and other representative bodies (e.g., an alphabetical list of candidates' names on the ballots and the opportunity for the voter to cross off some names). Furthermore there should be a broadening of the basis for recruiting candidates for seats in the Sejm, the people's councils, and other representative bodies, so as to secure wider representation and a genuine interplay of opinions (the representation of Catholic, nonparty specialists, and so on, should be increased). Finally, executive authorities should be made truly accountable to the representative bodies that have appointed them. In particular, this concerns the possibility of recalling incompetent representatives at the middle and top levels of power, as well as public control and supervision of their conduct."

This is, however, at most a bare minimum: experience has taught us that such requirements cannot in themselves lend credibility to the Sejm and the councils, since they can easily be turned into mere shams. For this reason many of the respondents go further in their proposals and call for major changes in the electoral system.[24] In addition to an alphabetical ballot and allowing people to cross names off it, they propose the creation of electoral districts with fewer seats, even one-seat districts, which would give elections a greater authenticity. Above all, however, the proposals center on the procedures for announcing candidacies. A minimal change would entail restoring to private citizen groups the right to place their own candidates on the list of the Front of National Unity[25] (as was possible in 1957) and the introduction of a more credible system of public control over the honesty of elections. Furthermore a set of procedural guidelines is needed for candidates put up by duly and legally registered public organizations and associations as well by private citizen groups.

One of the respondents writes: "This requires appropriately formulated legal regulations—and their observance—concerning the right of association and respect for the right of citizens to associate freely subject to no restrictions by the arbitrary decisions of administrative authorities. The sole reason that could warrant a refusal to register an association would be if the goals it had set for itself were in explicit contravention of existing law. . . ."

Other proposals particulary worthy of attention are:

—members of the government should be prohibited from holding a seat in the Sejm (similarly, administrative officials should not be eligible for seats in lower-level representative bodies);

—the United Peasants' Party and the Democratic Alliance,[26] as well as Catholic representatives should be granted autonomy, independence, and equal partnership with regard to the Polish United Workers' Party;

—the principle of rotation after a specified number of

years in office should be observed for top positions in the state administration;

——limits must be set on links between positions in the government and seats of power in the party (and at lower levels as well);

——the Sejm should have the right and the obligation to appoint supervisory and watch commissions staffed with investigative and intelligence personnel——absolutely independent of the government.

The principle of rotation of the highest governmental and party posts is especially important, inasmuch as under our present circumstances, this is the only effective way to prevent the feudalization of power.

Every respondent who took up this topic pointed out the need to make the Supreme Chamber of Control[27] independent of the government and subordinate to the Sejm, that is, restore it to its original status.

Furthermore, an organizational separation between the party apparatus and the state administration, the agencies running the economy, and the judicial system is generally held to be indispensable; the concentration of these functions in one set of hands makes real checks and controls impossible. The respondents felt that to interpret the "leading role of the party" as implying direct participation in administration at all leadership levels revealed a misconception of what the proper exercise of power entails. The party's role should be to perform control and supervisory functions and to chart in general terms paths for the country's economic, social, and political development. Some poll participants thought that an essential element in any new solutions should be a guarantee of a formal majority for the Polish United Workers' Party in the bodies of popular representation, i.e., enough seats to ensure the party the exercise of power. However, there must be a change in the way these seats are acquired if the institution of elections is to be taken seriously by the public.

To recapitulate, the key issues are to secure for the Sejm and other representative bodies a superior and supervisory role, to restore credibility to elections, and finally, to rebuild a genuine apparatus of Sejm control not subordinated to the government. It is not, after all, a normal and proper state of affairs when those who should be controlled are themselves the controllers.

The respondents agreed on the absolute necessity of a

thoroughgoing reform of the judicial system and the need to restore the rule of law and reestablish trust in law and order. The
present legal system and the whole administration of justice are
in deep crisis: there is a total lack of legal regulations for dealing
with such matters as the trade unions, workers self-management, censorship, the individual and civil rights of the citizenry,
the relationship between the state and church, etc. In place of
citizens' rights and the duties of the state, clearly formulated
and statutorily defined, we have shifting political declarations
or general and intentionally ambiguous regulations whose interpretation rests wholly with administrative bodies and personnel.
Such declarations are usually not spelled out in legal terms and
can contribute nothing to the establishment of a stable legal order, which must be based on clearly defined laws and duties
binding both citizens and state.

The respondents are of one mind as regards the course to
be followed in this area:

—a guarantee of proper conditions for the independent
operation of the judiciary. Supreme Court judges should be appointed for an unlimited term, instead of for five years, as is
currently the practice;

—all external pressure on the administration of justice
must be declared inadmissible and punishable;

—judges must be paid high salaries.

The party must spell out in precise terms its policy toward
the judiciary, guaranteeing their independence and respecting
the principle of equality of all citizens before the law.

The conduct of the security services and the police must
be accountable before the law at every stage of their actions and
in every case. Incidents of arbitrary conduct and breaches of the
law and the use of intimidation and force to extort confessions
go on constantly and are in fact multiplying; they must be un-
conditionally stopped. The right of citizens to defense must be
earnestly and fully upheld; any limitation on this right in any
way whatsoever must be made indictable and punishable by law.

The practices of prosecutors' offices must be subject to
permanent review by a parliamentary commission set up expressly for this purpose. Every citizen must be able to appeal to
this commission. It must have unrestricted access to the facts
and have the means to conduct its own investigations.

Refusal of a passport for political motives without indicating the reasons for rejection in each case must be declared inadmissible. A decision to refuse granting a passport must be sub-

ject to review by the courts in accordance with established principles.

An effective system of administrative courts must be established; the new administrative code now being drafted is inadequate to ensure the proper functioning of such courts. The reform of the Code of Administrative Procedure and the introduction of judicial control over administrative practices demonstrate through their inadequacies the attitude of those in the government toward independent control. The draft was finally approved only after having been demanded for years by public opinion (the legal profession called for judicial control over the administrative apparatus as far back as 1956). The code also specifies areas beyond the bounds of control: military and security matters, public order, control of the press, and passports. The code is therefore incomplete: whole areas and institutions of great importance for citizens' rights have been exempted from control. Legislative acts or general administrative ordinances and decrees are not subject to control, while the exemption of the administrative apparatus and its actions from public scrutiny, which actually dates back to the nineteenth-century monarchy, has remained intact. The glaring lack of any law making the acts of the administrative apparatus accessible to public scrutiny is particularly telling in a state where that administration is supposed to provide offices and services to the public. Finally, judicial control over the administrative apparatus is limited to examining the legality of its acts rather than exercising any direct influence on its efficacy.

We have no civil rights spokesmen, either in the person of an ombudsman, as in Scandinavia, or in the form of a Sejm appeals committee. Constitutional review of laws is another matter calling for solution; the resolution of the State Council of July 14, 1979, does not regulate this matter satisfactorily, inasmuch as it does not determine the basic rights of citizens under the law in this regard.

The current Labor Code must also be changed in those sections that leave room for arbitrary interpretation to the detriment of workers (e.g., regarding dismissal in general, dismissal for "work stoppages,"[28] questions of overtime in particular, etc.).

The existing state of affairs, in which, according to studies, a large percentage of citizens feel that genuine equality before the law does not exist, does grave harm to both society and state and can therefore no longer be tolerated.

The elimination of inequality before the law and of the

privileges, open and hidden, enjoyed by those within the struc-
tures of power, as well as the corruption that these things entail, ranks with the most important and the most difficult tasks
for any program. Placing these matters under public control
must be both the watchword and the guarantee of renewal.
Without such control it will be impossible to restore the system
of power to good health. One of the respondents speaks of:
". . . retaining existing and creating new privileged groups whose
doings are outside the control of society . . . the existence of
groups and individuals in a society calling itself socialist who are
'more equal than others' incites the growing criticism of the
whole of society and rules out in advance any tolerance for an
appeal for a 'socialist attitude toward work' or the 'upholding
of civic duties and the observance of a socialist life style.'"

Another respondent writes: "How do party, state, and economic functionaries purchase their villas, cars, and sumptuous
household furnishings? Certainly not with their salaries."

Complaints about concealed, albeit widespread, privileges
approaching the bounds of legality, and frequently overstepping
them, were voiced by many of the respondents. We also received
responses cautioning against demagogic slogans that in the name
of a falsely conceived egalitarianism, challenge the need for income differentials to reward labor of particular social value. In
short: concealed privileges, doled out away from the public eye
and acquired through abuse of power and position, are universally disapproved.

This is such a burning issue, provoking such a strong response among the public, that we must second the opinion of
the respondents that no public trust can be achieved without a
thorough housecleaning in these matters: the truth must be
made known, the most egregious examples of such practices
must be eliminated, and those guilty of breaking the law, defying the fundamental principles of public morality, and using
their official positions to extract personal advantage must be
brought to account.

There must be an investigation to determine the substance
of charges concerning the use of state-owned building materials
and the labor of state enterprises (as well as the army, convicts,
trade school students, transport workers, etc.) for private ends,
the obtaining of allotments of various material goods below the
prevailing market prices (special government coupons,[29] foreign
currency allotments,[30] etc.), and finally, taking advantage of
official position to procure scarce items and items imported for

hard currency and using them for private ends. Where evidence is presented concerning any infraction of the law or flagrant violation of the rules of communal life, judicial proceedings should be initiated against the offender.

Covert economic and other privileges and secret incomes must be eliminated. Every form of separate shops and service networks[31] (with the exception of the military) must be reintegrated into a public, open-access system, and those employed in the state and governmental apparatus should receive ample compensation to enable them to avail themselves of that system.

It is not a normal state of affairs, say the respondents, when the personal assets and incomes of individuals in positions of power are cloaked in secrecy by the censor, whereas such secrecy does not exist in capitalist states. It should be an iron rule that the earnings of people in positions of public responsibility must not be secret. The respondents repeatedly stress that in a state based on the rule of law, it is inadmissible for official salaries to be supplemented by covert benefits in goods and services, allotments kept from public scrutiny, supplemental facilities, and above all, unreceipted extra payments, add-ons that are not accounted for and are taken from undisclosed budgetary funds.

*   *   *

This is the package of political, legal, social, and other measures proposed by the respondents to break the current crisis of the Polish state, to create an atmosphere of trust, and to stimulate the public to action. The reform that would be effected by these moves is absolutely indispensable if the situation is to be improved and the creative forces inherent in our society are to be set free. They must, however, be supplemented by various measures of an economic nature, which we shall now go on to discuss.

II

In the poll responses economic issues did not top the list of "areas of social tension" in terms of importance. Political sources of tension dominated the discussion. However, the economic situation was described almost invariably as nearly catastrophic, and the urgent need for reform and remedies was argued.

1. *Rather than improving, the situation in planning and management has deteriorated.* The current phase is characterized by intensified market instability. The authorities have lost control of economic processes, and the country's economy resembles "a supertanker adrift" (the respondents note that the disproportions in the plan and the attempted switch to quarterly planning show how far things have gone). The margin for maneuvering has considerably narrowed, and genuine opportunities to reorient economic policy or modify the workings of the economic system have diminished.

2. As a result, *disorganization in the economy and in social life* has deepened, and social and individual productivity have declined. There still exists no mechanism to coordinate productive and nonproductive investments. Investment maneuvers proved illusory. The freeze on some capital investment projects very often went hand in hand with the start of new, even more costly ones, coordinated just as poorly. On the other hand, occasional correct decisions in this area were, and are, simply not implemented.

3. *The electric power shortage will grow worse.* The losses it inflicts on the national economy are reaching enormous proportions. Cutbacks in the energy supply will increase in the upcoming years. If energy is in short supply, production must fall (for example, a 16-point cutback in energy supply affects 25 percent of the industrial factories and 35 percent of municipal consumers).

4. *The supply of goods on the market has shrunk*, and by all indications will shrink further. The rate of decline in the purchasing power of our currency will be much greater than the disproportionally rapid increase in the nominal incomes of the population, further deepening the sense of crisis and leading to the pauperization of the groups with the lowest incomes.

5. Problems in food supplies will increase, since *a decline in agricultural output* can already be foreseen on both the cooperative and state farms as well as in the private sector. The drop is due, first, to import and energy cutbacks, and second, to the lack of capital investment funds in the countryside, to shortages of energy, fertilizers, feeds, and machinery, and above all, to the lack of a stable government agricultural policy.

6. Although, according to official statistics, the value of exports rose by 12 percent in 1979, *imports vastly exceed exports*. We have not fulfilled our foreign trade plan with the CMEA countries, and our trade deficit with the hard-currency

countries has considerably exceeded all indicators and projec-
tions, which have already been revised many times.

7. *The foreign debt* in hard currencies continues to grow
and, according to some figures, has reached $18 billion, while
according to others it is as high as $20 billion. The annual debt
service alone on these credits is currently around $2 billion. Our
current payments on this account amount to considerably more
than 60 percent of our receipts from exports to hard-currency
countries.[32] According to the views of economists cited in responses to the poll, it is permissible to have payments that are
always below or sometimes slightly exceed 25 percent of the
value of exports to a creditor's market; beyond this point danger signs appear. For the last two years we have lacked ready
funds to make current payments.

The dilemma facing us was succinctly summed up by one
of the respondents: "Without change we face calamity. Even if,
on the other hand, changes are made, we can expect nothing
good for quite awhile." "Barring a miracle, the upcoming years
will be extremely difficult from the economic point of view,"
writes someone else. Another person says: "Neither the authorities nor society are prepared, and they have never faced such
prospects before."

However, another recurrent, and even preponderant, view
was that our organizational and cadre reserves are so large, and
the inefficiency and faults in the system are so costly, that any
reforms, consistently implemented, could produce a tangible
improvement relatively quickly, within, say, two to three years.
Or to quote another view: "Theoretically—albeit very theoretically indeed—there is a chance for a sort of 'economic miracle.'
If a reform is carried out consistently, and a stabilized policy
vis-à-vis agriculture and small-scale manufacture is accompanied
by a resumption of public confidence, the effort will be worth
making; then we may well witness an outburst of initiative and
enthusiasm that in just one year could surprise us with its
achievements."

It is also stressed that an economic reform which broadened the role of working people in management and created a
sense of security among the peasants and craftsmen would hardly be of trifling political significance, since it would on the
whole have a salutary influence on relations between the apparatus of power and the citizenry.

In one way or another *carrying out a comprehensive economic reform in Poland is such a necessity* that the the re-

spondents all agreed on this score (although opinions vary with regard to scope and timing). This view is particularly characteristic for economists and management specialists. They oppose the view that during a period of crisis and major economic difficulties, reforms are impossible. They hold that the contrary is true: without reform there is no way out of our difficulties; without reforms there is no way to create any reserves.

On the basis of the poll responses, we have been able to sketch an *outline of a course of action*, a kind of *"scenario"* of remedies, beginning with the first steps.

A. *The First Phase—*
Political Measures and Immediate Steps

I. As a first step, say many of the respondents, a declaration must be issued concerning reforms that provide for changes in economic policy and in the way economic problems are solved in the power system.

The declaration should define who personally (the premier or the first vice-premier, or perhaps a group such as the Economic Committee of the Council of Ministers) will be in charge of the economy——disposing over the appropriate prerogatives and bearing responsibility for it——under the supervision and control of political representative bodies. Without such a measure "at the very top," it is difficult to avoid further inertia and the attrition of responsibility; and it is difficult to act flexibly, promptly, and decisively.

It would be incumbent on the person in charge of the economy to draft without delay a plan for economic reform, prepared in collaboration with, say, an economic council set up for that purpose, with advisory and conceptual tasks.

Such a body should be under the Sejm and independent of the state apparatus, especially the economic apparatus. Composed of experts enjoying general confidence, the proposed economic council would attempt to assess the planned reform, while preparing its own suggestions on the course, pace, and general nature of the changes to be made.

One of the products of the council's activities would be a draft bill for a law concerning the economic system in Poland, a kind of "economic constitution" for the state, to be presented to the next Sejm for approval. This law would be a guarantee of a stable and enduring state economic policy, safeguarding it against the frequent shifts of course and conception that have led in numerous areas, particularly agriculture, to chaos and uncertainty. Such a law would establish and spell out in detail the distribution of national economic management tasks, and indicate areas over which the Sejm, the Planning Commission, the government, and the party, respectively, had jurisdiction. The previous chaos and arbitrariness can no longer be tolerated.

Public opinion would have to have access to broad and reliable information about the activities of the council, about the discussions taking place in it, and about differences in views— in addition to the general debates and the discussions by the group working with the economic leadership. Economic problems would then take on the organizational and technical character appropriate to them, they would be relieved of the odium of politics, and there would be the freedom of analysis, criticism, and public discussion that is indispensable for a properly working economy (with the exception of military matters).

The state of knowledge concerning reforms and preparing alternatives is sufficiently far along among economists and management experts that a final drafting of the project would be easier today than is commonly believed. This view is fully supported by the materials made available to the editors of the present report from studies and discussions going on in the forums provided by the Polish Society of Economics and the Institutes of Management and Planning of the Polish Academy of Sciences.

Detailed reform proposals, according to the suggestions of the respondents, are not our concern at the moment. This is so, first, because a detailed plan of the various measures that together would constitute an economic reform can only emerge as a product of discussion and the weighing of suggestions directly against one another, not as a result of a questionnaire; second, because in the current phase the crucial point is the general courses of action proposed by the poll respondents and those participating in discussions at the institutions we listed (specific reforms may come in several versions). We will describe the most essential of these courses of action later on.

Announcing a reform, in the opinion of most respondents, would indicate the need to squarely face the current situation in the country. "An hour of truth" is needed, as we wrote in the introductory comments, following one of the respondents, "that is, society must have access to complete and unfalsified information about the state of the Republic." This means both the difficulties as well as the potential resources at our disposal.

It is an indispensable condition for proper preparation and execution of a reform as well as for its credibility in the public's eyes (a similar measure, suggest the respondents, might be equally suitable for factory and rural community and city forums).

Along with the message, or the announcement of a message, on the state of the economy, the economic council, in collaboration with the Supreme Chamber of Control,[33] should be entrusted with preparing an analysis of the reasons for the current state of the economy. Without an open analysis of the processes that led to this condition, no declaration will have any credibility. Some of the respondents call for making public incidents of carelessness, negligence, malpractice and wastefulness, and lack of discipline (independently of potential prosecution for criminal offenses).

However, it should be emphasized that there were other voices recommending moderation in tracing responsibility for the crisis, since, some say, doing so could hamper making decisions about the reform and its efficient implementation. ("It also happens that some offenders are brought to account for their actions with great fanfare, are made into scapegoats, after which everything returns to its previous state," wrote one respondent.)

II. Independent of work on the bases for reform and on changes in economic policy, some respondents propose *the adoption of several of the most urgent,* and in their view indispensable, *measures* (which is not to say that all or even most of the respondents advocated these measures):

1. The elimination of obvious, often absurd irritants in people's everyday lives, stemming mainly from disrepair, disorder, and organizational snags. These are problems that can be solved relatively easily, whether by a minor expenditure or by making full use of existing but wasted resources and facilities. For example:

a) the elimination of serious shortages in the stocks of medicines and medical instruments in pharmacies and hospitals. The urgency of the present situation accentuates the grave disproportions in the level of health care between different occupational groups in the population;

b) in education the supply of textbooks to schoolchildren and students has reached a state of urgency;

c) improvements in the operation of the retail shop system. A series of remedies should be applied, such as: expanding the commercial shop system where local manpower reserves exist or where the branch structure of retail shops is poorly adapted to people's needs; transfer of large segments of the retail-trade office work force to jobs in the commercial shop system; increasing the number of employees in the retail system by eliminating disproportions in wages; improvement in the organization of labor in wholesale warehouses and storehouses to eliminate food spoilage during transport and storage, etc.;

d) a public decision on whether meat rationing should be temporarily introduced to assure everyone the absolute minimum supply and to reduce the glaring disproportions between large urban areas and the rest of the country;

e) intervention to improve ground and municipal transportation.

2. Creation of a body with the suggested title "The Cost of Living and Living Standards Council," which, in cooperation with the Central Bureau of Statistics and other scientific institutions, public organizations, and in particular, trade unions, would continuously accumulate and regularly publish data on the cost of living and the living standards of the population, with special attention paid to the living standards and cost of living of the most disadvantaged and underprivileged social groups.

B. *Measures on Economic Policy and Management of the Economy*

Before even the first elements of economic reform can be implemented, there is a whole series of measures concerning economic policy and management of the economy that could be useful or are in fact indispensable. We should note that this list of measures largely coincides with the one covered by the changes first proposed by many of the economists who participated in the discussions at the Polish Society of Economists.

I. *Overhauling planning*

As one of the respondents described it: "An urgent need in the present situation is the return to a planned economy. The current problems of 'piecemeal' planning actually have nothing in common with planning and lead to huge losses and the uncontrolled generation of excess reserves." All those who touched on this question shared this view. Unrealistic plans, without sufficient funds, materials, and productive forces to back them up, must be brought to an end once and for all. We must instead set about creating the indispensable reserves to make plan fulfillment a realistic possibility.

II. *Overhauling the investment system and reconstruction of the investment program*

In an economy predicated on central direction, the system of investment has been transformed in practice into uncontrolled chaos. This is not just a question of the past few years, since as early as 1973 it was impossible to establish precisely what had been decided, what had been accomplished, and to what degree. Every attempt to set things straight under such conditions was preordained to fail; hence the steps taken in the interim, since 1976, have either been only for outward show (top-level decisions were not respected, the incompletion of projects was hidden in, for example, capital repair costs) or inadequate (many decisions limiting investments were withdrawn under pressure from industrial groups or local authorities; modernization projects were usually never completed because all the resources were swallowed up by new firms, etc.). On this score the respondents made a number of detailed recommendations that can be summed up in the following points:

1. Authorize the banks to maintain broad control over the use of short-term credits by producer enterprises to finance operations, so that they can get a full picture of work in progress.

2. Create a situation in which it will be possible to ascertain which cost calculations, material plans, and time schedules are binding and have been followed.

3. Revamp the system of investment planning so that the investment program can be coordinated with opportunities for completion and for obtaining materials and equipment, as well as to avoid projected investments later exceeding the future energy, transportation, and raw materials resources of the economy; as one of the respondents put it, "investments must be subject to planning."

4. Investment projects should be reviewed for possible material restrictions and reorientation of the investment program.

5. The right to make investment decisions in industry beyond a certain cost limit must be reserved for the central levels of administration, with the exception of the ministries and large production units.[34]

As regards future investment policy, the following are necessary:

1) allocate a smaller portion of national income to capital investment projects;

2) substantially rechannel funds into modernization projects and projects yielding quick returns ("investments aimed at economizing on the use of energy, material, and raw materials are incomparably more cost effective than investments aimed at increasing the production of these things");

3) substantially increase the development of energy and transportation to prevent new disproportions;

4) increase investment in agriculture, the food industry, and housing construction;

5) submit long-term programs to broad public discussion, so that the measures undertaken will actually yield tangible benefits to society.

III. *Measures aimed at containing inflation*

In the Polish economy demand has exceeded supply throughout the entire postwar period; however, since the price structure has been rather stable, this excess (in the form of extra money in the hands of individuals) has had no drastic consequences. But the current situation has become incomparably more serious. Price inflation has slipped from the center's control, to say nothing of control by society (for instance, out of a total of 73,000 administrative prices set in 1977 on new articles for the market, not including the prices of garden produce, 10 percent were set by the Council of Ministers and the State Price Commission, 24 percent were set by local sections of that commission, and 66 percent were set by the directors of associations and enterprises).

The respondents mention the following as some of the factors at work here:

a) The system of financing enterprises, which accelerates, as demonstrated by J. Seksiak and U. Libur in their analysis, a rise in the basic costs of production (including manpower costs). Independent of the growth in the wage fund for direct producers, price inflation sets into motion the classic wage and price spiral, since it generates a return pressure to raise wages in each enterprise.

b) A disproportionate share of the national income goes to investment projects.

c) Earnings from exports go mainly to service debt and the

interest on credits rather than for the expansion of imports, which on the domestic market would offset the costs of producing exported goods.

d) The economic bureaucracy, which in the institutions situated in the hierarchy of the administrative apparatus between the central authorities (Presidium of the Council of Ministers and the Planning Commission) and the boards of directors of enterprises, has accumulated more than 200,000 employees in industry, trade, cooperatives, and agriculture; the total annual income of this group is estimated at 25-30 billion zlotys, to say nothing of the funds it uses to serve various departmental, branch, or private interests.

For the time being, the only thing that can be done without economic reforms is to limit the inflationary effect of the excessive investment program. On the other hand, to prevent further inflation it is necessary:

1. To check the uncontrolled rise in prices by involving society in price controls as well as by any of various other means that would effectively contain any unwarranted or unjustified rises. A consumer protection movement could play a key role here.

2. To declare a temporary price and wage freeze until the economic reform is instituted—clearly stipulating what is to be exempted from this rule (the lowest wages, family allowances for families of the most disadvantaged strata, pensions, and retirement benefits). Along with an ongoing and honest analysis and publication of the costs of living and living standards, this should create the preconditions for other public compromises on these matters.

3. To establish clear guidelines for instituting price rises in the future, adopting as a working principle a conversion factor for the lowest wages, family allowances, pensions, and retirement benefits (automatic cost-of-living increases in wages, pensions, and retirement benefits, as well as upward valuations of savings deposits, which lose value as inflation goes on).

4. As supplies improve in the future, food prices should gradually be brought into line with the prices of durable goods, all the while maintaining the aforementioned principles.[35]

5. Money paid for being present on the job without actually working (we refer to plant stoppages for which the workers are not responsible) should be regarded as a relief benefit; the intention is to alter not the amounts paid but the public attitude toward them.

6. Some of the respondents also point out the need to cut

off certain "wage chimneys,"[36] to eliminate social and wage privileges, and to establish a reasonable tax on high incomes and
luxuries. This should contribute to the success of the reform by
creating a feeling that "things have gotten fairer," as one of the
respondents put it.

IV. *Changes in agricultural policy*

Actions in the realm of agriculture must, according to the respondents, be regarded as particularly pressing, since a long time
is naturally needed for the farming sector to respond. A variety
of measures is needed: political and legal, to stabilize conditions
in agriculture; organizational, to improve administrative efficiency; and economic, to facilitate better utilization of resources.

The authors would like at this point to diverge from the
principle they have been following thus far in this discussion,
namely, of merely presenting a concise recapitulation of the
specific suggestions made by the respondents, to present a more
general argument: we feel that it is especially crucial that there
be a public formulation of the theoretical foundations of farm
policy as far as measures of a political nature are concerned. In
other words, there should be a public disavowal of certain myths
and prejudices that have traditionally disfigured farm policy.
There must be a public realization that, as one of the respondents puts it, it is *not* true that under present-day conditions
only large farms can be up-to-date and productive, and that
small-plot family farms must necessarily be backward. This was
one of the arguments used to push through collectivization and
as a basis for calling farm cooperatives a higher form of farm organization than individual farming. It is also the source of the
view that state farms and cooperatives are a more "socialist"
form of farming which over the long run, as a result of "social
transformations" in the countryside, must ultimately prevail
over individual farming.

First, the claim that large-scale farming is superior finds no
confirmation in practice either in our country or in any other
socialist state. Every indicator to date has shown that the costs
of production on state farms are higher and their output is lower
than on individual farms; moreover, after the giant production
units in agriculture were introduced,[37] the differences became
so great as to defy comparison (even in crop output, where state
production might be expected to enjoy a clear advantage). The
efficiency of farming on cooperatives is obscured by various

kinds of subsidies and supports from the state, which the individual peasant does not enjoy, as well as by the nonagricultural production also performed by the cooperatives; however, even they are much less productive than individual farms. This survey draws on the experience of other socialist countries, e.g., Hungary, which is often cited as a successful example of collectivized agriculture, but where, however, nearly half of the agricultural output comes from private plots. In the USSR private plots were formally recognized in 1979 as an important foothold of a socialist economy in the countryside (let it be noted, however, that they account, for example, for 70 percent of the country's total potato production). On the other hand, the German Democratic Republic and Czechoslovakia can attribute their previously high level of agricultural production and supply to the fact that they have developed industry——these states can afford to subsidize every quintal of grain and every kilogram of meat, which is even more expensive in those countries than on our state farms. However, in both these countries the situation is deteriorating quite rapidly.

Second, the theoretical argument, which superficially seems reasonable enough, that the costs of production per hectare on large-scale farms are lower than on family farms (even considering that the output per unit of land falls at the same time) has proven to be true only within certain limits and for certain periods. This argument has been vitiated, on the one hand, by the increase in the price of energy and, on the other, by the growing shortage of arable land, which, as it becomes scarcer, must be maximally productive, especially in a small country still in the process of industrialization, such as ours. The example of Western Europe shows that family farming has always been——and still is——the basis of modern farming.

According to the data contained in a European Economic Community report, the average size of a farm in the Common Market countries is about 15 hectares, while in the Federal Republic of Germany it is 13 hectares. There is no need to mention the fact that Western European farming is the most productive in the world.

Without a public statement that the authorities consider the individual peasant holding to have a status equal in rights and rank as a form of property in the socialist system, the peasants will consider any organizational or economic measure as yet another attempt at manipulation; after temporary concessions, the policy of discrimination against the individual peasant will be resumed.

To increase the efficiency of agriculture, the following legal and organizational measures are necessary:

1. Once the administration of agriculture has been decentralized, there should be a maximum dismantling of the bureaucracy, which unproductively squanders the skills of thousands of people who have higher education in agricultural science—in the management apparatus, the farm administration, the "Peasants' Self-Help,"[38] purchasing agencies, cooperatives, supply and sales agencies, and so on.

2. To reduce and simplify operating costs, the purchase of agricultural products must be placed in the hands of genuine cooperatives and peasants' associations in order to abolish the costly role of middlemen between the state wholesale agencies and the countryside.

3. To ensure reliability in relations between agencies of local administration and economic institutions and the countryside, local institutions of public control should be created with the power to suspend the enactment of decisions that drastically infringe on the law; furthermore, there should be local arbitration boards authorized to settle disputes between farmers and economic administrative agencies in matters concerning decisions made by the latter.

4. It must be made easier for persons who promise to cultivate their land themselves to purchase land from the State Land Fund by means of a far-reaching credit system encouraging long-term planning. This ought to apply especially to regions with top-grade land, as well as to regions in the northwest provinces, where a proper settlement structure is important politically.[39]

5. Gigantomania—in organization, capital investment policy, and technology—must be eradicated once and for all from the administration of state farms. Huge farming enterprises, as experience worldwide (and in feudal times as well) teaches us, serve principally to conceal, through their aggregate output results, the unprofitability of the units under them and to multiply bureaucracy without any justification in terms of a commensurate improvement in administrative cost efficiency. In the same way, giant livestock superfarms that violate the technological limits of operational efficiency have not stood the test.

6. In agriculture cooperative forms can only develop organically out of the economic needs of the countryside, just as they emerged originally when the cooperative movement blossomed, and not as a result of government fiat. In its credit policy the state must be guided solely by the dictates of good

economic sense.) To increase the interest of state farm workers in the economic returns of their enterprise, certain forms of profit sharing, or even workers co-ownership, might be introduced.

7.(Cultivated land must be recognized as one of the basic resources of the nation. Its use for any other purpose should be permitted only in infrequent and exceptional cases, and should, moreover, be burdened with considerable costs) As regards the ever increasing arbitrariness of administrative conduct, the appropriate supervisory and control bodies (e.g., the Supreme Chamber of Control, the public prosecutor) should be granted special prerogatives, e.g., the power to suspend administrative decisions in this domain, even with the possibility of initiating punitive proceedings for destruction of arable land.

The respondents propose the creation of a "set of principles" for agricultural policy, to be put up for deliberation in the Sejm and adopted as "Statutes for the System of Agriculture in the People's Republic of Poland," which would do away once and for all with the uncertainty that has up to now weighed so heavily on Polish farming.

The paramount aim of any policy for the food industry, which must not be lost from view, is to make Poland self-sufficient in food production within a specified length of time; this goal should become the basis for a program of economic policy around which we can mobilize the concern, the efforts, and the imagination of society in both town and countryside.

V. *Promoting housing construction*

In the view of the respondents, housing construction should be a subject of particular concern for the state (considering the crisis situation in Poland in this area) and, indeed, a prime target of social policy.

Decentralization of the regional administration of housing construction, following the path taken long ago in the GDR, is only the first step, although an important one. It must be followed promptly by some basic changes in housing construction, statutory and organizational as well as economic. Here, briefly, is a list of such changes:

1. Housing cooperatives must regain their original, genuinely cooperative character to give future residents a say in determining the form of their dwellings (it is a paradox that in a country with economic planning, and moreover, with the extra

time allowed by long waits for housing, there is no way to let architects know for whom their designs are intended, and who will live in the dwellings they design; the positive exception to the rule in Poznan proves the absurdity of the predicament).

2. There should be a guarantee of fairness in the principles guiding the assignment of apartments (a return to cooperative principles); the state could conclude housing contracts with a cooperative society while reserving for itself a pool of apartments, or it could build them itself; on the other hand, a continuation of the current arbitrary practices, which generate tremendous social tensions, is unacceptable.

3. In the economics of housing construction, the policy of financing the producer (the enterprise doing the job) must be abandoned in favor of financing the purchaser (the cooperative investor), in order to maintain some constant control over the work done by construction enterprises by regulating the amounts due upon receipt and acceptance by the investor.

4. To reduce construction costs, local construction with locally available materials, mainly bricks and mortar, should be developed. In urban centers there should be a gradual switchover from the present excessively energy- and material-intensive system of large-scale fabrication to light prefabricated systems.

5. Regardless of the form of large-scale industrial production of building materials, there must be an effort to develop local production of the same materials and production of fixtures by local and cooperative manufacturers, as well as in a number of private factories.

The Sejm should maintain particularly close supervision of the progress of any program for the development of construction, and the mass media should maintain a keen interest and devote ample space to this matter.

VI. *The drafting and implementation of plans for*
    the reconstruction of the transportation and energy sectors

According to data published in the specialized economic and technical literature, only 60 to 70 percent of railroad shipments derive from real economic needs. A similar estimate applies to truck shipments. Without an economic reform it will be impossible to rectify these ills. A program for the reconstruction of transportation must be drafted, taking into account shipping routes as well as rolling stock and reloading facilities (especially at seaports), and the appropriate funds must be set aside for these things. The mere elimination of superfluous shipments will not solve the problem of those transport routes where bottlenecks arise, and where as a result of delays the economy suffers tremendous losses.

Similarly there can hardly be any hope for improving the cooperation between industry and the energy sector in the area of spare parts and fixtures as a result of instituting an economic reform; however, what can be done right now is to draft a program for investment and technical overhaul in the energy sector aimed at: (a) putting new capacities into service (quick decisions are necessary in this regard); (b) updating existing power plants (to provide them with complete systems of fittings so they do not shut down due to shortages, frozen coal, low-grade fuels, etc.); (c) reducing energy losses stemming from obsolete technology for transmission and use; (d) utilizing nonconventional sources of energy wherever possible.

VII. *A program for restoring a rational enterprise size structure*

There must be a real change with regard to licensing policies for the crafts and service agencies: they must be given a sense of security. Rural industry and small manufacturing plants, eliminated during the period of centralization, with its gigantomania, must be reconstructed (as one of the respondents noted, it is absurd to have a situation in which enterprises that employ fewer than 100 workers account for only 11.3 percent of the total number of enterprises in Poland, but 51.4 percent in the GDR, 80 percent in Japan, and 88 percent in the FRG).

A flexible policy with regard to public services, based on the assumption that a small "family" enterprise or a small private or private-state partnership is the most effective form of organization for a certain range of economic tasks, is a precondition for any chance to create a "bright spot," that is, workplaces and jobs for a large number of those persons now employed in the economic bureaucracy, and to halt the inordinate growth in the numbers employed in large enterprises. The creation of services would be an anti-inflationary measure as well. Up to now people with socially unjustified incomes have created an inflationary surplus demand, but the high-cost, high-paying services that would be provided if this sector were expanded could soak up the excess demand created by the earnings of other workers in the economy. However, care should be taken, by appropriate use of credit policy, that the green light for enterprises in this sector does not provoke increased migration from the countryside to the cities, especially of the young people who are needed in agriculture.

C. *The Drafting and Implementation of an Economic Reform*

In urging the need for prompt drafting of a detailed program of reform by the competent bodies, the respondents indicated some of the long-range objectives the reform should aim for. A wide-ranging and coherent reform must equally include:

1. Changes in the role of the main institutions of the economy along with changes in the planning system;

2. Changes in the methods of management;

3. Changes in organizational structures to give enterprises basic responsibility for conducting their own business.

The aim of the first set of changes is to help the central institution of economic management concentrate on planning development and on supervising the fulfillment of its plans, and subsequently, to define the long-range goals of the economy and coordinate activities aimed at attaining these goals. As regards current activities in production, services, and trade planned by the enterprises themselves, this central institution will perform supervisory and control functions, intervening with economic measures (credit policy, orders for goods by the ministries themselves, the creation of new enterprises, etc.) to counteract the difficulties and aberrations that can be expected to occur from time to time as part of the normal economic process. Administrative measures should be applied only in exceptional cases (allocation of scarce raw materials, etc.).

The second point would entail a shift from a command economy to management by economic instruments designed to enable the production units to function as efficiently as possible. The system of financing enterprises, which while rewarding profits would at the same time endeavor to reduce basic costs, would create the conditions for effectively containing inflationary tendencies and for putting the country's finances in order.

The third point would entail more than the mere simplification of organizational structures and the elimination of the unnecessary links that have sprung up in powerful layers of the bureaucracy and that are capable, through the resources at their disposal, of manipulating the decisions of the central agencies. More specifically, it means providing the instruments for effective and independent action to the production units at the base of the economy and real opportunities for control to the central institutions of economic management.

One of the most important tasks of a reform would be to work out a new model for a socialist enterprise enjoying some independence in its actions, based on enduring legal and economic foundations, and finally, endowed with an internal organization that ensured the optimal participation of its work force. A socialist enterprise should not be subordinate to any administrative body but should function as an independent economic unit whose relations with the administration are regulated by statutes protecting the enterprise against unlawful interference in its operations. The form and scale of these basic units of the economy can and must vary depending on what they do.

The ways that the central institutions of economic management go about exercising their supervisory functions must be subject to regulation. The economic ministries, which were created to conform to fields of technological specialization, do not hold up under examination. Many of the respondents felt that in the central seats of power there was an overriding need for a clear and precise delimitation of powers, duties, and responsibilities between administrative agencies (ministries) and the directors of economic units, who make decisions independently and are evaluated exclusively in terms of economic results. Some of the respondents call for a simplification of the structures of the ministries in accordance with the following principles:

a) Those in charge of the economy, in collaboration with the Planning Commission, should define the course and long-range strategy of general supervisory activities (as defined above), while a ministry should regulate activities in its particular sector and function as a "field marshal" in relation to those who are in charge of the economy.

b) The concentration of economic ministries, which has reached an advanced stage, and even the possible creation of a single ministry of industry. This concentration would badly cripple "branch vested interests" that are backed at the level of a minister or even a deputy premier.

c) A reduction in the number of top positions, particularly in the number of all sorts of deputies.

Another respondent, who also pointed out the need for a sweeping reduction in the ministerial apparatus and in the entire complicated bureaucratic hierarchy under it, rounded out the picture presented above with a further suggestion. In place of a multilevel bureaucratic structure that operates chaotically and inhibits economic development, we should set up bodies of a supervisory nature to check on individual enterprises; their members should be representatives of the public interest appointed by the central authorities along with representatives of the enterprise's work force.

According to some of the respondents, it remains to be decided in what branches of the economy and in what types of enterprise it would be expedient to introduce some economic and legal form of co-ownership between the work force and the state, with both partners being duly represented.

The decisive point, of course, is the carrying out of the reform. Not even the best plans can be fulfilled if conditions for their fulfillment are not provided. Some of these conditions were indicated by one of the respondents: "First, the main obstacles to reform must be removed. Second, the necessary resources must be secured. Third, the reform can be instituted quickly or gradually, but in either case it must be thorough. . . ." The main obstacle to be eliminated is the all-pervasive bureaucracy, with its manifold levels of central offices and large production boards. One of the first steps in the reform must be to limit the scope of their actions and decisions, since otherwise these inefficient bodies, sensing their very existence threatened, could inhibit any effective reform (the Hungarian reform included just such an insurance measure, which had some success at the outset). The monopolistic, overly powerful position of some enterprises will pose a serious obstacle. To counteract it other, smaller units should be allowed to produce the same items.

The reform will also need material resources and manpower. Where there is a lack of material reserves, the necessary means must be sought abroad, which, despite our considerable debt, is still possible. The human resources are the energy, initiative, and effort that the very idea of reform and change could elicit from society, just as it could rekindle hope.

Concerning our huge foreign debt, one of the respondents writes: "A policy aimed at correcting the balance of payments in our situation can have three objectives: (1) protecing the country's position on the international credit market; (2) clearing the country's debts by taking advantage of worldwide inflation; (3) clearing the debts by net payment of credits. The first of these goals is the most modest but, on the other hand, the easiest to achieve. It requires a reduction in the balance-of-payments deficit to a level that permits the debt to grow in proportion to the average level of world inflation, that is, so that its value in real terms does not grow. Once this point is reached, there should be no difficulty in obtaining the credits needed to regulate the most urgent credit obligations." The second goal would be harder to achieve. It would entail reaching a stable balance of payments such that the real value of the debt decreased as inflation continued. On the other hand, the third goal (eliminating the state's debt) could be achieved only through a reform and its consequences in the form of a revival of the Polish economy.

* * *

"'A clear vision of a new system' and of the ways to carry out a reform will help to persuade the public that the efforts and sacrifices stemming from our present difficulties will not once again be in vain," writes one of the respondents.

Another points out the need to elicit the public's interest and involvement in the economic reform, which "must be negotiated with society—only then can it succeed."

However, to create the necessary psychological climate for all these changes, to break through apathy and arouse belief in the possibility of achieving economic health, requires, according to the respondents, the demolition of a certain myth deeply rooted in both the public mind and segments of the power apparatus, namely, that Poland is a poor country. We possess huge stocks of raw materials and fossil fuels, even crude oil (even if the oil shortage has not, in the final analysis, been exaggerated). We are a country with huge agricultural potential. We are able not only to feed ourselves but to profitably export food. We have a huge industrial base. We are a society of vast but unexploited reserves of initiative and energy, which at present is exhausting itself either in a struggle to keep its head above water and satisfy basic needs or in the accumulation of goods, and not always by honest and moral methods. In a word, we are a country of huge but poorly utilized potentials.

On the other hand, the mobilization of these material and human potentials is an absolute necessity if we are to endure as a state capable of independent existence. To do so, a change in the political atmosphere is necessary. If we must put our reserves and our energies to work, we must be sure we are doing so for ourselves and not for others. In this period society's will to act has been paralyzed by the fear that our worldly goods and efforts would go to waste or to the benefit of others. An economic reform, therefore, must be coupled with broad transformations in the state and a change in the social atmosphere.

CHAPTER 3

Social Behavior

In this section we will address the problem of social behavior, which can be summed up in the question: What should Poles do to preserve and expand those values that have enabled us to become a nation with a sense of its own identity and culture? What should we do to go from being the objects of political manipulation to becoming total masters of our own country and the subjects of our own political life? The respondents expressed the conviction that society has certain obligations to itself independent of the behavior of the authorities.

These obligations concern the norms and rules of living together in a society, a tireless effort to expand the frontiers of truth, and the determination to restore a measure of autonomy to the affairs of public life. The ability to put these values into effect calls for determination and sacrifice. They must be applied to various aspects of actual social life: in situations in which a person's life depends to such an enormous degree on participation in institutions under state control, this task is an especially difficult one. To the principles of secrecy, mistrust, and an instrumental view of man, which are built into our political system, must be counterposed the principles of truth, good faith, and respect for the intrinsic worth of every individual. "Perhaps the world is actually heading toward disintegration of social ties, toward atomization and disintegration. But if this tendency is at hand, and the authorities in our country, or at least a decisive portion of them, therefore find it easier to rule a herd of isolated individuals, alienated, hostile, and mistrustful, our duty must be to oppose that tendency," writes one of the respondents. Society is not the sum of the individuals in it but the sum of the bonds that unite people.

In the most general terms we can say that as regards the attitude of Poles toward themselves, we must realize those positive values which derive from the solidarity and interaction with everything that unites us as the mutual heirs of the traditions of Polish culture, morals, and civilization. The passive acceptance of the decay of social ties indeed threatens those basic values which have enabled the Polish people to become what we are and to survive the most difficult times in our history. Poles have become immersed in a situation in which we stand alone not only with regard to the authorities but even to ourselves, indeed, we stand against ourselves. Yet just such a society, however discontent and dissatisfied it may be, is the easiest to manipulate. A society that considers itself powerless is therefore powerless.

If the authorities do none of the things that ought to be done, what, then, can society do? A dramatic question, and all the more so since almost none of the respondents sees any real chance of the authorities undertaking the requisite reform measures, while at the same time, all are aware of the limited prospects for any organized collective action not guided from above.

Despite the obvious imprecision in the distinction between the governors and the governed, it is unavoidable for descriptive purposes and as a language for phrasing recommendations. This dichotomy would perhaps not be charged with such significance if authority emanated from society and was answerable to it. However, as everyone knows, this is not the case. That is why the conceptual dichotomy of society versus the authorities which we used in our poll was de facto accepted by the respondents, despite the reservations it can and did prompt (the same people are active in a variety of social roles; the exercise of power is a function that is qualitatively different depending on where it has its seat in the hierarchical structure; the lowest levels of power are difficult to distinguish from "society," and so on).

Every Pole holding a public post must strive to make use of his position to serve the public interest in accordance with his sense of what is right and fair. The problem, however, is broader, affecting not only individuals but also social groups with ties to the ruling apparatus that are aware of what is improper and unfair in its workings. There can be no doubt that within and around the seats of power, there is no lack of people who are even today bound and motivated by the ideals that unite socialism and democracy; there is no lack of people with intense patriotic feelings; no lack of people, finally, disturbed by the malfunctioning and inefficiency of the system and ready and willing to support a program of remedies.

As one of the respondents wrote, commenting in particular on these latter motives, "The success of a program of reforms will depend on finding for it an ever increasing number of people and social groups not only ready to undertake a criticism of the existing state of affairs, but also resolutely determined to find ways to get out of it, and hence ready to lend active support to any reform effort. They are, above all, people working within the system of power or in economic life. One might suppose that for such people, ideological and general humanistic arguments for reform would be less important than simple logic."

But one might also therefore suppose that a large portion of those in the seats of power might be, and indeed ought to be, natural allies of any reform program. It follows then, as some of the respondents have concluded, that in addition to the keenly felt division of society into governors and governed, there is also a political division, perhaps not as sharp and clear as the first split, into those having a vested interest in the process of reform of the Republic and those opposed to such change.

The respondents' recommendations for society can be grouped under the following three main headings:

1. *Social self-education*, i.e., cultivation of the desirable attitudes of solidarity (to guard against the atomization widely discussed in the "Report"), the capacity for democratic action (considering the conditions under which such habits are absolutely indispensable), and civic responsibility (to guard against indifference and selfishness).

2. *Programmatic and diagnostic activities.* Analysis of the state of society and drafting a program for the future (and hence a task that now could not actually be accomplished under official auspices).

3. *Pressure for change.* It is not economic demands that are at issue here but rather a demonstration that society can no longer remain the passive object of manipulation.

These recommendations are exemplified and expanded in various ways, which we will have occasion to discuss later on. We should also mention that there were some voices that dissent from the general trend sketched here.

Social self-education

"I take the title question of the poll to be asking, what can and should society do in the situation in which we currently find ourselves, where the authorities can no longer rule in the old way without causing a national tragedy," writes one of the respondents.

Those respondents who replied to this question almost universally agreed that collective actions should be undertaken to alter the public's frame of mind. Here, for example, is one of the arguments presented to justify the need for self-educational measures: "Among the arts of politics, democracy occupies a place of high esteem for Poles, although it is little practiced. . . . An intermediate stage is needed in which the elementary conditions for the success of political and economic reform would be created. If this 'buffer' period is skipped, the attempt to switch course could end in either a fourth confrontation[40] or in a merely superficial, cosmetic change in policy, which, as past experience has shown, quickly reverts to the old routines if there are no political forces supporting the reform."

Most of the respondents did not share this lack of confidence in the capacity of Poles for democracy. Public experience has shown that both under conditions of acute political tensions and in urgent situations unfolding on a smaller scale, Poles have demonstrated good common sense and an ability to find ways to cooperate and compromise.

On what do specific measures aimed at restoring society's control of itself depend?

First of all, on the exercise of those rights with which the citizens are invested by law, but which have remained a dead letter, since their exercise has until now been effectively blocked. The right of assembly is cited by one of the respondents as an example: "This right, ensured by the Constitution of the PRP, must be fought for with a variety of initiatives, mainly social and cultural, and hence outside the trade unions. The broad utilization of this right is a necessary condition to develop social initiatives and a sense of popular control. A reminder: creation of clubs among the intelligentsia and of local and regional citizens' support societies altered the sociocultural landscape of Poland beyond recognitions after October 1956.[41] On the other hand, the destruction or bureaucratic ossification of this movement at the beginning of the sixties was symptomatic of the halt in the process of democratization." Another respondent writes, stating the case a bit more generally, that the first step in assuring a partnership between the authorities and the public is the "genuine activation of already existing institutions in the legal system as well as the propounding of new solutions, perhaps more apt than current ones. Institutions such as the right of appeal, the right to recall representatives, to say nothing of the right to express one's views, convictions, etc., do, after all, exist in our legal system; there are democratic provisions with regard to penal law, which is not to say that they are used to an adequate degree in passing sentences; and there exist institutions such as self-government or committees of public control. The very first step, therefore, should be to restore life to those provisions that already exist and to create the requisite conditions for existing institutions to properly function."

Among the institutions proposed as a forum for civic action, that is, genuine citizens' action, not the empty facade that is the current rule, the respondents mention the Sejm, the trade unions, scientific societies, artists' associations, people's councils, bodies of popular representation in general, cooperatives (especially housing cooperatives), youth organizations, and even the Central Committee of the Polish United Workers' Party! The point is made that formal opportunities exist for acting within the framework of these institutions. If these rights are to be taken seriously and are to become a vital force, it is necessary to break the social stereotype, with all the ensuing consequences. Civic courage and the ability to speak out are needed. As is the knowledge that one is not acting in isolation.

"The life of the average citizen is played out wholly within the framework of official structures. The possibility of bringing one's influence to bear on the shape of these structures and on the way they function is small, and pressure from administrative quarters is great. It is therefore important to safeguard independent thought and a dignified posture and to endeavor to alter one's own milieu in accordance with the dictates of reason and one's conscience, and of civic courage. We might call this the ethos of the common man. Guided by the principles of this ethos, and adopting an active posture, one can change a great deal without departing at all from official structures," suggests a group of respondents in a collective reply.

These authors, like a number of other respondents, also highly valued the activities of independent circles, which, in a situation where there exist no normal outlets for the citizen to claim his rights, have already initiated certain civic actions.

Social self-education should aim at restoring to fundamental values their guiding role in social life. One of the respondents had the following to say: "Under our circumstances the cultivation of the habits of forthright and intelligent cooperation requires a resolute and total divorce of the compromised methods of political education from the methods of social education. I believe another sort of education can come from the development of fundamental, timeless attitudes independent of any political circumstances. Also linked to realizing this viewpoint is the hope of fashioning new models for the personality, so much needed during the first stage of education, models that could instill in the hearts and minds of our youth the moral qualities of social man."

The respondents also mentioned some practical means for restoring to basic moral values their rightful place in social life. "Every professional and social group should give utmost consideration to a review of *its own ethical code*. Doctors and judges, engineers and administrators alike must have a clear idea of the 'ought nots,' of what is morally inadmissible in their professional conduct. Internal tribunals should be set up in professional and social circles; let all reprehensible conduct be liable to exposure before a group of persons whose moral authority passes a verdict weightier than any punishment," writes one of the respondents.

Diagnostic and programmatic study

Social self-education in an integral part of all diagnostic and programmatic proposals, the function of which is twofold. Their first task is to fill the gaping holes in our knowledge about present-day Polish society, about its aspirations and its needs. This knowledge, made public, will influence the shaping of public consciousness. At the same time, however, a collective concern for tasks of social self-education will help to forge solid ties between creative groups, cultivate the habit of resolving differences of opinion democratically, and satisfy the need for participation, which can never become a reality as long as all activity, meant only as an empty facade, flows from the top.

What would be the point of these efforts? Here are some sample opinions.

A detailed social diagnosis: "Drafting a general report on the state of our nation, reports on various aspects of social life, for example, the situation in public health services, the operation of higher education, the design and implementation of educational reform, the harm done by censorship, the productive use of foreign licenses, and other matters of importance for the nation. These reports should be subject to the broadest possible discussion in concerned circles," writes one of the respondents.

Economic matters especially require systematic and regular scrutiny. Another respondent calls for "setting up a research team on the national economy, the aim of which would be to perform independent investigations and diagnose the current state of the economy, as well as to draw up general plans of action for economic policy and planning that would stand as alternatives to the existing central plan. The team should include, in addition to a core of economists, sociologists and engineers who would tackle respectively the social and technological aspects. The real source of many problems lies in these two areas. In addition to this immediate, practical effort clearly needed in the present situation, an 'issues' team could be set up to examine long-range prospects and major problems of development."

Intellectual groups have a particular obligation in this respect, since they command a wealth of information and enjoy relative freedom of action. Despite their comparatively small numbers, these groups are able to exercise a certain, at times even fruitful, pressure on the authorities.

The Editorial Team feels that the idea of diagnostic and programmatic analyses can, with complete justification and in accordance with the spirit of the responses to the poll, be expanded. Let us quote one of the respondents: "Every enterprise, institution, local or professional society, or scientific and technical organization should, in its own interests and in the interests of us all, accumulate knowledge and information and analyze the state and situation of the social, scientific, or economic field it covers. Enlisting anyone who wants to join in this effort, excluding no one of good will, a program of action could be drafted that could and should be adopted wherever possible."

The same proposals would equally apply to developing discussion as an indispensable condition for intellectual life. "The avoidance of genuine discussion and confrontation of views on even the most trifling matters characterizes many milieus in Poland, including intellectual ones. The disappearance of the habits and skills of discussion and debate, the inability to debate and argue without insinuations and suspicion, and indeed, without any genuine discussion at all, make it impossible to arrive at a valid common consensus. The cultivation of the habit of ongoing discussion, both at the local level and throughout the country, should be undertaken with or without the approval of the authorities."

Here is another passage from the same writer: "A slogan, or even a set of slogans, has emerged that defines the civil status of a modern Pole: 'Do what you can to make things better. If you can only do a little, at least do what you can. If you can do nothing, then at least turn your thoughts to determining what ought to be done when it can be done, and be ready to do it.'"

The Editorial Team is aware that realizing these proposals, which represent a minimum list of citizens' duties, is not easy. For many specific situations in which the Poles of today find themselves, passivity instead of an open, critical, and demanding attitude, conformity instead of intelligent deliberation, and a shrug of the shoulders instead of taking the risk entailed in action can cost dearly. We believe, however, at the risk of being superficial, that pressure for change in this respect is possible and can even be effective; in the present situation it is the only path open to Poles.

It would be hard to list all the topics suggested for team study. We would like to take up, however, one more problem in the discussion of the present "ethical code of Poles," with particular emphasis on positive principles rather than a system of prohibitions. A number of respondents, declaring themselves Christian in outlook, advocated taking up the ethical and practical aspects of actions meant to morally renew society. The following comment is typical in this respect: "The Church is involved mainly in work with the teachings of religion and the moral education of youth, and secondarily with upholding morality in family life by encouraging adults to actively practice their religion and with a broad defense of its spiritual domain. On the other hand, the moral aspects of professional, social, and public life in general are not dealt with. Morality cannot be maintained, much less improved, without a principled attitude, a certain moral absolutism that views some moral principles as unshakable and, in extreme cases, requires heroism. Thus the Church demands from us adherence to its principles in our personal lives; but in social affairs not only does it not do so, it often adopts a pragmatic posture itself. An analysis of contemporary social relations from a Christian perspective is urgently needed. . . ."

Among the values whose role in the public mind is particularly threatened, truth certainly occupies a central position. This is a result of the instrumental attitude toward language, the manipulation of information and of public declarations, and even assertations that fly in the face of science. Perhaps it yields immediate advantages for manipulation, but over the long run such a course is harmful, since it destroys credibility in relations between the authorities and society and distorts the collective consciousness (for example, reliable information about the nation's past history). There must therefore be an examination of the state of affairs in this area and an analysis of the devastation wrought by the shortsighted policy of an offhanded attitude toward truth.

The rehabilitation of truth as a value of social life concerns society as a whole, but above all, those circles for which truth is a real tool of their trade, the cornerstone of their work. We mean people in science, culture, experts, those who inform public opinion.

Drafting a program of alternative models for a future society is another of the theoretical tasks we face. It would make possible a crystallization and fruitful confrontation of ideological stances whose dissimilarity cannot be made evident when any thought lacking official approval is suppressed. "Therefore one of the most important tasks of the day," writes one of the respondents, "is the need for groups that have rarely been active and circles that accept the 'Experience and the Future' Report as a platform, or that at least in the most general sense are socialist, to formulate programs. Also needed are studies and discussions, an encounter between different circles and views, and reaching a compromise on a platform. The quite valuable 'Experience and the Future' Report permitted a compromise in quite general terms, but again it was reached solely on the basis of criticism of the current situation. On the other hand, a positive program cannot at the same time be a compromise program. We must generate programs that stem from different ideological-political assumptions, as well as general issues, and that affect different specific aspects of social life."

Pressure for change

The third form of social conduct, along with self-educational and diagnostic and programmatic efforts, is pressure on the authorities to undertake the needed reforms that we discussed in the preceding section. Almost all the respondents were of the opinion that without systematic pressure from the public, there could be no counting on reform initiatives from above. One of the respondents writes: "I am very skeptical about the ability of any authority acting in the absence of an opposition. I therefore feel that society must exert constant pressure on the authorities, demanding its constitutional rights. Society must itself act against progressive stagnation and the sense of helplessness."

The three levels of action distinguished in this section overlap and intersect in practice. Therefore every attempt at self-education discussed above is at the same time a form of pressure on the authorities, and the scope and extent of such attempts will determine the effectiveness of the pressure. The same can be said about diagnostic and programmatic efforts. Various kinds of reports "should force the authorities to take up the problems posed in this way by public opinion," writes one of the respondents; "ultimately this would create among the leadership a feeling (the absence of which is one of the major shortcomings of the system) that the actions they initiate are subject to public assessment and response. Those in power do not feel themselves so firmly at the helm that they can wholly disregard public opinion. The examples of recent months show that the leadership feels itself compelled to react to widespread independent information concerning certain events.[42] An analysis of the range of problems touched on in the mass media and in speeches by the leaders shows that certain questions reached the center of attention not when they were most keenly felt by society, but when independent publications pointed them out."[43]

Another respondent writes: "There is no way to govern a developed, civilized country today while in conflict with the opinion of the world of science, culture, and technology. Its influence could therefore be considerably greater than it is today."

There are also some very radical proposals. In one response we read: "I think it is possible that people will be inclined to collectively defend their right to 'a good job' and refuse to take part in social actions that are detrimental from this point of view, as well as refuse to take part in activities whose preposterousness is evident to all, even if such participation would yield specious immediate benefits to the individual concerned. Such benefits are just hollow 'rewards,' since what an individual gains through his participation is taken away from him by all the other absurdities perpetrated without his knowledge and for which he pays as a member of society. I would say that today it is a civic duty to get a movement started to fight wastefulness or some other phenomena of this sort. Such efforts would gradually bear economic fruit—how great it is impossible to say, but surely considerable. Moreover, they would also help to bring about a gradual change in the whole atmosphere of public life and to forge natural links between social groups and circles. In the long run, finally, they would create ways to exert pressure on the authorities, forcing them to make changes in the existing system of government."

Fairness requires us to mention the doubt voiced by one of the respondents concerning the advisability of society's exerting any pressure on the authorities: "I am not at all sure that it is true that the greater and broader the mobilization of the public for direct involvement in political matters, the easier it will be to escape the present situation. Granted, the authorities should be subject to some pressure and control by society if they are to govern effectively; they cannot, however, govern effectively if they are backed up to the wall by a politically exasperated society."

We would like to end this very brief list of suggestions concerning social behavior with one last opinion, somewhat different from the rest: namely, that nothing at all should be attempted because any action would be doomed to failure from the outset. "The alternatives are: if we want to live in peace, we must support the system in its present form; if we want to live differently, we must change the system to its very roots. Since, however, it is impossible to effect such a transformation, there is no use wasting time and energy on piecemeal changes. I have no intention of expending my energy on reformist notions that no one is waiting for, that no one is asking for, that no one intends to carry out, and whose intensions and sources will be cast in a false light. . . . The only thing I could ask of anyone whom I am capable of influencing or who might ask my opinion is that they deny their moral support to the system and to the sort of argument that takes refuge in magical or rigid thinking, in a kind of thinking based on fear of destabilization and the desire to gain respite from history scot-free."

It would be surprising if in so numerous and diverse a group there were no differences of views, evaluations, and assessments of our chances. One such antinomy is particularly worth mentioning. It concerns the question whether in the current situation it might not be best to adopt a pragmatic approach, guided by realism or at least aimed at removing the most threatening dangers; or whether, on the contrary, an ideological approach, its sights set on a fundamental transformation of the system in accordance with some accepted prototype, might not be more in order. The latter alternative is supported by the argument

that only a program providing for a fundamental transformation
"has any chance of gaining broad public acceptance and counteracting the repeated attempts to divert Poles from the task at
hand with solemn promises and pleas for confidence."

Those who support the first option claim that the most important matter at present is "to create a common ground for
discussions among persons of differing social and political views
in order to decide how to make Poland a 'normal' country, i.e.,
a country in which people are more or less able to live on a level
corresponding both to Poland's place in the industrialized world
and to the traditions of Polish culture." The pragmatic approach
evidently had the most advocates among the respondents, as is
shown, for example, by a terminology that tended toward positivistic slogans: "organic work," "work at the root," and so on.[44]

There is undoubtedly some discrepancy between questions
concerning short-term preventive measures for tackling the crisis
the country is currently experiencing and the social responses
advocated, whose effectiveness is necessarily of a more long-
term nature. This can be explained by the conviction, stressed a
number of times, that a society deprived of subjectivity has no
modes of behavior that could effect a quick cure.

This is a rather disillusioned thought, although perhaps
only seemingly so. With regard to suggestions for theoretical efforts, one of the respondents had this to say: "It is a program
that might seem too modest considering the crisis in which the
country currently finds itself. Instead of concrete actions, idle
chatter is proposed. On the other hand, however, the task at
hand might be perceived as simply overwhelming: after all,
nothing short of restoring genuine social life in our country is at
issue. In my opinion it is only through such 'chatter' that we
will be able to work our way toward concrete solutions in the
various areas of social life that actually benefit society. Only by
revitalizing social life will we be able to overcome the egotism
of certain groups and the atmosphere of stagnation, the sense of
impotence, and the apathy now reigning in broad segments of
our society."

Another respondent writes: "We must nonetheless realize
that whatever our professions, whatever public function we perform, we are not, and never have been, mere appendages of the
state. If in following the dictates of our conscience we do what
we should in science, the arts, and the economy, we will only
reinforce those values which can restore a sense of dignity and
hope to a people now so endangered—values, we might add,

that are fundamentally opposed to those which derive their strength from a system of privileges obtained through obedience."

There is a certain profound truth in this. As one of the poll participants wrote: "A society that does not want to become its own master will never do so."

A Word from the Editorial Team

This analysis of the material from the second poll conducted by the "Experience and the Future" group merits a brief postscript from its editors, whose obligation and privilege it has been to sift through the accumulated material, which is incomparably richer in content than our brief discussion of it could possibly show. We use the term "privilege" because the compilation of such widely divergent responses is not merely their simple sum; their juxtaposition has yielded a new quality.

Every individual response begins its true life when it has been communicated to someone else. Not only is it disseminated and absorbed by other minds, it also serves to stimulate new thinking in the mutual pursuit of truth.

The spirit of democracy and coalition that inspired both polls was particularly valuable. It emerges at a time when our thinking is afflicted with prejudice and rancor, when a complex historical process that has influenced the fate of millions of people and even several generations has again and again tended to revert to a black-and-white scheme of things: either hostile rejection or resigned, unthinking acceptance.

The authors' rights to this text belong to a thinking, robust society that aspires to self-awareness; it is to such a society as well that it has been addressed. It is the product of many minds, and it is for the reader himself to decide how and to what extent it is to be used. We would like, however, once more to dissociate ourselves from any attempt to place a purely political interpretation on this document. "Experience and the Future" is not and cannot be a political group, nor will it ever become one. The diversity of opinions and attitudes represented in it precludes it assuming that role, while it invests the group with another, and in the eyes of many of the respondents, more important role: namely, that of expressing and promoting broad public opinion in our country.

As the reader makes his way through this document, therefore, he should bear in mind that it is the product of distilling the results of a poll in which over a hundred persons with different outlooks and political views and from different professions and organizations took part. It represents a summation of the individual views expressed in the poll, rather than one view accepted by everyone—as is the case with political programs.

The majority of the respondents were people whose function in the social division of labor was to formulate and disseminate ideas. To be sure, thinking about matters of public concern is the inalienable right of every human being; nonetheless the respondents, who had easier access to information or were to some degree privileged in this respect, were generally more independent owing to the nature of their work. However, theirs is more an obligation than a privilege, *for in a situation in which knowledge is accessible, ignorance is a crime*. Similarly, when one has the opportunity to communicate one's knowledge to others, to withhold it is unconscionable. Such people, therefore, are duty-bound to be concerned about the rights of everyone whose lot it is to grapple with things less pliant than words and ideas, and who by the nature of their work are forced into a thick web of relationships requiring dependency, conformity, and submission. Only through solidarity with them can words about freedom and responsibility convey any weight or value.

Not only our mounting objective difficulties, but our own impotence, our inclination to sterile contemplation of disappointments and defeats endured and suffered weigh heavily on us. A person who aspires to something, on the other hand, whose gaze is set on the future, will see the same problems, but in another dimension: in the dimension of opportunity and endeavor. It is this attitude, indeed, which appears in the vast majority of the responses to the poll.

At a more practical level, the conclusions from this enormous mass of material, representing wide-ranging perspectives and assessments, can be summed up in three recommendations: rejection of apathy, a sober assessment of realities, and a readiness to make reasonable compromises. To help these three recommendations take root in the hard soil of present-day Polish reality is no easy task. The reality in which we live is changeable and vague: its image is distorted by consciously falsified propaganda and by our own subjectivism, over which the shadows of the past, lingering resentments for wrongs suffered, and dashed hopes hang heavy. At the present juncture there is no substitute for a collective effort of thought and reflection; and it is to just such an undertaking that the "Experience and the Future" group has dedicated itself within the limits of its potentials, as one of several valuable initiatives.

It is no less difficult to do justice to the appeal for readiness to make reasonable compromises. In our tradition the very concept of compromise is repugnant; hence it becomes difficult, if not impossible, to perceive the fundamental difference between compromises concerning principles and values, which are to be condemned, and compromises made in practical matters, where they are a precondition for any collective action and a crucial component in any policy-making, especially democratic policy-making and democratic thinking. Rescuing this principle, even despite past habits and philosophies of power, is, we think, crucial for the future of democracy in Poland.

Thus in these pages, as in the pages of the earlier report, the words "negotiation" and "social consensus" appear rather frequently. Those who use these words are well aware that fruitful negotiations presume the existence of two sides willing to attempt them, which in turn requires an appropriate institutional framework as well as assurances that the outcome will be of an enduring nature. However, in a situation in which the greatest threat is atomization and the disintegration of social bonds, the paramount task is to resolutely reinfuse the whole of the social system with the spirit of cooperation and, moving beyond our acute differences, to forge a consensus in the name of society's more paramount goals.

From the outset no one should be left out of this community of understanding. Everything that even in limited measure and in only a rudimentary way could contribute to the rebirth of genuine social life merits recognition and thoughtful consideration; this applies equally to initiatives taken within the framework of officially functioning institutions, organizations, and societies, as well as to those attempted outside them.

Recognition of everything that could prevent wholesale submission of social life to the state is linked, in the editors' views, with the need for sober realism, social solidarity, and a common effort to attain realistic goals. Extreme tendencies are alien to us, and the principle "the worse the better" is not for the good of society as a whole.

All the vast material from the two polls, every consideration and proposal in them, is marked by a pervasive concern for the present and future fate of the community that has shaped us all. The national consciousness that has emerged in the process lies neither in patriotic platitudes nor in a shared aversion to outsiders, but in a sense of being a full member of this community and of bearing a full share of the responsibility for its future. Every attempt to confiscate this sense of responsibility, to monopolize it in the hands of a few, expecting nothing but passive acceptance from the majority, is a threat to national consciousness. A nation endures only as long as a sense of responsibility exists among its members, i.e., only as long as it is not merely an assemblage of subordinate subjects but a society linked together by a community of goals and composed of citizens who are fully aware of their rights and duties.

The poll responses reflected a whole range of variations on this common theme, but all were united in the way they understood our obligations to the national community. If we wanted to draw some lessons from our analysis in accordance with its spirit, we might sum them up in the following three supreme precepts.

The first is *to preserve a national identity*, which entails not only safeguarding the whole wealth of our past heritage, which is so much more than mere folklore and traditional costumes, but also creating conditions in which our national culture can develop and thrive unfettered and become a dynamic force in the spiritual and material aspirations of successive generations of our people.

Second, we must *develop the skills and talents of democratic cooperation*, of self-government, and the art of living together. In this way the conditions should be created and the moment should approach at which the people will begin to make their own history.

Third and finally, *the economic efficiency of society must be developed*; or put more broadly, we must forge the capacity to live and act under the conditions of modern civilization, for Poland's place in the world depends on doing so.

These three precepts are closely linked, and the areas of action they cover overlap and complement one another. It behooves each and every one of us to heed these three precepts to the extent of his strength and abilities. Only the collective aspirations and efforts of everyone, acting alone but persistently and conscious of the common goal, can create conditions in which the people "feel at home," the true masters of their country, free of complexes and not dreading the future.

Warsaw   May 3, 1980

Notes

Translators' Notes to the "Report"

[1] A rather obscure, state-run educational forum on social issues. The "Experience and the Future" group was to operate under its auspices. The first and only meeting of the discussion group took place on November 4, 1978, in Warsaw, under the auspices of the collegium. The collegium later withdrew its sponsorship, and no agreement has ever been reached on a new sponsor.

[2] Agreements were concluded between Poland and other Eastern European countries abolishing visa requirements, and the border between Poland and the GDR was opened in 1971. That year roughly one million trips abroad were made from Poland, and this figure rose sharply in the following years. The border between Poland and the GDR was effectively closed following the August 1980 wave of industrial unrest in Poland.

[3] A Sejm [parliament] bill of December 14, 1971, granted access to medical care for private farmers. The pension law for peasants did not go into effect until January 1, 1978 (Sejm bill of October 27, 1977). It met with strong resistance on account of the large amounts of money the farmers were required to pay into the pension fund, in some cases reaching 8.5 percent of their income (*Labor Focus on Eastern Europe*, 1978, no. 4).

[4] This reform was carried out in three stages from 1972 through 1975. The lowest regional administrative unit, the *gmina*, was doubled in size (it now averages 129 square kilometers, with 7,000 inhabitants) and reduced in number by 50 percent to 2,365. The number of the highest regional units, the voivodes, was, on the other hand, increased from 22 to 49, limiting the power of the regional leadership. The previous intermediate unit, the district (*powiat*), was abolished. As before, popularly elected people's councils exist at both regional levels, although their importance has evidently been reduced. The local party chairman is now automatically the chairman for the council as well and has now been invested with full executive power over the region. This, of course, has strengthened the party's leading role, as was to be formally acknowledged in a constitutional amendment (see Note 5).

Officially the reform was advertised as a decentralizing measure.

[5] The two largest worker upheavals prior to 1980 in Poland's postwar history took place in Poznań in October 1956 and in Szczecin in December 1970. In both cases one of the immediate results was the appointment of a new party first secretary—Gomulka in 1956 and Gierek in 1970. The change in the country's leadership was followed by an attempt to introduce broad changes in policy. Some of the measures undertaken immediately after the upheavals also obviously improved the population's living standards.

[6] "Poland's geopolitical situation" is a favorite euphemism for all the problems entailed in being a neighbor of the Soviet Union and Germany.

[7] Enacted into law on October 13, 1973, the educational reform provides for the institution of a ten-year comprehensive school, normally followed by two years of specialization prior to further education in a particular field if so chosen. One criticism of the reform has been that it neglects general education and is socially biased.

[8] The workers' upheaval of June 1976 centered in Radom and Ursus. As a result of repression by the authorities, a large number of workers were dismissed from their jobs, and many were beaten up, maltreated, and sentenced to prison on trumped up charges for up to ten years. This spurred the creation of the Workers' Defense Committee (KOR), which pressed for a parliamentary inquiry into the allegations of police brutality. Most of those arrested were freed as a result of the amnesty declared by the government on July 22, 1977.

[9] Petrys—a former employee of the security apparatus—worked as a research assistant at the Polish Academy of Sciences (PAN). In his thesis he copied parts of Hankus's thesis and presented it as his own original work. This case was taken up by Professor J. Groszkowski, chairman of the academy. Unable to help Hankus, Groszkowski resigned his post. Petrys was acquitted.

[10] Government vehicles carry "R" stickers.

[11] The Supreme Chamber of Control (NIK) performs supervisory control and auditing functions with regard to the administration of the state. It was created in 1956 and placed under the Sejm. In 1976 it was placed under the government (Council of Ministers). In September 1980 it was again placed under the control of the Sejm (see Richard Szawlowski, "Poland—a New Supreme Board of Control," *Osteuropa Recht*, 1979, no. 2).

[12] Adopted June 26, 1974, and in effect since January 1, 1975. One of its weak points is that a worker can be held economically accountable for damage to materials and for poorly done work. This is a provision that can be very easily abused. The abuse of the law exceeded all bounds in 1976, when strikers were fired without warning in accordance with Article 52, point 1, which refers to "serious neglect of a worker's duties, as for example leaving one's workplace without justification." Otherwise strikes are

neither forbidden nor allowed by this law. The Gdansk agreement, point 2, now explicitly permits strikes.

[13] There has been widespread public criticism of waiting lists for apartments and the way they are handled.

[14] June 1975.

[15] The event referred to was a major disaster, when a bank in the heart of Warsaw blew up on February 15, 1979. The cause was said to be a gas leak, which no one believed.

[16] The bitter cold winter of 1978-79, which to a great degree paralyzed Polish society and caused many deaths.

[17] Between 1968 and 1972 many influential members of the country's intellectual establishment emigrated. Most of them were Jewish. As a result the continuity of intellectual life was disrupted.

[18] The "second economy" is not just a black market. It extends to a wide selection of goods and services available only to selected groups of employees or at very high prices. Among the groups favored, which are usually allied somehow with the party, are the army, police, security services, some ministry employees, and so on. The goods and services available in the "second economy" include housing, cars, building materials, vacations, medical care, and even some basic foods.

[19] The price rises were announced on June 24, 1976, and revoked the next day after broad strikes and demonstrations. The price of high-quality sausage was to go up by 90 percent, of cheaper meat cuts by 50 percent, of poultry by 30 percent, of butter by 50 percent, of sugar by 100 percent, and of poppy seeds, beans, peas, and vegetables, each by about 30 percent.

[20] In 1954 and 1955 the grip of the secret police on the country loosened a bit. In 1968, as a result of a confrontation between the party and nonconformist intellectuals, the role of the secret police increased again. After 1970 public hostility to the secret police was largely economic in character. They were resented for their social privileges (allocation of apartments, holidays, access to material goods, better pay, etc.) more than for any particular repressive activity.

[21] See Note 4.

[22] See Note 4.

[23] In Polish *"wojewoda"* and *"naczelnik gminy,"* the two most important local administrative positions. They were reformed under Gierek (see Note 4) and are now appointive positions filled by the government under *"nomenklatura"* (see Note 23 in "Which Way Out?").

[24] Price increases, long anticipated, were announced by the government on June 24, 1976, during a "debate" in the Sejm. The following day the increases were rescinded, again in the Sejm, where face was saved by calling the price increases "projected." See P. Raina, *Political Opposition in Poland 1954-1977*, London, Poets and Painters Press, 1978.

[25] See Note 11.

[26] 1948-53.

[27] The case of prosecutor Bogusław Sliwa, from Kalisz in southwestern Poland, illustrates this point well. Sliwa was the district prosecutor, and in the course of his investigations he came to the conclusion that a murder had been committed by one of the local police officials. He could not proceed with the case; and when he complained to the Council of State, he was dismissed from his post (Helsinki Committee in Poland, *Document No. 1. Report on the Observance of Human and Civil Rights in the Polish People's Republic*, Warsaw, October 1980).

[28] Matejewski, general of the Ministry of Internal Affairs (MSW), an associate of Mieczysław Moczar and supposedly one of the organizers of the so-called "Olsztyn putsch" in 1972. During First Secretary Edward Gierek's visit to Czechoslovakia, Moczar called a meeting of top-ranking territorial party officials in his bid for power, which was unsuccessful. Soon afterwards Matejewski fell victim to a purge in the MSW, and he was accused of speculating in hard currency and other misdeeds. Many of his fellow employees also lost their posts.

[29] See Note 8. The best-known case is that of a laborer, Jan Brozyna, who died in police custody, apparently as a result of severe beating. See Raina for more details.

[30] See Note 12. The new labor law does not distinguish between workers and officials nor between types of employment, i.e., wage labor, work in cooperatives, or popularly elected councils.

[31] In the late sixties and early seventies there was a tendency to base energy supplies on oil. After the energy crisis of the midseventies, Poland's economic planners rediscovered the importance of coal for the national economy.

[32] The new economic maneuver was introduced by the PUWP's first secretary, Gierek, at the Fifth Plenary Session of the Party Central Committee on December 1, 1976. The objective was to reduce the rate of investment in the economy as a whole and to stimulate the consumer goods and foods sectors by increasing aid to agriculture, for example.

[33] The experiment with Large Economic Units (WOG) was first introduced in 1973. A year later it included 40 percent of industrial production. The units were given considerable incentives, which was supposed to simplify planning.

[34] The production associations function at a higher level than the state enterprises. They are usually organized by branch of manufacture.

[35] The Stalinist period is meant.

[36] The Katowice steel works is Poland's largest. It was a controversial prestige construction project carried out with the collaboration of the USSR, which also takes a large part of its output. It was criticized as a misguided investment project.

[37] Two large industrial areas. Silesia is in southwestern Poland, while Zagłębie Staropolskie is near Radom, 100 kilometers south of Warsaw.

[38] The winter of 1978-79.

[39] In 1977 state farms (PGR) produced only 17.5 percent of total agricultural output measured in value terms.

[40] Pseudo-cooperative associations that came into being in 1948, with regional branches trading with private peasants. In 1977 they accounted for 17.9 percent of total agricultural output.

[41] These fleets provide private peasants with collective agricultural machinery, financed partly by the land tax. Ninety percent of all peasants participate.

[42] State farms and farming cooperatives are the two major levels of the cooperative sector.

[43] The weekly *Tygodnik Powszechny* (General Weekly) and the monthly *Znak* (Sign), both published in Cracow, and the monthly *Wież* (Link), published in Warsaw. In addition to being Catholic, these three periodicals are also regarded as among the most readable in Poland.

[44] In Poland three parties formally exist: the Communist Party, which officially is called the Polish United Workers' Party (PZPR), the United Peasants' Party (ZSL), and the Democratic Alliance (SD), which is the party for private entrepreneurs and the intelligentsia. Until now the Communist Party has had total control of the other parties, but the latter have recently acquired a bit of autonomy.

[45] Numerous Western radio stations broadcast in Polish, such as Radio Free Europe, the BBC, Deutsche Welle, and others. The major Western newspapers are also relatively easy to obtain in Poland.

[46] Unofficial publications defying censorship sprang into being in 1977; the most important are *Biuletyn Informacyjny* (Information Bulletin), *Glos* (The Voice), *Opinia* (Opinion), *Spotkania* (Encounters), *Aspekt* (Aspect), and others. The samizdat press in Poland was and is much larger than in any other Eastern European country. Even before July 1980 there were about fifty periodicals, with *Rabotnik* (The Worker) the largest. Its circulation is about 10,000 copies monthly. Books have also been published; the NOWA publishing house is widely known. This report, for instance, was published in Poland by NOWA.

[47] During the first five years of Gierek's leadership (1971-75), real wages rose by 40 percent, and one Saturday off work per month was introduced.

[48] The constitutional amendment of February 10, 1976, conferred on the party a "leading role in the construction of socialism" (Article 3, para. 1). This amendment provoked a wave of protests in the fall of 1975.

[49] A Polish euphemism for such entrepreneurs as small-scale manufacturers, tradesmen, farmers, or craftsmen. These groups, although sometimes prosperous lead a precarious existence, depending on the whims of authority in applying single or multiple taxes, revoking licenses, and so on. The link

between "private initiative" and the state security apparatus has been noted by M. Tarniewski, *Ewolucja czy rewolucja*, Paris, Institut Litteraire, S.A.R.L., 1975.

[50] Well-known Polish sociologist and social thinker, born in 1897 and active during the prewar period; from 1959 to 1962 he was vice-president of the International Sociological Association. His *Class Structure and Social Consciousness* is available in English (Routledge Kegan Paul, 1979).

[51] During the period of the Polish partition (1772-1918), World War II, and the Stalinist policies that followed, the Church was the repository of national identity. See Leszek Kolakowski, in *Index on Censorship*, November-December 1979.

[52] Born 1913; member of the Council of State; head of the Department of Social Sciences of the Polish Academy of Sciences; former president of the International Sociological Association. His books include *Polish Society* (1970, in English), *Society and the Intelligentsia* (1957, in Polish), and *Reflections on the Republic* (1972, in Polish).

[53] In 1958 the workers' councils were formally placed under the control of the party and the trade unions. Factory committees were created in the aftermath of the 1970-71 conflict.

[54] "Commercial prices" were 100 percent higher than normal ones and were used in special shops that had a broader range of goods to offer. The price rises of July 1, 1980, which precipitated the strikes, were effected by further reducing the supply in the normal butcher shops and transferring it to the "commercial" shops. In the Gdansk agreement of August 31, 1980, point 11, the workers demand that such shops be abolished, while point 13 calls for the introduction of a ration card until supply matches demand.

[55] Teaching is one of the lowest paid occupations in the country. People who stay in the profession are often those who did not succeed elsewhere.

[56] See Note 18.

[57] Top-ranking party functionaries have access to selected information not available to the public at large.

[58] See Note 7.

[59] Gomulka had fallen out of favor and been out of office for nearly seven years; therefore the public did not hold him responsible for the misdeeds of the party. In 1948 he had been disgraced by the Polish Communist Party leadership of the time (with Stalin's approval) for having opposed collectivization of agriculture and for having displayed "nationalist tendencies." For his "right-wing" approach Gomulka was expelled from the Communist Party in 1948 and put under house arrest. For more details see Nicholas Bethell, *Gomulka, His Poland, and His Communism*, Penguin Books, 1971.

[60] Cardinal Wyszynski was held under house arrest in a monastery from 1953 to 1956.

[61] See "Which Way Out?" Chapter 1: "Possible Strategies."

[62] See Note 32.

[63] This refers to a wage system in which a very considerable portion of earnings comes not from direct pay but from bonuses, commissions, awards, etc.

[64] In an open letter to the Ministry of Health (April 12, 1978), the Committee for Social Self-Defense (KOR) threatened that it would ask the Polish emigration in the West to organize an aid program if conditions in this area were not improved within a month; they were improved. In early 1981 the Solidarity trade union distributed medicine provided largely by Scandinavian countries.

[65] After the retraction of the June 1976 price rises, the authorities began to introduce "back-door" price rises by withdrawing certain goods from retail outlets and replacing them with new, more expensive ones.

[66] See Note 54.

[67] Published in March 1973 and prepared by a group of experts appointed by the Minister of Education, headed by J. Szczepański. It was supposed to develop a framework for future educational reform. See Note 7.

[68] It fell on November 11, 1978.

[69] "*Sanacja*," which means "renewal" and comes from Latin, is the name given to Marshall Pilsudski's regime, which was set up in 1926 in the aftermath of a military coup d'etat.

[70] Stefan Rowecki (cover name Grot) was born in 1895; he was chief commander of the Home Army (noncommunist resistance movement during World War II) until June 30, 1943, when he was arrested. He was murdered at Sachsenhausen in 1944.

[71] *Dziady* (Forefathers' Eve), which portrays nineteenth-century Russian despotism and the Polish struggle for freedom, is an epic drama written by Adam Mickiewicz in the 1820s. It is considered one of the most important works of Polish romanticism and Polish literature in general. In 1968 its withdrawal from the National Theater (Teatr Narodowy) repertoire under pressure from the Russians provoked serious unrest among students and intellectuals.

[72] These are works by Stefan Zeromski that deal with Polish-Russian relations during the nineteenth and early twentieth centuries.

[73] Ruch is a state-owned chain of kiosks, reading rooms, and literary clubs.

[74] The Union of Polish Youth (ZMP) was an organization active in the Stalinist period. It was renowned for its unquestioning and enthusiastic adherence to the party line.

[75] See Note 16.

[76] A prominent Polish writer active in the prewar period; she was concerned with social issues of the day (1889-1964).

[77] See Note 48.

[78] Europe's first written constitution, which transformed Poland into a constitutional monarchy, was proclaimed on May 3, 1791.

[79] As a result of the Polish partitions of 1772, 1793, and 1795, Poland was erased from the map of Europe, not to appear again until 1918.

[80] Tadeusz Manteuffel Szoego, born 1902, medieval historian, organizer and first director (since 1953) of the Historical Institute under the Academy of Sciences.

[81] A committee of experts working under the auspices of the Polish Academy of Sciences since the early seventies. Its purpose was to analyze development trends to give the authorities an idea of what the country would look like in the year 2000 and of what should be done in the interim to correct some of the trends should they prove unfavorable.

[82] "Which Way Out?" deals with these issues.

[83] According to the Gdansk agreement between representatives of the striking shipyard workers and the government delegation, the authorities pledged to look into the matter of censorship more carefully than before and to draft legislation within three months. The "Experience and the Future" discussion group has started work on a new report devoted to the subject of social communication; many of its members played an active role in the public discussion on censorship.

[84] See Note 73.

[85] In accordance with current practice, the Council of State appoints judges. They can also be recalled from their posts.

[86] This was the major function of the trade unions before August 1980.

[87] Genuine trade union representation was envisaged in the Gdansk agreement of August 31, 1980. The independent self-governing trade union organization "Solidarity" was formally registered by a district court in Warsaw on October 24, 1980. A clause stipulating the leading role of the Communist Party was inserted into the union's statutes. This caused a serious political crisis, and the clause was removed by the Supreme Court on November 10, 1980.

[88] See Note 44.

[89] See Notes 40 and 41.

[90] A nationwide food cooperative and retail outlet with shops, restaurants, etc.

[91] Point 3 of the Gdansk agreement guarantees the Catholic Church greater freedom and access to the media.

[92] Karol Adamiecki, 1866-1933. Attached to the Polytechnical Teachers Institute in Warsaw.

[93] Such a discussion is stipulated in the Gdansk agreement, point 6.

[94] This too was secured in the Gdansk agreement (point 9).

Translators' Notes to "Which Way Out?"

[1] Piotr Jaroszewicz, who had been prime minister since 1970, resigned in the wake of severe criticism for the country's catastrophic economic condition at the Eighth Party Congress, held on February 11-15, 1980, His successor, Eduard Babinch, became prime minister at a special Sejm session on February 18.

[2] In Poland most of the weekly and monthly press deals with social and cultural issues.

[3] See Note 52 to the "Report."

[4] Tomasz Strzyzewski was employed by the Main Office for the Control of the Press, Publications, and Entertainment, i.e., the censor, from August 1, 1975, to March 10, 1977, when he managed to emigrate to Sweden, smuggling out a huge collection of the censor's internal documents with him. They have since been published by the opposition in Poland and by Polish emigrees in the West.

[5] In the late seventies "prosperity," fueled by Western credits, caused a crisis of rising expectations.

[6] In Poland the land is divided among state cooperative farms, agricultural cooperatives, and private farms. Although the latter occupy almost 80 percent of the land, the authorities clearly favor the state farms and discriminate against the private farms in investment and price-setting policies. Yet the large state and collective farms are the least productive, despite heavy subsidies. They produce, on average, 20 percent less than the private farms, which themselves are too small and too underdeveloped to be very efficient.

[7] See Note 54 to the "Report."

[8] The black market, where goods are far more expensive or available only for foreign currency, but are much more accessible. See Note 18 to the "Report."

[9] Youth organizations provide references for prospective job-seekers, engendering opportunistic attitudes among youth.

[10] The most serious worker uprisings in Poland's postwar history. All of them were violent. In 1980, however, both sides made great efforts to avoid violence.

[11] The reference here is to the problem, very acute in Poland, that there are not enough products to cover the amount of money in circulation. This is a special form of inflation in which money loses value not only because prices rise but equally because there are no goods on the market at all.

[12] Poland was forced to participate in the invasion of Czechoslovakia and to support materially the USSR's client states in the Third World. The result of this active bloc foreign policy could be to isolate the country from the West and from the nonaligned nations. Poland's leadership was sur-

prised at the Soviet decision to invade Afghanistan.

[13] In the aftermath of the latest wave of strikes, the threat of Soviet invasion was used by the country's leadership in an attempt to keep the strikers in check.

[14] This expression is used to describe the policies of the propaganda machine under Gierek's rule.

[15] See Note 83 to the "Report" and Note 4 above.

[16] The trade union law of July 1949. A short and rather vague document, its Article 2 specifies what groups of workers and state employees are allowed to set up their own unions. Private farmers, not mentioned in the law, have failed to register Rural Solidarity as a trade union, thus leading to increased tensions.

[17] Formerly an institution of supervision and control, introduced in the law of July 30, 1958, after the genuine workers' councils established in 1956 had been dissolved. See Note 53 to the "Report."

[18] This refers to the collectivization of agriculture.

[19] A 1974 law permits transfer of farmland to the state in return for old-age pensions and payments. See Note 3 to the "Report."

[20] According to the new constitution of 1976, Poland is a *socialist* state, and no longer a *people's democracy*, as stipulated in the 1952 Constitution. According to the *Worterbuch zum sozialistischen Stadt*, a socialist state is characterized by friendly relations between the classes and is working for the construction of a *developed* socialist society, which heretofore has existed only in the USSR. Communism is achieved only after this stage has been passed.

[21] The Popular Front period, before the Communist Party assumed total power (1945-48).

[22] Euphemism for the Stalinist period (1948-53).

[23] *Nomenklatura* (sometimes called *Berufsverbot*) is the list of posts that can be filled only with the consent of party organization (candidates must be approved by a local or national party organ). The list includes all key posts in the state administration as well as in other public institutions, such as, for instance, higher education. The importance of the post dictates the level of party organization involved.

[24] Under the existing electoral system it is bad for a person to do anything but put the ballot given him in the ballot box. If one goes behind a curtain to cross off a name on the list, it is interpreted as a protest.

[25] The Front of National Unity (FJN) is a nationwide social and political movement that has existed since 1952. Originally known as the National Front, it is dominated by the Polish United Workers' Party but includes representatives of other political groupings, such as the Democratic Alliance and United Peasants' Party (see Note 26 below), as well as a number of nonparty members. Its proclaimed aim is to work toward the socialist construction of Poland. It has the exclusive right to nominate candidates for

national elections to the Sejm and people's councils.

[26] The United Peasants' Party (ZSL) dates, in its present form, to February 27, 1949, although it claims antecedents in a much older populist tradition. The Democratic Alliance (SD), which has existed since 1938, is active among the intelligentsia and craftsmen. See Note 44 to the "Report."

[27] See Note 11 to the "Report."

[28] See Note 12 to the "Report."

[29] They entitle the possessor to skip the waiting list for buying a car.

[30] Since the early seventies a citizen wanting to make a trip to the West could apply for a hard-currency allotment. However, such an allotment was very difficult to obtain.

[31] This refers to special retail outlets accessible to high-ranking party members.

[32] This figure rose even more in the years that followed.

[33] See Note 11 to the "Report."

[34] See Note 34 to the "Report."

[35] Industrial goods are far more expensive than food.

[36] See Note 62 to the "Report."

[37] Associations of major state enterprises in selected branches of the national economy (steel, coal, etc.).

[38] See Note 40 to the "Report."

[39] As a result of the border adjustments after World War II, the major portion of the Polish population in the eastern territories of prewar Poland moved to the northwest, to the area that had been German territory.

[40] In this passage the editors express fear about the possibility of another workers' uprising, which indeed did take place a few months after the publication of "Which Way Out?" The three previous confrontations were in 1956, 1970, and 1976.

[41] The regional social associations that came into being in the aftermath of the October thaw of 1956.

[42] A widespread movement among the country's intellectuals against the amendments to the Constitution forced the authorities to retract some of the original provisions.

[43] The Committee for the Defense of Workers (KOR) publication on public health is a very good example.

[44] Polish positivism has a very special significance; born in reaction to the failed 1863 uprising against the tsar, it emphasized down-to-earth practical work, as opposed to emancipatory romanticism, and the need to create an economic infrastructure.